Diversification, Refocusing, and Economic Performance

Diversification, Refocusing, and Economic Performance

Constantinos C. Markides

The MIT Press
Cambridge, Massachusetts
London, England

This book was set in Palatino by Asco Trade Typesetting Ltd., Hong Kong and was printed and bound in the United States of America.

Library of Congress Cataloging-in-Publication Data

Markides, Constantinos C.
  Diversification, refocusing, and economic performance /
  Constantinos C. Markides.
  p. cm.
  Includes bibliographical references and index.
  ISBN 0-262-13311-3 (hc : alk. paper)
  1. Corporate divestiture—United States—Case studies. 2. Downsizing of organizations
—United States—Case studies. 3. Corporate reorganizations—United States—
Case studies. 4. Diversification in industry—United States—Case studies.
I. Title.
HD2746.6.M37   1996
338.7—dc20   95-22500
                                                                CIP

FTW
AJE 7146

To my parents, for they have been the giants on whose shoulders I have stood

Contents

Acknowledgments

For almost everyone engaged in academic research, intellectual debts accumulate fast. The research reported in this book was primarily carried out during my doctoral studies at Harvard Business School in the period 1986 to 1990. I would therefore like to thank the four members of my dissertation committee at HBS—Norman Berg, Richard Caves, Howard Stevenson, and Malcolm Salter. Without their continual intellectual and emotional support as well as advice and help, this research would never have been completed.

I am also grateful to several colleagues in the Academy of Management who read portions of this research and provided helpful comments. I'd like to thank George Baker, Robert Hoskisson, Cynthia Montgomery, Krishna Palepu, Robert Stobaugh, John Stopford, and Peter Williamson. Several anonymous reviewers—for The MIT Press as well as the academic journals where a lot of this research has been reported over the past five years—have also helped enormously in improving this book.

As is usually the case, friends and colleagues have been subjected to "conversations" on the research topic, especially at times they least expected it! For suggestions, criticisms, and research support, I'd like to thank Chris Ittner, Yolande Oyon, Seung-Joo Lee, Alvin Wint, and especially Daniel Oyon. Without their help and support, this research would (most probably) have been finished in half the time it took (but the quality of the research is another matter).

A special thank you to Mark Indelicato for numerous hours of computer assistance, to Barry Feldman for database support, to the staff at Baker Library at Harvard and the staff at the London Business School library for research support, to the Division of Research at Harvard Business School for financial support, and to Terry Vaughn, Dana Andrus, and the rest of the team at The MIT Press for excellent editorial help.

A portion of this research has already been reported in academic journals. Much in chapters 1, 2, and 4 is based on material that appeared in highly condensed form in *Multinational Business*, winter 1991, no. 4, pp. 12−25; and *Business Strategy Review*, vol. 4, no. 1, spring 1993, pp. 1−15. Some of the results in chapter 4 have appeared in *Strategic Renaissance and Business Transformation* (H. Thomas, D. O'Neal, and J. Kelly, eds., John Wiley & Sons, 1995). Chapter 5 is based on a paper that appeared in the *British Journal of Management*, vol. 2, no. 2, June 1992, pp. 91−100, while chapter 6 is based on a paper that was published in the *Academy of Management Journal*, vol. 35, no. 2, June 1992, pp. 398−412. Finally, chapter 7 was originally published in the *Strategic Management Journal*, vol. 16, no. 2, February 1995, pp. 101−18. I am grateful to the several publishers who have granted their permission for me to elaborate and integrate these materials in this book.

Diversification, Refocusing, and Economic Performance

1

Introduction and Statement of the Phenomenon

While headlines proclaim megamergers, hostile takeovers, and proxy fights, something far less visible but just as noteworthy is occurring at hundreds of American companies. Much like overweight people ... these corporations are working off excess weight. They are shedding unwanted and often unlucrative divisions, subsidiaries, and product lines in order to concentrate on what they do best and most profitably. When they do buy another company now, it's done to enhance the "core" business. This is conglomeration in reverse.

U.S. News & World Report, April 15, 1985

There is rising evidence, especially in the business press, that over the past decade many U.S. corporations have "restructured."[1] For example, Lewis (1990, p. 43) estimates that "nearly half of large U.S. corporations have 'restructured' in the 1980s." Earlier, a special report on corporate restructuring published in the *Wall Street Journal* (1985, p. 12) found that out of the 850 of North America's largest corporations, 398 (47 percent) of them restructured.

A serious problem with many of these studies on restructuring is that they are not precise enough about what they mean by "restructuring." Corporate actions such as reducing corporate staff, eliminating management layers, decentralizing the corporate structure, repurchasing stock, rationalizing operations, consolidating plants, forming alliances, and refocusing can all fall under the general term "restructuring." A researcher needs to look at these forms of restructuring separately if any generalizations are to be made.

---

1. See, for example, F. W. Budd (1986): Hostile acquisitions and the restructuring of corporate America, *The Freeman* (May): 166; *Midland Corporate Finance Journal* (1984): The restructuring of corporate America: An overview, Summer; *Dun's Review* (March 1981): 111–14; *Business Week*, August 24, 1981, pp. 68–73; *The Wall Street Journal*, November 2, 1983, p. 33; *Business Week*, July 1, 1985, pp. 50–55; *Euromoney*, February 1987, pp. 106–17; *Fortune*, March 2, 1987, pp. 38–46; *Business Week*, June 20, 1988, pp. 116–30; and *The Wall Street Journal*, January 16, 1990, p. A16.

Table 1.1
General Mills' business structure

Business segment	Revenues as a % of total sales				
	1970	1978	1982	1986	1989
Food processing	78.5	53.5	50.9	66.7	71.1
Crafts, games, toys	10.2	19.9	12.3	0.0	0.0
Specialty retailing/fashion	0.0	15.2	20.9	10.3	0.0
Restaurants	0.0	11.4	15.8	22.9	28.9
Specialty chemicals	3.6	0.0	0.0	0.0	0.0
Other	7.7	0.0	0.0	0.0	0.0

Source: Company annual reports and Donaldson (1990).

In this study I will focus on a type of restructuring known as corporate refocusing. By this I mean the voluntary (or involuntary) reduction in the diversification of U.S. firms that is usually, but not necessarily, achieved through major divestitures (Bhagat, Shleifer, and Vishny 1990 call it "the return to corporate specialization"). Specifically in this study I use the term "refocusing" to mean the company decision to reduce the scope of its activities in order to concentrate on the "core" business (i.e., to reduce its diversification). In the business press this practice has had different labels like "de-conglomerating," "de-diversifying," and "getting back to basics." I have chosen to discuss this type of restructuring because corporate refocusing has proved to be by far the most common and most beneficial form of restructuring undertaken by firms (e.g., Lewis 1990; *Wall Street Journal* 1985).

A good example of a refocused firm is General Mills, which undertook most of its restructuring in 1985 to 1988. The company began in 1928 as a national network of flour mills, diversified into a variety of unrelated industries in the 1960s and 1970s, and then refocused itself around packaged foods in the late 1980s.[2] The evolution of the firm's business structure is shown in table 1.1.

According to the company's 1985 annual report:

the history of the company to date [can] be divided into five strategic phases: an emphasis on flour milling (1928–45); a maturing milling business coupled with growth in packaged foods and experimentation in other areas (1945–59); a shift from a commodities to a consumer orientation, which included closing over half the flour mills and exiting from the formula feed business (1960–66); and an

2. A detailed discussion of General Mills' history and restructuring can be found in Donaldson (1990a) and (1994).

aggressive diversification phase into many new consumer industries that began in 1966.

By 1976 the company was competing in thirteen different industries, and had sales of $2.6 billion. Despite the 1977 sale of the chemicals business and the gradual exit from some other peripheral businesses such as travel, jewelry, luggage, coin and stamps, wallpaper, and furniture, General Mills entered the 1980s with a widely diversified business structure.

Following a disappointing fiscal 1984 during which the firm's profitability (return on assets, *ROA*, and return on equity, *ROE*) was at a fifteen-year low, and its *P/E* ratio was less than half the 1968 rate, General Mills embarked on an "historic restructuring plan," marking the firm's fifth strategic phase. The major element of the plan, which was announced in January 1985, included the spin-off of the toy and fashion companies, and the sale of some specialty retailing units. In all, twenty-six individual companies or divisions which accounted for about 30 percent of General Mills' assets were divested. According to *Business Week* (2−11−85, p. 31): "Wall Street practically cheered the news … the company's stock jumped $5\frac{3}{8}$ points to $55\frac{1}{4}$, the day after the announcement." The planned refocusing was completed in May 1988 with the sale of the Specialty Retailing Business (Talbots sold to Jusco Ltd., Japan, and Eddie Bauer to Spiegel, Inc.). The company's major divestments are shown in table 1.2.

From a company competing in thirteen separate industries in the 1970s, General Mills has transformed itself into a focused company competing in two industries: Consumer Foods and Restaurants. The dispositions of the period 1985−88 accounted for more than 38 percent of sales and nearly 53

Table 1.2
General Mills' major divestitures, 1977 to 1989

Business segment	Years	Final year sales ($ millions)
Chemicals	1977	127
Foods	1979−87	456
Fashion	1979−85	595
Toys	1982−85	715
Restaurants	1985−88	167
Retailing	1985−88	738
Other	1982−86	117
		2,915

Source: General Mills' 1988 annual report.

Table 1.3
Selected financial statistics for General Mills

	1980	1982	1984	1985	1986	1989
Total assets ($1,000)	2,012	2,702	2,858	2,663	2,086	2,888
Total sales ($1,000)	4,170	5,312	5,601	4,285	4,587	5,621
ROS (%)	4.1	4.2	4.2	2.7	4.0	7.4
ROE (%)	16.7	18.3	19.1	−7.1	26.9	56.6
ROA (%)	8.4	8.3	8.2	−2.7	8.8	10.9
Debt/equity (%)	37.0	26.9	29.6	43.9	67.2	73.3
P/E ratio—close	8.3	8.9	10.0	23.3	18.9	17.0
Price/book—close	1.4	1.6	1.8	2.6	5.1	7.2

Source: Donaldson (1990) and company annual reports.

percent of assets. The results of this strategy appear to have been positive (see table 1.3).

In the four years since the announcement of General Mills' refocusing, its return on sales (ROS) increased from 2.7 percent to 7.4 percent and its ROE from −7.1 percent to 56.6 percent; the stock price has increased nearly 2.4 times; and earnings per share in 1989 were more than 2.5 times the levels in 1985. In March 1990 General Mills' president and CEO, Mark Willes, in a speech at the Harvard Business School, attributed the firm's success to three things: a *focused corporate strategy*, a continually renewing product strategy, and the attraction of good people. In his own words, "A company cannot be successful with the strategy of being all things to all people."

Another example of a refocused company is Gulf & Western (now Paramount). The company was founded in 1958 and over the next twenty-five years grew into a broadly diversified, multi-industry enterprise with annual sales of about $7.5 billion (in 1982). However, in August 1983 the company announced a major refocusing program whose goal was to transform G&W into a "focused, services-based company" with leadership positions in its markets. The evolution of the company's business structure is shown in table 1.4.

According to the firm's own annual reports, over the period 1983−85:

Gulf & Western divested companies with sales of $4 billion, liquidated a $900-million marketable securities portfolio, reduced debt by $765 million, [and] repurchased 19.3 million of its common shares ....

The refocusing program was completed in September 1985 with the sale of the Consumer and Industrial Products Group to Wickes Companies, Inc. for $1 billion. According to the *Wall Street Journal*:

Table 1.4
Gulf & Western's business structure

Business segment	Revenues as a % of total sales			
	1979	1982	1986	1988
Natural resources	7.6	0.0	0.0	0.0
Consumer and agricultural products	7.4	0.0	0.0	0.0
Apparel and hosiery	18.5	20.1	0.0	0.0
Bedding and home furnishings	18.5	11.7	0.0	0.0
Manufacturing	21.2	13.0	0.0	0.0
Auto parts distribution	8.6	6.4	0.0	0.0
Entertainment	15.6	15.3	30.4	36.4
Publishing/information	15.6	3.7	25.1	23.3
Consumer/commercial finance	20.9	23.2	44.5	40.2
Other	—	6.3	0.0	0.0

Source: Gulf & Western's annual reports.

Table 1.5
Selected financial statistics for Gulf & Western

	1981	1983	1985	1987	1988
Revenues ($ million)	$7,409	$2,522	$3,321	$4,701	$5,107
Total assets ($ million)	5,893	4,554	4,064	4,929	5,378
Net earnings ($ million)	290.9	(191.7)	247.8	356.1	384.7
ROS (%)	3.9	(7.6)	7.4	7.6	7.5
ROA (%)	4.9	(4.2)	6.1	7.2	7.1
Stock Price—close	$15\frac{7}{8}$	$30\frac{1}{8}$	$49\frac{6}{8}$	$71\frac{1}{8}$	$81\frac{2}{8}$
Book value per share	27.5	24.5	29.15	35.05	39.0
S&P 500 composite—close	122.55	164.93	211.28	247.08	277.72

Source: Gulf & Western's annual reports.

the sale [of the group] shrinks G&W in half; the $1 billion cash sale completes Martin Davis' transformation of G&W from a volatile giant into a streamlined entertainment, communications and financial firm.

Over the period 1984–88 the company tried to build its three remaining core businesses with intensified internal growth efforts as well as acquisitions. The most significant of several acquisitions in publishing were Esquire, Inc. and Prentice-Hall, Inc. in 1984, and Ginn & Company in 1985.

The strategy appears to be a success (see table 1.5). In the period 1981–88 the firm's ROS increased from 3.9 percent to 7.5 percent, while its ROA went from 4.9 percent to 7.1 percent. In the same period the company's stock increased by more than five times.

According to the company's 1988 annual report:

Our restructuring since the beginning of 1983 established a framework for our earnings uptrend and parallel rewards for long-term investors. Shareholders who owned our common stock over the five-year period through October 31, 1988, earned a 239% return on their investment (the increase in our stock plus cash dividends paid). By contrast, the Standard & Poor's Composite Index of 500 stocks showed a return of 96% over the same period.

The experiences of General Mills and Gulf & Western are not unique. Other examples of companies refocusing abound: Outlet Co. got rid of most of its department and clothing-store holdings to concentrate on broadcasting; Esmark sold its energy holdings and spun off its meat-packing division to concentrate on consumer goods and specialty chemicals; Banner Industries sold its trucking business; Exxon divested its office-systems division; Gulf & Western sold more than 147 units and divisions worth $2 billion; ITT has divested at least 85 subsidiaries in recent years; Dravo Corp. sold all of its operations except its natural resources business; Baton Broadcasting got out of the printing and packaging industries so as to concentrate on its core broadcasting business.

Although it is difficult to pinpoint a particular year as the turning point in diversification, all available evidence suggests that 1980 may well be that year. For example, Williams et al. (1988) report that whereas in the period 1976–79 American conglomerates were increasing the scope of their activities, the period 1980–84 saw a reversal of this diversification trend. Specifically they found that the average number of business groups managed by a sample of 80 U.S. conglomerates increased from 4.79 in 1976 to 5.04 in 1979, but the holdings began to decline after 1980, reaching 4.58 in 1984.

Needless to say, this de-diversification effort represents a dramatic change in the evolution of the American corporation that begs for an explanation. It was only twenty years ago that the elite of corporate America was fully immersed in diversification and conglomeration. In fact all statistical evidence suggests that throughout the postwar period (1945 to 1980) American firms were diversifying (e.g., see Dugger 1985, p. 694; Mariotti and Ricotta 1987; Rumelt 1974, p. vi; Ravenscraft and Scherer 1987a, pp. 28–32). What has prompted the emergence of refocusing, and what has been its effect on the modern corporation? Furthermore, are *all* diversified firms refocusing, and if that is the case, why are they doing it *now*?

Refocusing has received prominent exposure in the business press where it has been heralded as a managerial revolution that will forever change the organizational structure and product mix of American companies. The 1980s have been dubbed the "era of restructuring," and the claim has been made that out of this turmoil have emerged companies that are "leaner and meaner" and are therefore more efficient vehicles for creating and distributing stockholder wealth (e.g., see *Business Week*, July 1, 1985, p. 50; *Fortune*, March 2, 1987, p. 37).

On the other hand, it is only very recently that the refocusing phenomenon has begun to appear in the academic literature (especially the strategy literature). Traditionally academic research had focused on issues such as the motivations for divestment (e.g., Duhaime and Grant 1984; Lewis 1983; Maupin 1987; Ravenscraft and Scherer 1987a,c) and divestment implementation (e.g., Bettauer 1967; Clarke and Gall 1987; Duhaime and Patton 1980; Harrigan 1980, 1981; Hayes 1972; Nees 1978, 1981; Porter 1976; Wright 1985). Furthermore the study of the effects and consequences of divestment (and refocusing) on the U.S. corporation had clearly remained the province of finance experts (see Markides and Berg 1988 for a survey of this literature). For example, of the 36 studies dealing with the consequences of divestment that I have identified in the academic literature of 1970 to 1990, 33 had been undertaken by finance specialists and 34 had used the event-study methodology based on financial assumptions. Only one study (Montgomery and Thomas 1988) had looked at the consequences of divestment from a strategy perspective or without using the event study methodology. Recently, however, strategy researchers have begun to explore the strategic implications of refocusing in a systematic way. Prominent examples of this research are the papers by Bethel and Liebeskind (1993), Bhide (1990), Comment and Jarrell (1991), Geroski and Gregg (1994), Gibbs (1993), Hoskisson and Johnson (1992), Hoskisson and Turk (1990), Hoskisson, Johnson, and Moesel (1994), Johnson, Hoskisson, and Hitt (1993), Lichtenberg (1992), Liebeskind and Opler (1992), Liebeskind, Opler, and Hatfield (1992), Liebeskind, Wiersema, and Hansen (1992), and Singh and Chang (1992).

Despite this recent research activity, there are still many questions about the specific strategy of refocusing that remain unanswered. At the most basic level, we still have very little systematic evidence on the extent of refocusing (e.g., Comment and Jarrell 1991; Lichtenberg 1992; Liebeskind and Opler 1992). Nor do we know the nature of the firms that are refocusing and the reasons they do so. The effect of refocusing on firm profitability and firm value is another area that needs exploration.

The purpose of this research is to study the extent and effect of refocusing in the period 1981–87. Some of the questions that I will try to answer in this study are the following:

1. Is there more refocusing taking place in the 1980s as compared to the 1960s? How prevalent is this phenomenon?

2. What are the characteristics of the firms that are refocusing?

3. Why are firms refocusing, and why do we observe this behavior now?

4. What is the effect of refocusing on firm value?

5. What is the effect of refocusing on firm profitability?

6. How do firms adjust their organizational structure to accommodate the new strategy of refocusing?

The study will be empirical in nature and will therefore be data driven. Given the importance of the phenomenon and the relatively scarce information on it, the goal will be to learn as much as possible about the causes and consequences of refocusing. Only then will we be able to offer informed opinions.

Summary of the Findings

The major findings from the study are the following:

• More firms were refocusing in the 1980s than in the 1960s. For example, in the 1960s only 1 percent of the top American companies were refocusing, while fully 25 percent were diversifying. By contrast, in the 1980s more than 20 percent of these firms were refocusing, while only 8 percent were diversifying. As a result the trend toward diversification that began more than fifty years ago is now reversing itself. In particular, there was a significant increase in the single-business firms, and a decrease in the unrelated-business firms within the population of Fortune 500 firms. This represents a major evolutionary change for the American corporation.

• Even though many firms refocused, a large number of firms continued to diversify. Consistent with profit-maximizing behavior, the firms that refocused were the "overdiversified" firms, while the firms that diversified were the "underdiversified" firms. The net effect of some firms diversifying and some refocusing was a relatively small change in average diversification and concentration levels in the economy as a whole. Thus the fear that all the restructuring of the 1980s would lead to higher concentration levels did not materialize.

• Firms refocused primarily by divesting unrelated businesses and acquiring related ones. For example, I estimated that the top 100 U.S. firms undertook 431 acquisitions and 302 divestitures in the period 1981–87. More than 65 percent of the acquisitions were related to the core business and almost 58 percent of the divestitures were unrelated to the core business.

• Significant refocusing activity was displayed by the conglomerates and the Fortune 100–200 firms.

• The firms that refocused were characterized by high diversification and poor performance relative to their industry counterparts. This implies that firms refocus in response to a performance crisis, possibly brought about by "excessive" diversification. In addition a firm is more likely to refocus the higher the profitability, size, concentration ratio, and advertising intensity of its core industry—that is, the higher the "attractiveness" of its core business. Firms whose managers feel they are a possible takeover target are also more likely to refocus, and this suggests that a lot of the restructuring of the 1980s was brought about by the threat of hostile takeovers. On the other hand, the higher the R&D intensity of the firm's core business, the lower is the likelihood that the firm will refocus. A change in the top management of the firm, as well as the firm's debt-to-equity ratio, have no effect on the refocusing decision.

• Refocusing announcements were associated with statistically significant positive abnormal returns, which implies that reductions in diversification create market value. On average, a firm's market value goes up by about 2 percent on the day it announces its refocusing. A firm's refocusing announcement is valued higher, if the firm is highly diversified and unprofitable. That is, the firms most in need of "surgery" gain the most from it. The capital market's expectation for improved performance after refocusing is not fulfilled in the short term, and this implies that it may take some time before refocusing's beneficial effects materialize.

• Consistent with event study interpretations, refocusing by the over-diversified firms is associated with profitability improvements. The effect of refocusing on profitability is not fully realized until after three to four years.

• The relationship between diversification and profitability is curvilinear. At low levels of diversity there exists a positive relationship between diversification and profitability; at high levels of diversity the relationship is negative. This means that a firm contemplating diversification can start from zero diversification and diversify *profitably* up its optimal limit. After this point the costs outweigh the benefits of additional diversification, so it doesn't pay for the firm to diversify any more. Every firm has a limit to how much it can diversify, but the optimal point differs according to a firm's resources.

• Refocusing is a necessary but not sufficient condition for improved performance: Firms must also adjust their organizational structure to accommodate the new strategy if the benefits of refocusing are to be fully realized. More specifically, refocused firms are better served by a centralized M-form structure, while high-diversity firms do better by adopting a more decentralized M-form structure,[3] which facilitates the exploitation of the advantages of an internal capital market.

• Along with the trend toward reduced diversification, there is a trend away from the M-form structure, toward the CM-form structure.

These results are consistent with the following scenario of diversification: At any point in time a firm has a limit to how much it can diversify. This limit is a function of the firm's resources and its external environment. For a variety of reasons many firms have diversified beyond this limit. As a result their profitability and market value have suffered. Primarily because of a stronger market for corporate control but also because of organizational learning, the overdiversified firms are now reducing their diversification to return to equilibrium. They are thus able to raise their profitability and market value. At the same time the underdiversified firms are following a profit-maximizing strategy by diversifying in an attempt to approach their optimal diversification limit.

Organization of the Book

The book is organized as follows: Chapter 2 provides the theoretical foundation of the research and presents the hypotheses that have emerged from this theory. Chapter 3 describes the sample and the research design. Chapter 4 presents a general overview of the refocusing phenomenon. Chapter 5 identifies the characteristics of the refocusing firms. Chapter 6 examines the ex ante valuation consequences of refocusing. Chapter 7 investigates the ex post profitability consequences of refocusing. Chapter 8 analyzes the relationship between organizational structure, refocusing, and profitability. Chapter 9 concludes with a summary and discussion of the results.

---

3. The centralized multidivisional structure (CM-form) differs from the M-form structure in that a CM-form company's head office gets involved in the operating decisions of the divisions.

2

Diversification, X-Inefficiencies, and the Optimum Size of the Firm: An Explanation of Corporate Refocusing

With Wall Street in the grip of merger mania, an equally significant trend (in the opposite direction) has gone almost unnoticed: America's oldest and biggest companies are busy divesting themselves of unwanted businesses. In the 1960s, rich big companies diversified widely and often wildly. Now conglomerates are keen to sell off many of their earlier acquisitions and to concentrate their efforts where the rate of return is highest.

The Economist, May 2, 1981, p. 74

Systematic evidence on the extent and effects of U.S. firms reducing their diversification is scarce. Even more scarce are plausible explanations of the refocusing. Why is the refocusing phenomenon taking place at all, and why is it taking place *now*?

The prevailing popular view is that firms are now getting rid of all those so-called bad acquisitions they made in the 1960s. However, such an explanation goes against existing evidence. For example, Montgomery and Wilson (1986) reported that of the 434 acquisitions made in 1967–69, more than 76 percent were still in place in 1982. Even if the acquisitions of the 1960s are now being divested, it is hard to see how investments that lasted for more than twenty years could be characterized as bad. It is even harder to understand how and why so many firms came to the same realization (that their acquisitions were mistakes) at the same time.

There are economic reasons why firms diversified in the 1960s, and there are economic reasons why they are trying to reduce their diversification in the 1980s. Our task is to find these reasons. This chapter will attempt to provide a possible economic explanation of refocusing, by making the following propositions:

1. Every firm has a limit to how much it can diversify. This limit is a function of the firm's characteristics (more specifically its nontransferable specific assets) and its external environment.

2. Some firms (but not all) have (for a variety of reasons) diversified beyond this limit. As a result their profitability and market value have suffered.

3. Primarily because of a stronger market for corporate control but also because of organizational learning, the overdiversified firms will be reducing their diversification to return to equilibrium. As a result their profitability and market value will improve.

A Limit to Diversification

According to Baysinger and Hoskisson (1990), Bhagat et al. (1990), Hoskisson and Turk (1990), and Shleifer and Vishny (1990, 1991), the refocusing of the 1980s can be understood as attempts by firms to reduce their excessive diversification, most of which occurred in the 1960s perhaps as a result of a strict antitrust policy in the United States. For example, Hoskisson and Turk (1990, p. 469) state that: "Restructuring actually provides the firm with a number of opportunities to restore value that has been dissipated through excess diversification." This line of reasoning implies two things: First, there is an optimal limit to how much firms can diversify (and hence firms that diversify beyond their limit have excessive diversification levels), and second, many firms (or at least those firms that are now refocusing) had actually diversified beyond their limits during the period 1960–80—an action that suggests non-profit-maximizing behavior.

That there is a limit to how much a firm can diversify is still a controversial issue in the economics literature (e.g., see Calvo and Wellisz 1978; Mueller 1987, pp. 26–29; Williamson 1967). In the strategy literature, on the other hand, it is now accepted that a firm cannot diversify indefinitely without running into diseconomies—especially managerial diseconomies to scale. For example, in their survey of the existing literature on diversification, Hoskisson and Hitt (1990, p. 474) argue that "research and theory ... suggest an overall curvilinear relationship between performance and diversification." Similarly, in their examination of diversification in Britain, Grant and Thomas (1988, p. 73) report that "the relationship between product diversity and [profitability] was quadratic in form."

Intuitively it would seem that in a world where transaction costs are not assumed away, there must be a limit to how much a firm can grow in size (i.e., that coordination costs lead to U-shaped average cost curves). Had this not been the case, the world would have been dominated by a single megafirm. That the world is not ruled by a huge monopolist implies that a firm cannot grow indefinitely without running into some form of diseconomies—especially managerial diseconomies to scale (see Keren and Levhari 1983).

The issue of whether there is a limit to how much a firm can diversify can be formulated in terms of marginal benefits (MB) and marginal costs (MC) to diversification. On the one hand, we know from the literature that there exist certain benefits to diversification. For example, transaction cost economists (e.g., Caves 1971; Gorecki 1975; Montgomery and Wernerfelt 1988; Teece 1982) have emphasized the benefits that arise when a firm diversifies to exploit its excess firm-specific assets (brand names, managerial skills, consumer loyalty, technological innovations, etc.), whose markets are characterized by imperfections. These assets cannot be traded in the market because of a variety of imperfections such as transaction costs in transferring the assets and externalities in the use of the assets (e.g., Gorecki 1975). The firm therefore diversifies so as to exploit these assets in other markets.

Other benefits to diversification include market-power advantages emphasized in the industrial organization (IO) literature (e.g., Berry 1971, 1974; Caves 1981; Gort 1962; Markham 1973; Rhoades 1973), tax benefits and other financial advantages conferred by diversification emphasized in the finance literature (e.g., Conn 1976; Galai and Masulis 1976; Lewellen 1971), the benefits associated with growth emphasized in the strategy literature (e.g., Guth 1980), and other miscellaneous benefits associated with reductions in agency problems (e.g., Aron 1988; Marshall et al. 1984). The existence of these benefits to diversification have been well-emphasized in the literature. Perhaps more important, the literature also tells us that the marginal benefits to diversification tend to decrease as the firm diversifies further away from its basic business. For example, Montgomery and Wernerfelt (1988) argue that a firm contemplating diversification will first try to apply its excess assets to the closest market it can enter. If excess capacity remains, the firm will enter markets even further afield. But as these factors are applied in more distant fields, they lose their competitive advantage and thus earn lower rents. This implies that the marginal benefits to diversification tend to decrease as the firm diversifies. This relationship between diversification and the marginal rents to diversification is shown graphically in figure 2.1.

These benefits to diversification are not achieved without cost. Penrose (1959), for example, has emphasized the long-run constraints associated with recruiting, training, and assimilating new managers as the firm grows. Williamson (1967) looked at the costs to diversification in terms of information processing. He argues that top management must gather information from the operating layers of the firm and send down directions based

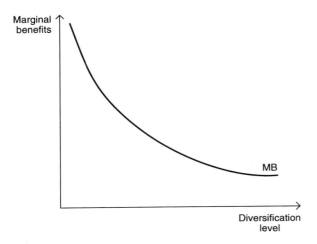

Figure 2.1
The marginal benefits of diversification

on the information gathered. Some of this information gets lost or gets distorted as it passes from one layer of the hierarchy to another. The loss of information and the inefficiencies that are created as a result constitute the costs of diversification.

Other types of costs emphasized in the literature include control and effort losses arising from increasing shirking as the firm diversifies (e.g., Calvo and Wellisz 1978), coordination costs and intrinsic diseconomies of scale in the expansion of the firm's hierarchical structure (e.g., Keren and Levhari 1983), X-inefficiencies created when managers continue to apply their existing "dominant logic" on newly acquired, strategically dissimilar businesses (e.g., Prahalad and Bettis 1986), disproportionate increases in the costs of coordination and control relative to real output as a result of limited managerial spans of control (e.g., Sutherland 1980), and the costs created when a "detached" corporate staff makes inappropriate and untimely interventions in the operations of the units (e.g., Ravenscraft and Scherer 1987a). The presence of such costs in today's firms has been demonstrated by many researchers (e.g., Finkelstein 1986; Kitching 1967; Ravenscraft and Scherer 1987a; Yavitz and Newman 1982). But again the literature also tells us what kind of functional relationship we should expect between diversification and the marginal costs of diversification: As the firm diversifies, the costs to diversification increase. For example, Williamson (1967) argues that as the firm diversifies, its hierarchy becomes steeper (i.e., more managerial layers are created) and as a result more infor-

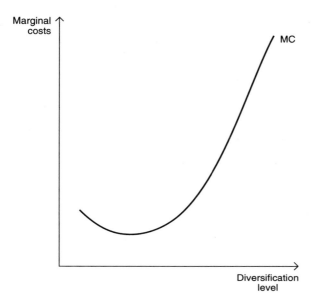

Figure 2.2
The marginal costs of diversification

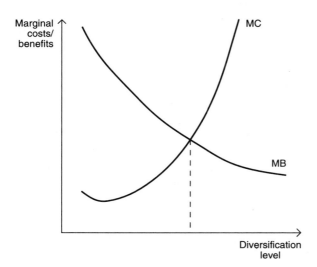

Figure 2.3
The optimal point of diversification

mation gets lost or distorted. Hence the costs of diversification increase. Similarly Prahalad and Bettis (1986) argue that as the firm diversifies into more strategically dissimilar businesses, the costs of applying an inappropriate dominant logic in a variety of businesses rise disproportionately. This discussion suggests that the relationship between diversification and the marginal costs of diversification is an increasing function as shown in figure 2.2.

Given the nature of these two curves, the existence of an optimal limit to diversification becomes immediately apparent when we put the two curves together, as in figure 2.3. The optimal diversification level is point D^* on the graph, where the marginal benefits to diversification equal its marginal costs. A firm that starts from zero diversification level can diversify profitably up to point D^*. After point D^* the costs outweigh the benefits of additional diversification, so it doesn't pay for the firm to diversify any more. Even though every firm has a different optimal point D^* (according to its resources), the important issue to note is that every firm has a limit to how much it can diversify.[1]

Even though this discussion has not explicitly addressed the issue of related versus unrelated diversification, the basic ideas presented here should not be affected by such distinction. For example, consider a firm that is primarily engaged in unrelated diversification. All that this implies is that the marginal benefit and marginal cost curves facing this firm are steeper than the curves facing a firm engaged in related diversification. This means that the unrelated diversifier will have a much lower optimal diversification level D^* and will find itself in an overdiversified position much sooner than the related diversifier. Note, however, that both firms still have a limit to how much they can diversify, and both will suffer if they go past their limit (but see also Markides and Williamson 1994, 1994a, for a more elaborate discussion of the strategy of related diversification). The same argument applies to firms that learn how to manage diversification as they go along: Organizational learning affects the slope

---

1. Every firm has a different optimal limit depending on its resources, its external environment, the type of diversification it is following (related versus unrelated), the caliber of its management team, its past diversification experiences, whether any learning occurred from other diversification experiences, and so on. For example, we would expect that a firm that has tried diversification in the past and has learned something from the experience would be able to manage more diversity (and hence have a bigger optimal diversification level D^*) than a "novice" diversifier. Similarly a firm that has good managers should be able to manage diversification better than a firm with bad managers. Identifying a firm's exact optimal diversification level is an impossible task—the optimal diversification limit for a firm is really a theoretical concept, much like the utility concept in economics, and cannot be measured precisely.

of their *MB* and *MC* curves but does not prevent firms from having a limit or from running into diseconomies once they pass this limit.

It is possible, however, that organizational learning does more than affect the slope of these curves. It may cause the *MB* and *MC* curves to curve upward or downward (raising the possibility of multiple optimal points for each firm), or it may cause continual shifts in these curves (raising the possibility that a firm may actually have no optimal point). Both of these scenarios are possible, but we do not believe they affect the analysis or the empirics that follow.[2]

Why Firms Diversify beyond D*

If a firm is profit maximizing, it should diversify up to the optimal point D^* (assuming it knows what this is) and then stop. According to Montgomery and Wernerfelt (1988), this is what all firms do: They stop diversifying when the marginal rents from an additional diversification move become subnormal (i.e., when they reach D^*). In their own words: "We envision a firm ... as having a queue of potential diversification opportunities. We argue that a firm, in electing to diversify, will begin with the most profitable opportunities and move toward the least profitable ones. Our expectation is that this process will end when marginal rents become subnormal" (Montgomery and Wernerfelt 1988, p. 631).

---

2. The *MC* and *MB* curves have been drawn monotonically rising and declining, respectively. This is probably an oversimplification: As a firm learns over time how to manage diversification, *MB* can curve upward before coming down again, while *MC* can curve downward before rising again. So there can be multiple optimal points for a firm. Furthermore, if learning by the firm leads to continual shifts in the curves (rather than simply affecting their slopes), a firm might have no optimal diversification limit. Finally, since both *MB* and *MC* are path dependent, a firm might not just have one (or multiple) optimal diversification points but rather a continually evolving (with time and experience) frontier of optimal diversification. Overall we have the possibilities of multiple equilibria, no equilibrium, or a continuously shifting frontier of equilibria (which ultimately implies no equilibrium).

All three scenarios are theoretically possible, but I do not believe that they affect the empirical analysis that follows. The existence of multiple equilibria does not prevent the outcome of overdiversified firms. All I want is to identify firms that are overdiversified and see what happens when they reduce their diversification. I am not concerned if firms are overdiversified because they went past their first, second, or third optimal point. Moreover, since this is a cross-sectional (rather than time series) study, I expect to capture at least some firms in an overdiversified position (even if in a few years time their optimal point increases and they become optimally diversified again). Finally, even if theoretically some firms have infinite learning abilities and manage to continually shift their optimal limit (and hence have no optimal limit), it is unlikely that too many such firms exist.

This line of reasoning implies that we should not expect to find any firms in the region beyond D^* because that is a region where no profits can be made and no rational firm will go there. Yet, as I will argue below, there are at least two reasons why we should expect to find some firms in the region beyond D^* (i.e., in an overdiversified position): Some firms have overinvested in diversification over the past thirty years primarily because of agency problems (but also for other reasons given below), and even firms that have invested optimally will find themselves in a disequilibrium when the optimal diversification level shifts to the left (mainly because of improvements in the external capital market).

Overinvestment in Diversification

Agency Reasons
Firms will overinvest in diversification (i.e., invest in projects whose net present value, NPV, is less than zero) when their managers pursue maximization of their own utility function rather than shareholder-value maximization (e.g., Hoskisson and Turk 1990).

According to agency theory (e.g., Jensen and Meckling 1976; Marris 1964; Williamson 1964) there is a natural divergence between managerial and shareholder utility functions: Shareholders want their firms to pursue profit maximization, whereas managerial interests are more aligned to a firm's continual expansion (because growth reduces managerial employment risk while increasing managerial compensation and nonpecuniary rewards; e.g., Murphy 1985, 1986). This means that in cases where managers retain substantial control over the allocation of company funds and can use these funds without any external monitoring, they will not return these funds to the shareholders but invest them—even in unprofitable projects —so as to sustain the firm's growth and increase its size. (This is consistent with the finding that management-controlled firms are more diversified than owner-controlled firms; Amihud et al. 1983). According to the free–cash flow hypothesis (e.g., Jensen 1986) as well as the firm life-cycle hypothesis (e.g., Mueller 1972), the conditions for such behavior are ripe for firms in mature industries that generate more earnings than can be profitably reinvested. As a result managers can use these retained earnings to finance their "wasteful" investments without resorting to the external capital market, which can monitor and discipline them. This discussion suggests that in mature industries we should expect to find *some* firms that systematically overinvest (in diversification).

The validity of this theory has been tested by comparing the rate of return of projects financed by retained earnings, versus the rate of return of projects financed by outside capital. The theory predicts that since retained earnings can be invested without outside monitoring, they will be used to finance low or even negative NPV projects. Thus the *marginal* rate of return on retained earnings will be low compared to the return on new capital.

Mueller (1987, pp. 35–43) reports several studies that have looked at the *marginal* returns on investment and tend to support this prediction: Baumol, Heim, Malkiel, and Quandt ([BHMQ] 1970) divided investment into its three sources—new debt, new equity, and ploughback—and estimated the returns on each. They found that (1) the rate of return on new equity (14.5 to 20.8 percent) was higher than the return on new debt (4.2 to 14 percent), and substantially higher than the rate of return on ploughback (3 to 4.6 percent), and (2) the rate of return on ploughback was substantially lower than what shareholders could have earned by investing in the market (Fisher and Lorie 1964).

In a subsequent exchange between the authors of this article and Friend and Husic (1973), it was established that overinvestment behavior is especially pronounced in mature firms that do not rely on the external capital market for financing. For example, BHMQ (1973) estimate that for firms that did not issue any equity, the returns to ploughback are all negative. In a direct test of this proposition, Grabowski and Mueller (1975) estimated the returns on investment out of all sources of finance for "mature" firms versus "young" firms. For young firms the returns ranged from 13.7 to 26.3 percent. For mature firms the corresponding returns ranged from 9.2 to 12.5 percent, which were still lower than the average stock market returns in the period.

Similar results have been reported by Hiller (1978) for the United States, McFetridge (1978) for Canada, and Brealey, Hodges, and Capron (1976) for the United Kingdom. A recent study by Kallapur (1990) also reports supporting results that are not sensitive to the method used to calculate return on retained earnings and fresh capital. Overall, the proposition that in the absence of external discipline, firms in mature industries will tend to overinvest in diversification appears to be supported by the empirical literature. Thus we would expect that from a random sample of firms, some of them will be overdiversified.

Another way to determine whether firms overdiversify is to look at the market reaction to reductions in diversification: If a firm is pursuing diversification for profit-maximization purposes, then an efficient capital market should evaluate this behavior in a positive way (unless real information asymmetries exist; Myers and Majluf 1984). Put differently, a firm that invests in diversification up to the optimal point should experience a reduction in market value when it reduces its diversification. Yet the exact opposite happens. As I show in chapter 6, refocusing announcements create statistically significant positive abnormal returns, implying that a reduction in diversification creates market value. Similarly an abundance of event studies on divestitures (e.g., Markides and Berg 1988) find that all types of voluntary divestitures create value. These results suggest that some firms have overinvested in diversification.

The same conclusion emerges when we look at the number of firms reducing their diversification. If firms diversify optimally, then at any point in time only a small number of firms would deviate from equilibrium (by accident). Yet, as it will be shown in chapter 4, roughly 50 percent of the 205 firms in the sample are reducing their diversification in the period 1981 to 1987. It's very unlikely that so many firms found themselves in disequilibrium by accident.

The Hubris Hypothesis

It is not only non-profit-maximizing firms that may have overinvested in diversification. It is also possible for a profit-maximizing firm to overinvest in diversification. This will occur in a systematic way if managerial and shareholder *expectations* (rather than objectives) differ systematically. Such a disequilibrium will arise if (for whatever reason) managers are overoptimistic of their ability to transfer assets across industries. That is, if managers have excessive faith in their ability to manage all kinds of businesses, they will (mistakenly) assign a higher value to D^* than what it really is for their firms, and will therefore diversify beyond the optimum.

This is, in essence, Roll's (1986) hubris hypothesis. It seems to be especially applicable to managerial behavior on diversification in the 1960s: Given that diversification was a relatively new phenomenon for which little information existed, and keeping in mind that the 1960s were years of general business euphoria, it is very likely that managers—armed as they were with the latest portfolio techniques developed in consulting firms—felt especially confident of their abilities to manage a diverse portfolio of businesses. Encouraged by the need to grow to attract new managerial talent, they therefore diversified beyond what was prudent.

This argument implies that as time went by, more information about diversification became available, and organizational learning occurred. Thus we would expect these same managers to have learned from their mistakes and to be now willing to correct them. The recent emergence of refocusing may signify exactly this.

The Role of the Capital Market

Systematic overinvestment in diversification will also have occurred if the capital market provided wrong signals and incentives to profit-maximizing firms (e.g., Matsusaka 1990; Morck, Shleifer, and Vishny 1990; Shleifer and Vishny 1991). For example, both Matsusaka (1990) and Morck et al. (1990) found that in the 1960s the stock market reacted positively to diversifying acquisitions, a fact that encouraged firms to engage in such activities. However, the ex post evidence on these diversifications shows that the capital market's reaction may have been a mistake (e.g., Kaplan and Weisbach 1990; Porter 1987; Ravenscraft and Scherer 1987). According to Shleifer and Vishny (1991, p. 58): "... the mistaken market enthusiasm about particular events such as conglomerate mergers is a commonplace equilibrium occurrence in financial markets. The fact that the market thought that conglomerates were a good idea does not mean that they were."

Why was the capital market sending "wrong" signals? This could have been the case either because the market was inefficient or because the information it had at the time led it to the wrong signals. Both of these reasons may have been in operation in the 1960s. It is now widely accepted that the stock market systematically "overvalued" the stock price of companies that grew by acquisition in the 1960s. The game (which came to be known as the chain-letter effect) went like this: A "growth" company whose stock is selling at a high multiple acquires a low P/E company. As a result the earnings per share (EPS) of the acquiring company increase (by simple arithmetic). The market applies the high multiplier on the new EPS, and so the stock price of the firm goes up. As Jacoby (1969, p. 9) argues: "This makes further acquisitions through exchange of stock attractive. They are the basis of a further expansion in reported earnings per share and further inflation of the price of the stock."

The question is, Why would a company made up of (say) six zero-growth components be valued so highly by the market? In other words, why did the market continue to apply the high multiple on a company that's made up of nongrowing acquired parts? One could argue that the capital market in the 1960s was not as sophisticated nor efficient as it is now, but this line of argument does not resolve the issue.

Another explanation has been offered by Jacoby (1969) who argues that promoters and bankers take advantage of the optimism of the public during stock market booms to generate profits for themselves. Thus the above game "... can continue until the public recognizes that there is no growth in the operating earnings of the acquired companies. The price of the conglomerate's stock then plummets to a point where the *P/E* ratio is normal. At this much lower price, further acquisitions are unattractive and cease. Meanwhile, promoters will probably have unloaded their shares on *less sophisticated* investors, and bankers will have pocketed their commissions" (Jacoby 1969, p. 9, my emphasis). Again this explanation rests on the assumption that less sophisticated investors exist and can be taken advantage of. This goes against the notion of efficient capital markets (but the similarity of this story with the recent rise and fall of the junk-bond market cannot be overlooked).

The existence of sophisticated investors who knowingly buy an overvalued stock can be explained, within the framework of an efficient capital market, by the speculative bubble argument: Investors knowingly pay more for a stock than it is worth, in the belief that they can pass it on for even more. Investors know full well that the bubble may burst, but they are willing to take this risk given the high rewards of selling the stock at a high price. For the investors this is just a high-risk/high-reward gamble, but the effect on the firm could be harmful: It creates incentives for the firm to continue its diversification (through acquisitions), even beyond the optimal level.

A final explanation for the overvaluation of conglomerate stocks in the 1960s may be that the market didn't know better, given the information it had at the time. Conglomerate diversification was a relatively new phenomenon at the time, so it is perfectly possible that the market favored diversification during this period given the information it had. When ex post diversification did not prove as profitable as expected, the market adjusted its valuation. This explanation is consistent with the results of Morck, Shleifer, and Vishny (1989). They find that while diversification in the 1970s did not reduce shareholders' wealth, returns to diversification declined substantially in the 1980s. Nevertheless, whatever the causes of the overvaluation of conglomerate stocks, its effect has been to provide incentives to firms to overinvest in diversification.

A Shift in the Optimal Level

So far we have argued that primarily because of agency problems (but also because of other reasons), many firms have overinvested in diversification. All available evidence supports this view. Even casual observation of the diversification (mis)adventures of the oil, steel, and tobacco industries lends support to this proposition. Certainly the very existence of diversified firms whose breakup value is bigger than their market value lends support to this proposition (e.g., *Business Week*, July 8, 1985, p. 80).

In this section we will argue that over the past twenty years, changes in the real and financial markets have reduced the optimal level of diversification for most firms. Thus even firms that were optimally diversified a few years ago are now in a state of disequilibrium. A reduction in the optimal level of diversification will occur either because the costs of diversification have increased or because the benefits of diversification have decreased (these shifts in the *MB* and *MC* curves of a diversified firm and the resultant decrease in D^* are shown graphically in figure 2.4). We will argue that both of these events may have taken place over the past twenty years.

Reduction in Benefits
Over the past twenty years the external capital market has become more efficient. Therefore the main function of a diversified firm—that of acting

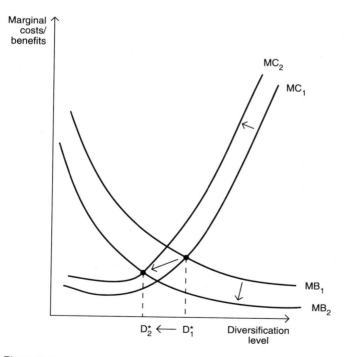

Figure 2.4
Shift in the optimal level of diversification

as an internal banker to its divisions—does not create (as much) value any more.

One of the advantages of diversification emphasized in the literature has been the informational advantages of a diversified firm's "internal capital market" relative to the external capital market (Weston 1970; Williamson 1975). For example, a firm can draw capital from slow-growing divisions to supply high-growing ones without having to disclose sensitive information to the outside world. In addition corporate managers tend to have information advantages over outside investors in evaluating and disciplining divisions, as well as in deciding what division needs cash and what division can supply this cash (Salter and Weinhold 1979). It has been argued (Bhide 1989) that the relative advantages of the internal capital market over the external one have been eroded, as a result of changes and improvements in the external capital market over the past decade.

Bhide (1989, 1990) argues that in the past, business on Wall Street was based on personal relationships (rather than merit) and competition was limited. In addition investment banks were small and thinly capitalized. However, the deregulation of the industry (e.g., "Mayday" 1975 and SEC rule 415 in 1982) introduced competition into a sedate industry, and competition brought with it innovations and improvements. For example, banks were forced to develop professional research departments and hire young talented individuals to analyze companies. These analysts came from the best business schools and specialized on specific companies or industries. As a result the external capital market was now in a better position to do a good job in evaluating companies.

At the same time companies were forced to disclose more and better information about their businesses. For example, Bhide (1989, p. 23) points out that: "By the end of 1986, FASB had issued more than 80 opinions requiring public firms to disclose, among other things, line of business information, unfunded pension liabilities, foreign currency exposures and their replacement cost accounts." The result of all this has been to erode the informational advantages of the internal capital market relative to the external one.

The rising sophistication of the external capital market may have eroded another advantage of the diversified firm. Although it has been argued that corporate diversification is of no service to individual investors because they can diversify their risk through portfolio diversification (Levy and Sarnat 1970), we can now argue that optimal portfolio diversification may not have been possible in the past, given the uncompetitive nature of the industry. Hence corporate diversification may indeed have been of value to investors in that it allowed them to diversify their risk. However, with the elimination of fixed commissions in 1975 and with the increasing competition among brokers, commission fees have dropped dramatically and portfolio diversification became a cheaper and easier alternative. As a result corporate diversification has lost some of its usefulness. Overall, the improved sophistication of the capital market has eroded the traditional advantages of corporate diversification and has therefore reduced the optimal level of diversification.

Increases in Costs

The downward shift of the marginal benefits curve has been accompanied by a similar upward shift of the marginal costs curve. The main proposition advanced here is that the marginal costs of diversification have increased significantly as a result of a more volatile and uncertain economic environment.

Several authors have identified and examined the various costs associated with diversification (e.g., see Hill and Hoskisson 1987; Mueller 1972, 1987; Penrose 1959; Prahalad and Bettis 1986; Slater 1980; Sutherland 1980; Williamson 1967). Penrose (1959) was the first to propose that the main limitation to a firm's growth is a *managerial* one: The firm's growth is constrained by its ability to recruit, train, and assimilate new management. When it diversifies, existing management must be diverted to the training and supervision (control) of new managers. In addition the increased number of managers must learn how to work together as a team. As a result current production costs increase, and these constitute the opportunity costs of diversification (Slater 1980).

Williamson (1967) looked at the limits to diversification in terms of information processing. He argues that top management must gather information from the operating layers of the firm and send down directions based on the information gathered. Some of this information gets lost or gets distorted as it passes from one layer of the hierarchy to another. Hence there is an optimal size to the firm, beyond which the distortions caused by information loss outweigh the benefits of diversification.

Another problem of complex hierarchies involves the monitoring of employees. Calvo and Wellisz (1978) argue that at any level in the hierarchy, employees (and managers) work less than maximum (they shirk) because they know that their efforts are not monitored perfectly by their superiors. Because perfect monitoring is costly, if not impossible, the best a firm (team) can do is to invest in monitoring up to the point where its marginal costs equal the marginal benefits from reduced shirking (Alchian and Demsetz 1972). This implies that some degree of residual shirking will always exist. In the Calvo-Wellisz model the control or effort loss arising from shirking is assumed to be noncumulative (in direct contrast to the Williamson model where information loss is assumed to be cumulative). This assumption leads the authors to conclude that there is no optimal limit to firm size.

Mueller (1987) has reconciled these two views by arguing that some types of information (e.g., information on shirking) may have to pass through one or a few layers of hierarchy as Calvo and Wellisz argue, while other types of information (e.g., R&D inventions) may have to pass through all the layers of the hierarchy, as Williamson argues. Mueller (1987, p. 28) concludes: "If this view is accurate, there may exist finite limits to a company's ability to expand and process some kinds of information efficiently, but not with respect to other kinds of information."

Another type of diseconomy arising from diversification has been proposed by Prahalad and Bettis (1986). They argue that at a given point in time, a management team has an inbuilt limit to the extent of diversity it can manage. Every management team operates under a "dominant logic," which is defined as "the way in which managers conceptualize the business and make critical resource allocation decisions" (Prahalad and Bettis 1986, p. 490). This logic consists of "beliefs, theories, and propositions that have developed over time, based on the manager's personal experiences" (p. 489). Similar businesses can be managed using a single dominant logic, but as the firm diversifies, its "strategic variety" increases and multiple logics are required for effective management. The firm's size is therefore limited by the ability of management to develop and handle a variety of dominant logics. What usually happens is that managers continue to apply their existing dominant logic on newly acquired, strategically dissimilar businesses, and as a result inefficiencies (X-inefficiencies) are created.

A formal analysis of some of these inefficiencies has been undertaken by Sutherland (1980). They include (1) "inordinate increases in the costs of coordination and control relative to real output (procedural diseconomies), usually as a result of limitations on the 'span of management' associated with any existing protocol," and (2) "unfavorable discontinuities in the expected value of decision errors, these forcing an acceleration of the positive opportunity costs or losses associated with investment decisions" (Sutherland 1980, p. 964).

In simpler language, the inefficiencies created by organizational complexity can be explained as follows: To function properly, a corporation needs to understand and process information efficiently. The information-processing requirements of a corporation are a function of the number of divisions relevant for decision making and the amount of interdependence between divisions (Hill and Hoskisson 1987). As the number of divisions increases, and as unrelatedness increases, so does the information processing requirement. This leads to more reporting requirements, more layers of management, bigger corporate staffs, more bureaucracy, more delays, and rising organizational sclerosis (e.g., see Wright and Thompson 1987).

At the same time, since corporate management doesn't really know its business units, it has to rely more and more on short-term (quarterly) reports to evaluate its units. This leads to "management by the numbers" (Ravenscraft and Scherer 1987, p. 139), which leads to short-term orientation, misguided investments or disinvestments, inappropriate and untimely interventions in the operations of the units, resentment, loss of morale, and so on (the situation is even worse if the accounting numbers used to evaluate the units are inappropriate; see Johnson and Kaplan 1987). Furthermore, as the number of units increases, and as the information processing requirement increases, bounded rationality sets in—a particular executive can manage only a small number of diverse businesses. His/her span of control is small, and this in itself creates inefficiencies and prompts the creation of additional management layers and more complex reporting requirements.

Finally, the interaction of the multidivisional structure with the ever-expanding size of the firm further retards the integration of the different units (Lawrence and Lorsch 1967), which creates conflicts and loss of direction, and leads to mechanistic "portfolio management." All these inefficiencies can be classified under the umbrella of X-inefficiency (Leibenstein 1966). That they exist in today's firms has been demonstrated by many researchers (e.g., Finkelstein 1986; Kitching 1967; Ravenscraft and Scherer 1987; Yavitz and Newman 1982).

Given the above analysis on the costs of diversification, it is easy to take the next step and argue that they are all a function of the external complexity facing the firm. Since the external environment has now become more uncertain and complex (because of technological, economic, social, and political changes), these costs must have gone up. For example, as Mueller (1987, p. 29) argues: "In a rapidly changing environment, or in areas in which change is inherent in the task, as in the introduction of innovation, the relevant information to be gathered and the criteria for monitoring performance are so varied that information and control loss problems must loom large."

As another example of the effects of environmental uncertainty on the costs of diversification, consider the way top management usually evaluates division managers. Since corporate management doesn't really know the business of its divisions, it has to rely on general indicators of performance (e.g., ROA and ROS) to evaluate its division managers. In the short run, or when the environment is stable, these indicators may be reliable. But if the environment is changing, these indicators will be inadequate.

That external volatility accentuates the costs of diversification is also directly derived from the "dominant logic" argument: As the environment changes, so does the "strategic variety" that a given management team has to face. As a result top management has to revise its dominant logic or face the additional diseconomies of applying an inappropriate logic on "new" businesses. Revising the dominant logic (or adding a new one) is extremely difficult—and almost impossible without some outside stimulus. Thus the result of external volatility is mismanagement. As Mueller (1972, p. 204) argues: "The decisions regarding what data are to be collected and what rules of thumb are to be employed to formulate the orders must be based on the past experience of the firm. But it is precisely in situations in which change plays a significant role that past experience is an inadequate guide to the future and rules of thumb frequently break down."

Not only does environmental uncertainty increase the costs of diversification, but it can also limit the exploitation of synergistic economies among divisions, as well as limit the overall flexibility of the firm. Hill and Hoskisson (1987, pp. 339–40) argue:

Environmental uncertainty places a premium on flexibility. Using linkages between divisions to realize vertical or synergistic economies may be a major cause of inflexibility and poor responsiveness. If divisions are tied to each other by investments in specific technological assets, then in circumstances where technology is rapidly changing (when uncertainty is high) the advantages of being closely linked may become outdated overnight. In such circumstances, flexibility is better maintained by not emphasizing linkages. This implies that potential synergistic and vertical gains will be lost as firms switch their focus to realizing financial economies.

Overall, we can conclude that the volatile environment of the 1980s has increased the costs of diversification and has thus reduced the optimal level of diversification of firms.[3]

---

3. The development of new and improved Management Information Systems in the 1980s may have counterbalanced the effect of environmental uncertainty on diversification. For example, better information systems could allow better monitoring of divisional managers and may have therefore reduced shirking. This suggests that firms might have diversified more, not less, for the same level of organization costs.

The Market for Corporate Control

If firms are overdiversified (either because they have overinvested in diversification or because the optimal level of diversification is now lower), it follows that their profitability and market value must suffer. (That this is indeed the case is evidenced by the big gap between the market value of many firms and their breakup value.) This implies that the appropriate remedial action will be for firms to reduce their diversification levels. A firm can proceed to do this either voluntarily (e.g., Donaldson 1990), or by "force"—some outside disciplinary force may prompt firms to take the necessary actions (e.g., Hoskisson and Turk 1990; Shleifer and Vishny 1990).

Although we cannot rule out the possibility that in the 1980s the costs of overdiversification became so great that firms voluntarily undertook the necessary restructuring (e.g., Donaldson 1990), it is highly unlikely that they did so without some outside impetus (e.g., see Hoskisson and Turk 1990; Jensen 1993). A bigger and more sophisticated market for corporate control may have provided the necessary impetus (e.g., Shleifer and Vishny 1990). Indeed, as is reported later in this book, from a questionnaire survey of 149 of Fortune 500 firms, we find that among the firms that restructured in the 1980s, more than 72 percent did so because their CEOs felt that the firms were a possible takeover target. In other words, even though these firms may have not actually been takeover targets, they still restructured because they were afraid of the market for corporate control. Similarly Mitchell and Lehn (1990) report that the takeover targets of the 1980s are those firms that had made value-destroying acquisitions in the past. Hence takeover-induced restructurings appear to represent a significant portion of all the restructurings taking place (see also Bethel and Liebeskind 1993; Johnson, Hoskisson, and Hitt 1993).[4]

The market for corporate control (also known as the *takeover market*) has been defined as "a market in which alternative managerial teams compete for the rights to manage corporate resources" (Jensen and Ruback 1983,

---

4. This is not to deny the importance of product-market discipline or the influence of the Board of Directors on restructuring. In a recent paper Gibbs (1993, p. 66) argues that "... since firms with strong governance restructured, it does indicate that factors in addition to agency costs are driving restructuring." It can therefore be argued that as global competition intensified in the 1980s, more and more firms were "forced" to refocus (in response to poor financial results) by their boards of directors. However, our questionnaire results seem to suggest that even in cases where the restructuring appears to be voluntary (e.g., brought about by the board), the fear of takeover may have been the primary catalyst for the board to act (e.g., Markides and Singh 1994).

p. 6). Black and Grundfest (1988) credit this market for creating $162 billion in shareholder value in the period 1981–86. Jensen (1989) estimates that transactions associated with this market created gains of more than $500 billion between 1977 and 1988 (for target companies alone). The merits and achievements of this market have been trumpeted enough in finance journals. Here I will only be concerned with an explanation for why this market emerged as such a dominant force in the 1980s. In other words, why did this market remain "idle and ineffective" all these years, and what prompted its sudden emergence now?

Jensen (1989) credits the emergence of the market for corporate control to the "rebirth of active investors." These are investors such as the entrepreneurs Carl Icahn and Ronald Perelman as well as LBO firms such as KKR and family funds such as those controlled by the Pritzkers and the Bronfmans, all of whom became more active in the running of companies in which they held large equity stakes. The main reason they decided to "all of a sudden" become more involved in the running of these companies was the fact that these companies were managed very inefficiently by their existing managers as a result of a real separation between ownership and control in the modern corporation.

But why did the rebirth of active investors occur in the 1980s? Jensen argues that managerial inefficiencies became so large, and the lost value so great, that it was inevitable that someone would try to take advantage of the situation. However, certain other changes took place in the 1980s that facilitated the emergence and growth of the active investors. Jarrell, Brickley, and Netter (1988) and Jensen (1988) provide a list of some of these factors. They include:

1. The relaxation of antitrust regulations under the Reagan presidency.

2. Deregulation of several industries such as airlines, oil and gas, financial services, broadcasting, and transportation.

3. "Improvements in takeover technology, including a larger supply of increasingly sophisticated legal and financial advisers" (Jensen 1988, p. 24).

4. The growing availability of debt primarily due to financing innovations such as the junk-bond market whose size in 1989 was estimated to be at least $200 billion (Light 1989).

5. "The retreat by the federal courts and regulatory agencies from protecting besieged target firms" (Jarrell et al. 1988, p. 50).

6. A growing awareness of the potential benefits of takeovers.

Other changes that may have contributed to the growth of the takeover market were, on the one hand, a higher concentration of stock ownership, primarily because individual investors withdrew from the stock market and their place was taken by large institutions, and, on the other, the support that new institutional investors such as pension funds and the venture capital arms of commercial banks provided to buyout promoters. For example, in the case of stock ownership, Bhide (1989) reports that in 1986 stocks accounted for only 21 percent of individuals' financial assets as compared to 43 percent in 1968; by contrast, institutional ownership of stocks grew from 31 percent in 1970 to 39 percent in 1986—institutional ownership of the top one hundred industrial firms was about 53 percent in 1986. These changes increased shareholder power and provided incentives for them to become more active and aggressive in the management of their firms. In the case of institutional investors, Bhide (1989) reports that by 1987 a total of $15 billion of institutional funds had been committed to the buyout business.

The power of investors over management may have also been strengthened by a sour economic climate that threatened the financial self sufficiency of corporations. Despite their general aversion of the external capital market, many firms had to turn to it for financing as their profits suffered during the 1982 recession.

Back in 1972 Mueller had observed that "management's pursuit of growth is presumably limited only by the availability of investment funds, the threat of takeover by an outside stockholder group should the market price of the firm fall very low, and compassion for the stockholders" (Mueller 1972, p. 206). Given the conditions that existed at that time, Mueller concluded that none of these three factors was strong enough to constrain management. However, as argued above, things changed in the 1980s. At least the first two constraints given by Mueller were strong enough to encourage management to take corrective actions or face unemployment. A strong market for corporate control implies that management no longer has the luxury of maintaining an inefficient organization.[5]

Implications

For the reasons given above, we would expect many firms to have over-diversified in the period 1960 to 1980. Their profitability and market value

---

5. See also Fligstein and Markowitz (1994) for a sociological explanation of the emergence of restructuring in the 1980s.

have suffered as a result. External pressures are now forcing these firms to reduce their diversification to a more manageable level. This return to equilibrium should help firms improve their performance and market value (see also Hoskisson and Turk 1990 for very similar propositions). Therefore

PROPOSITION 1   Compared to the 1960s there will be a significantly larger number of firms that are refocusing in the 1980s.

PROPOSITION 2   Relative to their industry counterparts the refocusing firms will be characterized by high diversification and poor performance.

The rationale for these propositions derives directly from the notion of the existence of an optimal limit to diversification: Most firms set out on their diversification programs in the early 1950s (Rumelt 1974). It is therefore likely that at the beginning of this diversification effort, most firms are moving toward their optimal region and very few will have gone over it. Even if a few firms have overdiversified so early in the process, they will be under little pressure to refocus, given the state of the market for corporate control in the 1960s. So we should not expect too much refocusing in the 1960s. As time went by, however, firms diversified more and more, and a larger number of firms passed their optimal region. These are the firms that are under pressure in the 1980s to refocus. They are under pressure precisely because their overdiversification has created a performance crisis for them (hence proposition 2). We should therefore find more firms refocusing in the 1980s.

    If refocusing is the appropriate remedial action for the overdiversified firms, we should expect that by refocusing they will improve their profitability and market value. As long as we can define ex ante who the overdiversified firms are

PROPOSITION 3   For the overdiversified firms reductions in diversification will lead to profitability improvements.

PROPOSITION 4   For the overdiversified firms reductions in diversification will lead to market value increases.

Since all that the theoretical analysis has established is that a lot of firms may be overdiversified, propositions 3 and 4 do not say that all firms that reduce their diversification will improve their performance, nor do they imply that all firms should be reducing their diversification. Rather they point out that from a random sample of firms there will be many that are in equilibrium with appropriate diversification as well as many that are just

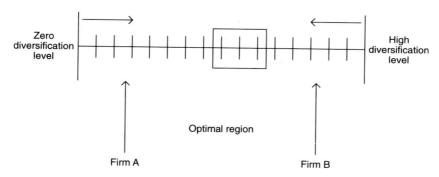

Figure 2.5
The spectrum of diversification

beginning on their diversification programs. It would be a mistake to argue that these firms will derive no benefits from diversification.

More specifically, the analysis on the "optimal" level of diversification suggests the following: Think of firms as located along a finite diversification spectrum that is normalized for each firm's structural environment and assets (see figure 2.5). At one end of this spectrum we find undiversified firms such as firm A. On the other side we find overdiversified firms such as firm B. Somewhere in the middle lies the hazy region of "optimum" diversification.

Looking at this spectrum in a dynamic way, we would expect that in the *population* of diversified firms (or from a *random* sample of these firms), some will be below their optimal diversification level while others will be above theirs. Assuming profit-maximizing behavior on the part of these firms, we should find that the underdiversified firms will be *increasing* their diversification, moving toward the optimal region, while the overdiversified firms will be *decreasing* their diversification, also moving toward the optimal region. Therefore

PROPOSITION 5   In the 1980s the *single-business* firms will be on average increasing their diversification, while the *unrelated-business* firms will be on average decreasing their diversification.

PROPOSITION 6   At low levels of diversity there exists a *positive* relationship between diversification and changes in profitability, while at high levels of diversity the relationship is *negative*.

The importance of proposition 6 cannot be overemphasized. It implies, as figure 2.6 shows, that the relationship between diversification and profitability is not linear but curvilinear (see also Grant and Thomas 1988;

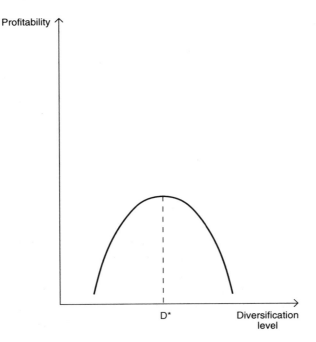

Figure 2.6
Relationship between diversification and profitability

Grant, Jammine, and Thomas 1986; Hoskisson and Hitt 1990). At low
levels of diversity the marginal benefits to diversification exceed the marginal costs, so increases in diversification lead to profitability improvements. Maximum profitability is achieved at point D^*, which is the optimal
point of diversification ($MB = MC$). Any movement beyond D^* will lead
to a profitability deterioration because in the region beyond D^* the marginal costs to diversification exceed its marginal benefits.

Summary

In this chapter I have tried to provide a possible economic explanation of
corporate refocusing by proposing the following "story" of diversification:
At any given point in time, every firm has a limit to how much it can
diversify. This limit is a function of the firm's resources and its external
environment. For a variety of reasons many firms have diversified beyond
this limit over the past thirty years. As a result their profitability and
market value have suffered. Primarily because of a stronger market for

corporate control in the 1980s, but also because of organizational learning, the overdiversified firms are now reducing their diversification to return to equilibrium. This should improve their profitability and market value.

Recent empirical evidence seems to support this notion. For example, research by Hoskisson and Johnson (1989) suggests that corporate restructuring increases with high levels of corporate diversification. Markides (1992a) and Montgomery and Wilson (1986) have found that restructuring is associated with a firm's poor performance. Bhagat, Shleifer, and Vishny (1990), Markides (1990), Mitchell and Lehn (1990), and Shleifer and Vishny (1990) present evidence that the market for corporate control accounts for a lot of the restructuring of the 1980s. And Comment and Jarrell (1991) and Markides (1992) have found that refocusing is generally associated with statistically significant positive abnormal returns, which suggests that refocusing creates market value. Similarly Lichtenberg (1990) has found that diversification has a negative effect on productivity.

Of course there are other possible explanations for why firms refocus. For example, Turk and Baysinger (1989) proposed that changes in the tax rates in the 1980s could account for some of this restructuring. However, as argued by Hoskisson and Turk (1990, p. 460), since the incidence of restructuring increases with high levels of corporate diversification, then the most likely explanation of refocusing must be overdiversification.

The test of any theory is how well its implications fit real life data. The rest of this book is therefore devoted to the testing of the implications outlined above against existing data. Further refinements to the theory can be made only when we have more empirical evidence available.

3   Research Design

Given the diversity of propositions outlined in the previous chapter, a *variety* of methodologies and samples will be used to test them. For example, the effect of refocusing on profitability will be examined through regression analysis, using a sample of 250 Fortune 500 firms. By contrast, the market value consequences of refocusing will be studied through event-study methodology, using a sample of forty-five refocusing announcements. The details of the different methodologies and samples used will be elaborated in the individual chapters that follow. This chapter will present the "main" sample of 250 firms, give a small summary of the different methodologies used in the study, and describe in detail the two most important variables in the whole study—refocusing and profitability.

The Main Sample

A sample of 250 firms was randomly selected from the 1985 Fortune 500 list, in the following fashion: Fifty firms were drawn from the Fortune 100, 50 from the Fortune 100–200, 50 from the Fortune 200–300, and so on. The population of Fortune 500 firms was selected for study because it contains most of the firms that engaged in refocusing activities in the period. A stratified sample is used to make sure that firms from the whole size spectrum are represented in the sample. The 1985 list was chosen as a convenient midpoint in the decade; unfortunately, a few firms were lost from the original sample because they ceased to exist after 1986 (due to acquisitions, mergers, and liquidations). All in all, thirty-one firms were lost after 1986 (five from the Fortune 100, eleven from the Fortune 100–200, five from the Fortune 200–300, six from the Fortune 300–400, and four firms from the Fortune 400–500).

This fact should be kept in mind. As we will see later in the statistical analyses, additional firms will be dropped from the base sample because of missing information on Compustat, the Center for Research in Security Prices (CRSP) tapes, and the TRINET tapes. Thus for different analyses different-sized samples will be used. It should be noted, though, that the smallest the sample ever gets is 200 firms.

Methodologies

Four basic methodologies will be used to test the propositions raised in the previous chapter:

1. The characteristics of refocusing firms (proposition 2), will be identified by a logit analysis on the full sample of 250 (now 219) firms.

2. The ex ante market valuation consequences of refocusing (proposition 4) will be examined through event-study analysis on a sample of forty-five refocusing announcements. In addition regression analysis is employed to find the reasons why the market reacts positively for some firms and negatively for others. Finally, the event-study methodology is again used to study in more detail the strategic moves undertaken by four firms.

3. The ex post profitability consequences of refocusing (propositions 3 and 6) will be studied through regression analysis, on the full sample of 219 firms.

4. The interactions between a firm's organizational structure, refocusing and profitability will be examined through a questionnaire survey. A questionnaire was sent to 457 firms and 136 valid replies were received. The information from these questionnaires will be analyzed using ANOVA and regression analysis.

Again more details about the methodologies and the samples used will be given in the individual chapters.

The Variables

The numerous variables operationalized for the study, as well as the data sources used will be described later, within the context of the discussions on methodologies. In this section we will only discuss the two most important variables in the analysis—refocusing and profitability.

The Refocusing Variable

Refocusing is basically a reduction in diversification. To measure its extent, we need measures of firm diversification. Although a variety of diversification measures exist (e.g., Pitts and Hopkins 1982), refocusing is a multi-dimensional concept that cannot be measured exactly with a single index. I will therefore use five measures to capture the different dimensions of refocusing. The five measures are the entropy index of diversification, Rumelt categories, SIC numbers, press announcements, and the restructuring index.

The Entropy Index of Diversification
This is a Standard Industrial Classification (SIC) based index traditionally used by economists (e.g., Jacquemin and Berry 1979) imported into the strategy literature by Palepu (1985). To see how this index can be constructed, consider a firm operating in N industry segments, where an industry segment is defined as a 4-digit SIC industry. These industry segments aggregate into M industry groups, where an industry group is defined as a 2-digit SIC industry (and $N \geq M$). Let P_i be the share of the ith segment in the total sales of the firm. Then the entropy measure of total diversification (DT) is defined as follows:

$$DT = \sum_{i=1}^{N} P_i \log\left(\frac{1}{P_i}\right).$$

This measure takes into consideration two elements of diversification: the number of segments in which a firm operates and the relative importance of each of the segments in the total sales of the firm. To include a third dimension of diversity, namely the degree of relatedness among the various segments in which a firm operates, we assume that products from different 2-digit SIC industry groups are unrelated, and that products belonging to different 4-digit SIC industry segments but in the same 2-digit industry groups are related (Palepu 1985). Let P_{ij} be the share of the segment i of group j in the total sales of the group. If we define DR_j as the related diversification arising out of operating in several segments within one industry group j, then

$$DR_j = \sum_{ij} P_{ij} \log\left(\frac{1}{P_{ij}}\right).$$

Since the firm operates in several industry groups ($j = 1 \ldots M$), its total related diversification (DR) is equal to

$$DR = \sum_{j=1}^{M} P_j DR_j,$$

where P_j is the share of the jth group sales in the total sales of the firm.

Consistent with the definition of DT, the firm's unrelated diversification (DU) is defined as

$$DU = \sum_{j=1}^{M} P_j \log\left(\frac{1}{P_j}\right).$$

From the above definitions it can be shown that the sum of the related and unrelated components equals the total diversification:

$$DR + DU = DT.$$

The index has a lower limit of zero ($=$ a single-business company) but no upper limit. However, if DT is over 3, then the company is considered "very diversified."

Like any other index that is based on SIC codes, the entropy index is subject to criticism, especially because it (presumably) fails to capture the dimension of relatedness between a firm's units. This is an old criticism of SIC-based indexes, but we now know that this is not true (Montgomery 1982). The index is objective, time-efficient, and does a pretty good job in measuring a firm's diversification over time. Its strength lies in the fact that it allows us to decompose a firm's total diversification into its related and unrelated parts.

The index was constructed using data from the TRINET tapes. This database basically lists a firm's sales by SIC. The three components of the index (DU, DR, and DT) were calculated for each of the 219 firms in the sample for the years 1981, 1983, 1985, and 1987.

Rumelt's Categories

The entropy index is a continuous measure of diversification. Another way to measure changes in diversification is through a categorical measure such as Rumelt's (1974) categories. I undertook this classification exercise, but my classification differs from Rumelt's in one important respect: Instead of going through each firm's annual report to determine the businesses in which it is competing (as Rumelt did), I used the TRINET tapes to get a breakdown of the SICs that each firm is competing in. Then using a slightly modified SIC table, and some judgment (like Rumelt), I classified the firms following Rumelt's criteria. A clarification of the exact steps taken for this procedure is provided below:

First, I obtained a breakdown of each firm's sales by 2-digit and 4-digit SIC from the TRINET tapes. Next, I used a slightly modified SIC table to calculate each firm's *specialization* ratio and *related* ratio (as defined in Rumelt 1974). The SIC table I used is basically the same as the one developed by the U.S. government, the only exception being that five 2-digit SICs were "too aggregate" and I therefore further broke them down as follows:

SIC 34

3410–3419 = Metal cans and drums
3420–3429 = Hand tools and hardware
3430–3439 = Plumbing and heating metal
3440–3449 = Structural and sheet metal
3450–3479 = Stampings and forgings
3480–3489 = Guns and ammunition
3490–3499 = Springs and pipe fittings

SIC 35

3510–3519 = Turbines and engines
3520–3529 = Farm, lawn, and garden equipment
3530–3539 = Construction equipment, industrial
3540–3549 = Machine tools
3550–3559 = Industrial machinery
3560–3569 = Industrial pumps, fans, etc.
3570–3579 = Typewriters, calculators, office equipment
3580–3599 = Machines, not elsewhere classified

SIC 36

3610–3619 = Transformers and switchgear
3620–3629 = Motors, controls, etc.
3630–3639 = Household appliances
3640–3649 = Residential and commercial wire
3650–3659 = Radio, television, phonograph
3660–3669 = Communications equipment
3670–3679 = Electronic components
3680–3699 = Batteries, etc.

SIC 37

3710–3719 = Cars and trucks
3720–3729 = Aircraft
3730–3739 = Ships
3740–3749 = Railroad equipment
3750–3759 = Motorcycles and bicycles
3760–3769 = Missiles and space vehicles
3770–3799 = Other transportation equipment

SIC 73

7310–7319 = Advertising
7320–7329 = Collection and credit
7330–7339 = Direct mail and graphic arts
7340–7349 = Cleaning services
7350–7359 = News syndicates
7360–7369 = Employment agencies
7370–7379 = Software and data processing
7380–7399 = R&D, consulting, public relations

To calculate a firm's specialization (SR) and related (RR) ratios, I had to determine whether the different SICs the firm was competing in were related in any way. Basically I started out with the assumption that two different 2-digit SICs were unrelated and then tried to determine whether they had anything in common in terms of production technology, customer base, and marketing/distribution requirements (Rumelt 1974). If they did, then they were reclassified as related. Unavoidably, this exercise required some value judgment but the exercise proved to be much more straightforward than it sounds on paper. When difficulties were encountered, the firm's annual report was consulted. Once these two ratios were calculated for each firm, the classification proceeded as follows:

If $SR > 95\%$, the firm was classified as Single Business.

If $70\% \le SR \le 95\%$ = Dominant.

If $SR < 70\%$ and $RR > 70\%$ = Related.

If $SR < 70\%$ and $RR < 70\%$ = Unrelated.

In these equations SR is the specialization ratio and RR the related ratio.

To test the construct validity of this classification, I picked forty firms at random and reclassified them using information from their annual reports. Thirty-four firms were placed in the same categories as before. For the other six there was disagreement as to whether they were Dominant or Related. The problems arose at the stage where I had to decide what the firm's businesses were (and not at the stage of deciding whether they were related). If I were to take management's words at face value, all of their businesses belonged to a single, closely related business. The SIC breakdown seemed to be a more objective breakdown of a firm's businesses, so I decided to follow my original classification.

Number of SICs

A third way to measure a firm's diversification is by simply counting the number of 2-digit SICs that the firm is competing in. This is arguably a crude measure, but comparing the 1981 count with that in 1987 can be revealing. I obtained this information from the TRINET tapes.

Announcements in the Press

Similar to Hoskisson and Johnson (1992), I took as refocusing those firms that publicly announced in the *Wall Street Journal* their intention to refocus and actually divested at least 10 percent of their asset base. The number and size of the divestitures undertaken by the sample firms was collected from a variety of sources such as the SDC Database on Mergers and Acquisitions; the journal *Mergers & Acquisitions*; Predicast's *Index of Corporate Change*; Quality Services Co, *Merger and Acquisition Sourcebook*; W.T. Grimm & Co, *Mergerstat Review*; and Cambridge Corp., *The Merger Yearbook*. I used multiple sources because during the research I could find no single source to be reliable or complete.

Restructuring Index

Hoskisson and Johnson (1992) found that restructuring firms were of two types: Unrelated-business firms that were increasing their diversification (DU/DT increasing, DR/DT decreasing) to exploit internal capital market economies and Related-linked firms that were decreasing their diversification (DU/DT decreasing, DR/DT increasing) to improve their control systems. For my sample firms I therefore calculated the related (DR) and unrelated (DU) components of their entropy index of diversification (DT) for 1981 and 1987. Then I considered as restructuring, those Unrelated-business firms that increased their DU/DT and decreased their DR/DT or decreased their DU/DT and increased their DR/DT and those Related- or Dominant-business firms that reduced their DU/DT and increased their DR/DT. Hence restructuring firms were classed as not only those decreasing their diversification but also those increasing their diversification to exploit capital market economies. However, since I was only concerned with refocusing firms, out of this subsample of restructuring firms I took as refocusing those that decreased their DU/DT and increased their DR/DT. In addition, to avoid "accidental" refocusers being selected, I considered only firms that changed the above diversification ratios by more than 0.1.

The Profitability Variable

Following a long tradition of industrial organization (IO) and business research, I intend to use mostly accounting-based measures of profitability (rather than market-based measures as I do in chapter 6). Accounting measures have come under attack lately for being biased measures of economic performance. For example, Benston (1985, p. 64) claims that accounting data "are of doubtful value for the purposes of economic analysis." Similarly Fisher and McGowan (1983, p. 90) claim that "there is no way in which one can look at accounting rates of return and infer anything about relative economic profitability."

The issue, however, is not whether accounting data are subject to error. Of course they are (as are market-based data). If, however, these errors are unsystematic or uncorrelated with the phenomenon under investigation, "... they merely add noise to any underlying profitability relationships, making them more difficult to detect. To extract such relationships from noisy data is what statistical technique is all about" (Ravenscraft and Scherer 1987, p. 16). Problems arise when the errors present in accounting data are systematically associated with the phenomenon under study. In such a case the researcher must try to explicitly control for these biases. This is what this study does.

The biggest bias present in the data arises from the accounting method a firm uses to account for an acquisition. Under *pooling of interest* accounting, the assets of the acquired firm are recorded at their preacquisition book value. The shares that the acquirer issues are entered at their par value, and an additional "paid-in capital" entry is made so that par value plus paid-in capital equal the target's common stock entry. By contrast, under *purchase* accounting, the acquired assets are entered at the effective price paid for them. If a premium is paid over the acquired entity's book value (usually the case), the acquired assets are "stepped up" relative to their preacquisition book values, and/or an addition is made to the acquirer's "goodwill" account, which is of course amortized.

These accounting differences boil down to a simple fact: Since in most cases the acquirer pays more for the acquired assets than their book value, then under purchase accounting, profitability measures such as return on assets end up systematically smaller than under pooling of interest accounting. To see this, consider the measure return on assets. Under purchase accounting the denominator of this ratio (assets) is always bigger than under pooling accounting because under the purchase method the acquired assets are entered at the price paid which is bigger than book value. Furthermore the numerator of this ratio (profits) is smaller under the purchase method since the premium paid has to be amortized.

If the profitability measures are to make any sense, the researcher has to remove these systematic biases. Since my unit of analysis is the firm rather than the acquisition transaction, I could not simply separate the pooling of interest acquisitions from the purchase acquisitions as Ravenscraft and

Scherer (1987) did: The same firm may account for one acquisition with the purchase method and then account for another acquisition with the pooling of interests method. Another way out of this dilemma is to go through the annual reports of every firm and year by year convert every acquisition that has been accounted by the pooling of interests method into a purchase acquisition. This would involve two adjustments: On the balance sheet, one would have to step up the value of the acquisition from its book value to its "price value" and then adjust the goodwill account; on the income statement, one would have to amortize the premium over book value. This is certainly a complicated and time-consuming exercise. Furthermore, in many cases it simply is not possible to obtain the price of the acquisition needed to make the adjustment.

Perhaps the easiest way around this problem is the following: The accounting method used to record an acquisition affects the balance sheet by influencing the total assets entry; on the other hand, it affects the income statement by influencing the depreciation and amortization entries. Therefore, instead of using return on assets as the profitability measure, one can use return on sales, where return is defined as the operating income of the firm. That is, the profitability measure is

PROF = (Sales − Cost of goods sold − SG&A expenses
        + Depreciation and amortization expense)/Sales.

This measure is not affected by the accounting policies of acquisition recording and is therefore free of the above-mentioned biases. It does suffer, however, from another bias: ROS will differ systematically from industry to industry due to differences in input structures. In addition, in times of heavy acquisition and divestiture activity, a firm may change its industry composition drastically. As a result its ROS may change dramatically, reflecting the firm's new industry composition rather than its operating efficiency. If, for example, a manufacturing firm with an ROS of 12 percent acquires a supermarket whose ROS is traditionally low (e.g., 2 percent), the firm's new ROS will drop to about 7 percent by simple arithmetic. To remove this bias, each firm's ROS must therefore be adjusted by industry. This adjustment will also make the ROS figure comparable across industries.

For each firm I therefore calculate its DROS, which equals the firm's ROS minus its industry-weighted ROS. To calculate the industry-weighted ROS, the following procedure is followed: First, a Compustat program is used to identify all the firms assigned to each SIC and to calculate their ROS. Then, using their sales as weights, the average ROS of every SIC is estimated. Next, a breakdown of each firm's sales by SIC is obtained from the TRINET tapes. The percentage of the firm's sales in each SIC is then calculated. The industry-weighted *ROS* for every firm is estimated by multiplying the share of the firm's sales in each SIC by the corresponding *ROS* of that SIC and adding the results. In my study, each firm's *DROS* was calculated for the years 1981, 1983, 1985, and 1987. (For each year the profitability of each SIC was recalculated and so were each firm's sales breakdowns).

A final bias that may affect the profitability figure has been identified by Meeks and Meeks (1981). Following an acquisition or divestiture, the firm's sales figure no longer includes those sales that were made to the acquisition target before the acquisition. Whereas before the acquisition was made these sales were external, they are now internalized and do not appear on the firm's income statement. The exact opposite occurs following a divestiture. This bias is serious only when firms undertake acquisitions or divestitures that are vertical in nature. Since very few of the transactions in the period 1981 to 1987 were vertical (see Williams et al. 1988), this bias was not a major problem for this research.

The Contours of
Refocusing Activity

This chapter begins the analysis with an overview of historical patterns in refocusing, and a detailed look at the activity in 1981 to 1987. Although my primary objective is to test propositions 1 and 5 from chapter 2, I include additional exercises to provide a better feel of the phenomenon. All of the analyses are based on the main sample of 219 Fortune 500 firms.

Historical Overview

Proposition 1 argues that compared to the 1960s, there will be more refocusing in the 1980s. As I argued before, the rationale for this is simple: Most firms set out on their diversification programs in the early 1950s (e.g., Rumelt 1974). It is very likely therefore that at the beginning of this diversification effort most firms were moving toward their optimal region and very few had gone over it. Even if a few firms had overdiversified so early in the process, they were under little pressure to refocus given the state of the market for corporate control in the 1960s. As a result we should not expect too much refocusing to have occurred in the 1960s. As time went by, firms diversified more and more, and a larger number of firms must have passed their optimal region. These are the firms that were under pressure to refocus in the 1980s. We should therefore find more firms refocusing in the 1980s.

Table 4.1 provides support for this proposition. Using Rumelt's classifications, we have calculated (for three time periods) the proportion of firms

Table 4.1
Refocusing and diversification, 1949 to 1987 (in %)

	1949–59	1959–69	1981–87
Firms refocusing	1.3	1.1	20.4
Firms diversifying	21.7	25.0	8.5

Table 4.2
Distribution of firms by strategic category, 1949 to 1987

	From Rumelt's (1974) study			This study	
Strategic category	1949	1959	1974	1981	1987
Single business	42.0	22.8	14.4	23.8	30.4
Dominant business	28.2	31.3	22.6	31.9	28.1
Related business	25.7	38.6	42.3	21.9	22.4
Unrelated business	4.1	7.3	20.7	22.4	19.0

Source: Data for 1949, 1959, 1974, reprinted by permission of Harvard Business School Press from *Strategy, Structure and Economic Performance* by Richard Rumelt. Boston: 1974, p. vi. Copyright © 1974 by the President and Fellows of Harvard College.
Note: Percentage in each category ($N = 210$)

that refocused (e.g., by moving from the Unrelated-business category to the Dominant-business category) versus those that diversified (by moving, for example, from the Single-business category to the Related-business category).[1] The numbers for the period 1949 to 1969 come from Rumelt's sample. The numbers for 1981 to 1987 come from my sample.

Overall, the table shows that whereas in the 1950s and the 1960s there was a negligible number of firms refocusing (about 1 percent), the number increased dramatically in the 1980s (to 20 percent). The exact opposite happened with diversification: Approximately one-quarter of the Fortune 500 firms were diversifying in the early period 1949 to 1969, but the number declined to just over 8 percent in the 1980s.

The dramatic effect of these changes can be seen clearly in table 4.2 which shows the distribution of firms by strategic category. It appears that in the 1980s the trend toward unrelated diversification that so dominated the postwar era was arrested. Its place has been taken by a significant jump in the Single-business and Dominant-business firms. Overall, in the period 1981–87 there were 43 sample firms that changed their classification to a less-diversified category, 18 firms that increased their diversification, and 149 firms that remained in the same category over the period (see table 4.3). Given the short time period under study, these are dramatic changes.

Evidence in support of these findings has been reported in a recent study by Lichtenberg (1990). Using a sample of more than 6,500 firms, he

---

1. Specifically, firms diversified when they changed from Single business to Dominant business (2 firms in the sample), from Single to Related (0), from Single to Unrelated (0), from Dominant to Related (6), from Dominant to Unrelated (6), and from Related to Unrelated (4). On the other hand, firms refocused when they changed from Unrelated to Single (0), from Unrelated to Dominant (6), from Unrelated to Related (11), from Dominant to Single (14), from Related to Dominant (10), and from Related to Single (2).

Table 4.3
Changes in diversification, 1981 to 1987

	Number of firms
1. Firms that increased their diversification	
From Single to Dominant	2
From Single to Related	0
From Single to Unrelated	0
From Dominant to Related	6
From Dominant to Unrelated	6
From Related to Unrelated	4
Total	18
2. Firms that refocused	
From Unrelated to Single	0
From Unrelated to Dominant	6
From Unrelated to Related	11
From Dominant to Single	14
From Related to Dominant	10
From Related to Single	2
Total	43
3. Firms with no change	149

finds that in the period 1985–89 there was a substantial reduction in the degree of industrial diversification: The mean number of industries in which firms operated declined by 14 percent, the proportion of companies that were highly diversified declined 37 percent, and the proportion of single-industry companies increased 54 percent during the five-year period. Similar results have been reported by Jarrell (1991): He finds that in the period 1978–88 the percentage of companies (in the Federal Trade Commission's Line of Business Survey) operating in only one business segment, increased from 35.6 to 54.3 percent. This is the exact opposite of what happened in the period 1950–75: The same companies had increased their number of business lines from an average of about three to more than seven, and the top 200 companies had increased their average number of lines from 4.8 to 10.9 over the same period (Jarrell 1991). Results documenting the emergence of refocusing in the 1980s have also been reported by Hoskisson and Johnson (1992), Lichtenberg (1992), Liebeskind and Opler (1992), and Liebeskind, Opler, and Hatfield (1992).

Overall, these findings support proposition 1 and provide strong evidence of a significant change currently under way in the United States. This is the first study that provides systematic evidence of the refocusing phenomenon, documenting the reversal of the diversification trend in U.S. industry. The finding that refocusing is not the small-scale, isolated event that it was in the 1960s provides justification for this study.

The Period 1981 to 1987

As I argued before, when we look at diversification in a dynamic way, we would expect to find (1) some firms increasing their diversification and some firms decreasing it. More specifically, we should find (2) profit-maximizing underdiversified firms increasing their diversification and profit-maximizing overdiversified firms decreasing their diversification. In addition, if the distribution of changes in diversification is symmetric, we would expect that (3) these opposing forces will counterbalance each other so that, on average, overall industry diversification will not change by much. If the distribution is not symmetric, then we should observe changes in aggregate diversification. We have no a priori reasons for expecting a symmetric distribution. Empirical support for proposition 1 is provided in tables 4.4–4.9. The first two tables use the entropy index as a measure of diversification, the next three tables use SIC counts, and the last table uses the Rumelt categories.

Table 4.4 shows the distribution of changes in the entropy index of total diversification (DT) in the period 1981–87. According to this index, 105 firms increased their diversification while 104 firms decreased it. The distribution of changes in DT looks normal, and the two groups (refocusers and diversifiers) appear to have changed their diversification by similar degrees. For example, 55 percent of the refocusers decreased their diversification by less than 0.3. The corresponding number for diversifiers is 48 percent. An examination of changes in DT by company size (table 4.5) reveals that both the refocusers and the diversifiers are spread pretty evenly over the five *Fortune* groups.[2]

---

2. Interestingly the results presented in table 4.5 also seem to refute the accepted wisdom that only conglomerates engaged in refocusing (e.g., Lee and Cooperman 1989; Lichtenberg 1990; Williams et al. 1988). Although the theory presented above predicts that the conglomerates will indeed engage in refocusing—since they are the most likely firms to be overdiversified—the theory also predicts that they should not be alone in doing so: Every overdiversified firm should be refocusing. As shown in table 4.5, the refocusing firms are distributed quite evenly among the Fortune 500 groups: for example, there are 22 refocused firms in the Fortune 100 versus 21 refocused firms in the Fortune 400–500. In fact it appears that most of the refocusing occurred in the Fortune 100–200 group. Furthermore, of the 104 firms that refocused, only about one-third were classified as conglomerates by *Forbes* in its annual survey of American business. These results suggest that along with the conglomerates, other overdiversified firms were also refocusing.

Table 4.4
Distribution of changes in DT, 1987 to 1981

DT87−DT81[a]	Number of firms
−1.26−−∞	0
−1.00−−1.25	5
−0.9 −−0.99	1
−0.5 −−0.89	12
−0.4 −−0.49	12
−0.3 −−0.39	16
−0.2 −−0.29	11
−0.1 −−0.19	22
−0.0 −−0.09	25
Total refocused	104
0 −0.09	17
0.10−0.19	18
0.2 −0.29	16
0.3 −0.39	10
0.4 −0.49	10
0.5 −0.89	26
0.9 −1.00	3
1.0 −1.26	2
1.3 −1.4	2
1.4 −1.77	0
1.78−+∞	1
Total diversified	105
Total firms	209[b]

a. DT = the entropy index of total diversification.
b. Ten firms were lost from the base sample of 219 firms because of missing information in the 1987 TRINET tape.

A very similar story emerges when refocusing is measured using the number of 2-digit SICs that firms are competing in. According to table 4.6, 121 firms decreased their diversification, 57 increased it, and 31 firms had no change. The proportion of companies competing in ten industries or less increased from 48 percent in 1981 to 53 percent in 1987 (table 4.7). By contrast, the proportion of companies competing in twenty industries or more decreased from 10 to 8 percent in the period (results similar to those of Lichtenberg 1990). It appears that most of the refocusing occurred in the Fortune 100–200 group where, on average, firms decreased their industry participation by two industries (table 4.8). Overall, the sample firms decreased their industry participation from an average of 12 industries in 1981 to 11 industries in 1987.

Table 4.5
Distribution of refocused firms by size, 1981 to 1987

	Firms with higher:			Firms with lower:		
	DT[a]	DR[b]	DU[c]	DT	DR	DU
Fortune 100 (45)	23	29	22	22	16	23
Fortune 100−200 (36)	14	14	14	22	22	22
Fortune 200−300 (44)	22	26	23	22	18	21
Fortune 300−400 (41)	24	23	21	17	18	20
Fortune 400−500 (43)	22	28	19	21	15	24
All firms (209)	105	120	99	104	89	110

Note: Number of firms in each Fortune group in parentheses.
a. DT = entropy index of total diversification.
b. DR = entropy index of related diversification.
c. DU = entropy index of unrelated diversification.

That some firms were refocusing while others were diversifying was also evident when refocusing was measured using the Rumelt categories (as shown in table 4.3). Two additional insights emerge when the Rumelt classifications are subdivided by firm size (table 4.9): First, it appears that in both 1981 and 1987 the Single-business firms are primarily "small" Fortune 400−500 firms. By contrast, the Dominant-business firms seem to occupy the top two Fortune groupings. The Unrelated-business firms seem to be evenly distributed. Given any scale economies at the "business" level, we naturally expect diversification to change with size. Second, all five size groups show an increase in Single-business firms, especially the Fortune 400−500 group. On the other hand, the Fortune 400−500 group is the only group to show an increase in Unrelated firms. The least amount of change in any category is displayed by the mid-sized firms, the Fortune 200−300.

Movement toward the Optimum

How do we know that the overdiversified firms are refocusing and the underdiversified firms are increasing their diversification (proposition 5)? To test this proposition, we have to account for the "regression to the mean" problem: Simple convergence of the diversification index toward a middle value may signify simple regression to the mean rather than proof of the proposition. We try to remove this bias by using two different indexes of diversification: We compare the 1981 entropy index (DT) of the Single- and Unrelated-business firms with their corresponding index in 1987.

Table 4.6
Distribution of changes in SICs, 1981 to 1987

Change in SICs	Number of firms
−13	1
−10	1
−9	2
−8	3
−7	3
−6	4
−5	9
−4	18
−3	18
−2	22
−1	40
0	31
1	19
2	15
3	6
4	8
5	3
6	2
7	0
8	0
9	2
10	1
13	1
Total	209

Note: Total number of firms with fewer SICs = 121. Total number of firms with more SICs = 57. Total number of firms with no change = 31.

The results, presented in table 4.10, provide tentative support for the hypothesis: The entropy index of total diversification (DT) for the Single-business firms increased from 1.211 in 1981 to 1.42 in 1987; by contrast, the entropy index for the Unrelated-business firms decreased from 2.603 in 1981 to 2.479 in 1987. This implies that the low-diversity firms are increasing their diversification, while the high-diversity firms are decreasing their diversification, which is exactly what proposition 5 predicts. The same story emerges when the related (DR) and unrelated (DU) components of the total diversification index are examined.

Table 4.7
Distribution of SICs, 1981 to 1987

	Number of firms		
2-digit SICs	1981	1987	1987 − 1981
1−5	33	42	+9
6−10	67	69	+2
11−15	54	53	−1
16−20	34	28	−6
21−25	13	10	−3
26−30	3	5	+2
31−35	4	2	−2
36−40	1	0	−1
Total firms	209	209	
Total SICs	2,504	2,306	
Number per firm	12	11	

Table 4.8
Number of 2-digit SICs, 1981 to 1987

	1981		1987		1987 − 1981	
	Total SICs	Average	Total SICs	Average	Total SICs	Average
Fortune 100 (45)	826	18.35	774	17.2	−52	−1.15
Fortune 100−200 (36)	533	14.80	456	12.66	−77	−2.1
Fortune 200−300 (44)	466	10.6	446	10.1	−20	−0.45
Fortune 300−400 (41)	365	9.02	345	8.4	−20	−0.50
Fortune 400−500 (43)	314	7.3	285	6.6	−29	−0.67
All firms (209)	2,504	11.98	2,306	11.03	−198	−0.946

Note: Number of firms in each *Fortune* group in parentheses.

No Change on Average

If some firms are increasing their diversification while others are decreasing it, then on average we should not expect a big change in overall diversification. This is especially the case in a symmetric sample such as the one that emerged in table 4.4, where 50 percent of the firms are diversifying and 50 percent are refocusing. Table 4.11 shows the diversification levels of the 219 sample firms over the study period. The most prominent result to emerge from the table is the fact that overall diversification levels have

Table 4.9
Rumelt classification by firm size (number of sample firms in each category)

	1981				1987			
	S^a	D^b	R^c	U^d	S	D	R	U
Fortune 100	7	17	8	13	9	18	8	10
Fortune 100–200	5	19	5	8	9	15	6	7
Fortune 200–300	8	10	14	12	10	10	14	10
Fortune 300–400	12	12	8	9	13	9	13	6
Fortune 400–500	18	9	11	5	23	7	6	7

a. S = Single-business firms.
b. D = Dominant-business firms.
c. R = Related-business firms.
d. U = Unrelated-business firms.

not changed much. The only group of firms to display any noteworthy refocusing activity is the Fortune 100–200, whose total diversification (DT) dropped by 0.127 in the period. It is interesting to note, though, that unrelated diversification has decreased while related diversification has increased. In fact it is the relatively "big" increase in related diversification that has produced the increase in total diversification.

As expected, the conglomerates and the multicompanies show quite big decreases in both unrelated and total diversification. Although part of this decrease can be attributed to a "regression to the mean" effect, there is no denying the fact that many conglomerates have actively reduced their diversification. For example, in its annual survey of American business, *Forbes* classified 73 firms as conglomerates in 1981. In 1987 the list included only 41 firms. According to *Forbes* (1987), these "vanishing" conglomerates are "going back to concentrate on one or two major industries. You'll find Sybron and Corning Glass Works, for example, in health care now."[3]

The major implication of table 4.11 is that overall there exists no massive refocusing trend in U.S. industry, as several reports in the business press would have us believe. Individual firms may be refocusing, but the refocusing efforts of these firms are counterbalanced by the diversifying moves of other firms. Therefore, on average, there is little change in

---

3. A recent *Wall Street Journal* (March 1, 1994, p. A1) article argues that conglomerates have not been restructured out of existence. Rather, they are still quite popular but now follow a more "focused" strategy. In other words, they are still quite diversified but not as diversified as in the 1970s or early 1980s.

Table 4.10
Movement toward the optimum

	1981 ($N = 209$)				1987 ($N = 209$)			
	S	D	R	U	S	D	R	U
Average number of SICs	6.48	12.95	11.74	16.78	6.18	11.64	11.31	15.15
Average DT	1.211[a]	1.980	2.249	2.603[b]	1.420[a]	2.051	2.268	2.479[b]
Average DU	0.545	1.116	1.470	1.828	0.637	1.155	1.413	1.705
Average DR	0.666	0.862	0.779	0.775	0.783	0.896	0.855	0.774

Note: 1 = as classified in 1981. DT = entropy index of total diversification. DU = entropy index of unrelated diversification. DR = entropy index of related diversification. S = Single-business firms. D = Dominant-business firms. R = Related-business firms. U = Unrelated-business firms.
a. Increase the diversification of Single-business firms is statistically significant at the 1 percent level ($t = 2.45$).
b. Decrease in the diversification of Unrelated-business firms is not statistically significant ($t = 1.02$).

Table 4.11
Entropy index of diversification, 1981 to 1987

	1981			1983			1985			1987[a]			1987–1981		
	DU	DR	DT	DU	DR	DT	DU	DR	DT	DU	DR	DT	DU	DR	DT
All firms (219)[b]	1.214	0.790	2.004	1.199	0.800	1.999	1.213	0.766	1.979	1.209	0.833	2.042	−0.005	0.043	0.038
Fortune 100 (45)	1.386	0.950	2.336	1.398	0.989	2.387	1.357	0.956	2.313	1.409	1.043	2.452	0.023	0.093	0.116
Fortune 100–200 (39)	1.346	0.939	2.285	1.301	0.924	2.226	1.312	0.887	2.199	1.264	0.894	2.158	−0.082	−0.045	−0.127
Fortune 200–300 (45)	1.262	0.736	1.999	1.257	0.764	2.021	1.294	0.745	2.039	1.259	0.752	2.012	−0.003	0.016	0.013
Fortune 300–400 (44)	1.106	0.677	1.783	1.067	0.658	1.725	1.135	0.603	1.738	1.154	0.720	1.874	0.048	0.043	0.091
Fortune 400–500 (46)	0.989	0.669	1.658	0.987	0.682	1.669	0.985	0.653	1.638	0.955	0.753	1.708	−0.034	0.084	0.05
Conglomerates[c] (18)	1.904	0.927	2.831	1.927	0.955	2.882	1.815	0.936	2.751	1.772	0.927	2.699	−0.132	0.000	−0.132
Multicompanies[d] (13)	1.738	1.104	2.843	1.672	1.084	2.756	1.693	1.000	2.693	1.471	0.955	2.427	−0.267	−0.149	−0.416
Diversified[e] (31)	1.834	1.001	2.836	1.820	1.009	2.829	1.764	0.962	2.726	1.637	0.939	2.577	−0.197	−0.062	−0.259

Note: DU = entropy index of unrelated diversification. DR = entropy index of related diversification. DT = entropy index of total diversification.
a. For 1987, $N = 209$.
b. Number of firms in parentheses (except in 1987 when the numbers in parentheses are 209, 45, 36, 44, 41, 43, 16, 13, 29, respectively).
c. A group of 18 firms classified as conglomerates by Forbes in its 1981 survey of American business.
d. A group of 13 firms classified as multi-industry by Forbes in its 1981 survey.
e. The sum of conglomerates and multicompanies.

overall diversification. Simply put, some firms are refocusing while others are diversifying.[4]

The correctness of this finding can be tested in another way. If most U.S. firms are refocusing, one would expect aggregate concentration ratios to increase. That is, if everybody is divesting peripheral businesses while acquiring businesses close to their core (horizontal diversification), soon every industry would be dominated by a few big firms, thus driving concentration ratios up. This has not been the case: for every U.S. industry I calculated its four-firm concentration ratio in 1981 and again in 1987. I measured concentrations with the standard Herfindahl index, which is the sum of the squared market shares of the four largest firms in every industry:

$$H = \sum_{i=1}^{4} S_i^2.$$

The data to calculate this index came from the TRINET tapes: I developed an SAS program that produced a list of all the SICs and their firms, plus the sales of every firm and the total sales of the industry. Then I used the equation above to calculate the index for every industry.

From the data I could see virtually no change in the overall concentration of the U.S. economy. There was some increase in the concentration of manufacturing industries, but that was extremely small. If the tobacco industry (whose concentration nearly doubled) is excluded, manufacturing concentration actually declined.

A More Detailed Look at *DT*

According to the entropy index, there were 100 firms that decreased their diversification in the period. The average drop in *DT* for these firms was 0.3033. There were 42 firms that decreased their *DT* by more than this mean, and they have been classified as "heavy refocusers." The remaining 58 refocusers decreased their DT by less than this mean, and they have been classified as "light refocusers." In the diversifying group (101 firms) the mean increase in *DT* was 0.407. Forty firms increased their *DT* by more than this mean and were classified as "heavy diversifiers." The remaining 61 firms increased their *DT* by less than this mean and were

---

4. Since the sample of firms comes from the Fortune 500, the firms under study are among the biggest firms in the U.S. economy. This sample bias implies that my finding that "overall diversification levels have not changed much" may be biased. In fact Lichtenberg (1992) and Liebeskind and Opler (1992) report results that are not consistent with those reported here.

classified as "light diversifiers." Panel *A* of table 4.12 shows this break-down along with the average diversification (*DT*) and profitability (*DROS*) of each group.

As can be seen by the table, those firms that were the most diversified at the start of the period were also the worst performers, and it is exactly these firms that undertook most of the refocusing in the period. As a result by 1987 they are the least diversified. Could it be that these firms decided to refocus *because* of their poor performance? Similarly, note from the table that those firms that were the least diversified at the start of the period were also among the most profitable in the group. It is exactly these firms that undertook most of the diversification in the period so that by 1987 they are the most diversified of the lot. Again this suggests that these firms decided to diversify *because* they were profitable (see also Grant and Thomas 1988; Grant, Jammine, and Thomas 1986). These results imply that profitability drives diversification, and not vice versa, and this refutes the accepted wisdom in the field (e.g., Rumelt 1974). This result also suggests a negative relationship between diversification levels and profitability.

Looking now at changes in profitability, it is interesting that all firms were doing much worse in 1987 than in 1981. By far the worst deterioration was displayed by the heavy diversifiers, followed by the light diversifiers, the light refocusers, and the heavy refocusers (in that order). Again this result suggests that firms that decreased their diversification did not do as badly as those that increased their diversification.

When the 1987 profitability levels are compared, the heavy refocusers come out the worst performers. This may be a reflection of the turmoil these firms went through as a result of refocusing. It may take some time before these firms return to a stable equilibrium.

In panel *B* of the table, a different subdivision of firms is shown. The "early refocusers" are those firms that did most (more than 50 percent) of their refocusing in the period 1981–83, the "middle refocusers" did most of their refocusing in 1983–85, the "late refocusers" did most of their refocusing in 1985–87, and the "even refocusers" did their refocusing over the whole period. The most striking result is how much better the "even refocusers" were doing relative to all other groups. This group of firms also did more refocusing than the other groups (it had the biggest drop in *DT*). These observations suggest that it is better to have a major surgery and spread the pain over time than to do a half-hearted job all at once. The table also seems to support the previous statement that it may take some time before the turmoil created by refocusing is fully absorbed by the firm: The "early refocusers" that did most of their refocusing in 1981–83

Table 4.12
Refocusers versus diversifiers, 1981 to 1987

	1981				1987		
	Number	DT	DROS[a]	Percent Unrelated	DT	DROS	Percent Unrelated
A							
Heavy refocusers	42	2.28	0.169	31.0	1.73	−0.698	16.6
Light refocusers	58	2.24	0.464	29.3	2.11	−0.058	22.4
Light diversifiers	61	1.87	1.288	11.4	2.06	−0.108	18.0
Heavy diversifiers	40	1.46	1.174	15.0	2.21	−0.206	17.5
B							
Early refocusers	14	2.16	2.687	21.4	1.87	1.326	7.1
Middle refocusers	39	2.21	−0.370	33.3	2.01	−0.823	23.0
Late refocusers	39	2.28	−0.058	33.3	1.90	−0.930	23.0
Even refocusers	8	2.48	1.644	12.5	2.05	2.136	12.5

a. $DROS = ROS −$ Industry-weighted ROS.

seemed to have recovered by 1987, whereas the middle- and late-refocusers were still feeling the effects.

Methods of Refocusing

Reports in the business press suggest that firms were refocusing on their core businesses primarily through acquisitions and divestitures rather than internal investments and product extensions: By divesting unrelated units while acquiring related ones, firms were now competing in fewer but related businesses. In the period 1981–87, for example, U.S. firms undertook 6,921 sell-offs and 825 leveraged buyouts, with a total transaction value of over $275 billion (W.T. Grimm 1988).

The large number of acquisitions and divestitures taking place does not by itself constitute evidence that this is how firms refocus. After all there were more divestitures and acquisitions in the 1970s than in the 1980s, and yet no refocusing took place at that time. What (supposedly) differentiates the current transactions from those in the past is the belief that there is a systematic underlying logic to the more recent transactions: Whereas in the 1970s firms were making mostly conglomerate acquisitions (Ravenscraft and Scherer 1987, p. 55), in the 1980s they were making more horizontal acquisitions, perhaps as a result of the relaxed regulatory environment. And whereas in the 1970s firms were divesting units in a basically random fashion (i.e., *any* unprofitable unit), in the 1980s they were divesting mostly unrelated units even if they were profitable.

Apart from repeated case examples in the press, there is no systematic evidence in the literature of the existence of such a logic. There is a research paper (Williams et al. 1988) that shows that conglomerates have followed this logic in the period 1980–84, but there is no evidence that a broad spectrum of firms was acting in this way.

To test the validity of this belief, a sample of 100 firms was randomly selected from the 1985 Fortune 200: 50 firms from the Fortune 100 and 50 from the Fortune 100–200. An attempt was then made to discover every acquisition and divestiture that these firms made in the period 1981–87. At first this information was collected from the SDC database on Mergers and Acquisitions (SDC.MRG and SDC.LTD). It soon became evident, however, that this database was incomplete. Further information was therefore collected from the journal *Mergers & Acquisitions*, Predicast's *Index of Corporate Change*, Quality Services Co.'s *Merger & Acquisition Sourcebook*, W.T. Grimm & Co.'s *Mergerstat Review*, and Cambridge Corporation's *The Merger Yearbook*.

In total 1,221 transactions were identified, averaging just over 12 transactions per firm. (This average number hides a lot of variation. For example, GE had 57 transactions while Kellogg had 1.) For each transaction we
also collected its SIC classification and the year it took place. An attempt
was also made to identify the "value" of each transaction (price paid or
received), but for 30 percent of the transactions the information was simply not available.

Once this list was compiled, each transaction was classified as related or
unrelated to the firm's core business in the following manner: Each firm's
"core" business was defined as the 2-digit SIC in which the company had
the largest percentage of its sales (information from TRINET). The classification then proceeded in the same manner as the Rumelt classification
reported before: Any transaction belonging to a SIC different from the
firm's core-SIC was initially classified as unrelated. I then tried to determine
whether the two SICs had anything in common in terms of production
technology, customer base, and marketing/distribution requirements. If
they did, the transaction was reclassified as related.

Table 4.13
Methods of refocusing, 1981 to 1987

	Acquisitions		Divestitures	
	Related	Unrelated	Related	Unrelated
All firms (100)	393	306	207	315
Fortune 100 (50)	249	207	136	218
Fortune 100–200 (50)	144	99	71	97
Conglomerates (19)	67	98	50	85
Multicompany firms (10)	47	57	30	55
All others (71)	279	152	127	175

Note:

$$\frac{\text{Total acquisitions}}{\text{Total divestitures}} = 1.34.$$

$$\frac{\text{Related acquisitions} + \text{Unrelated divestitures}}{\text{Unrelated acquisitions} + \text{Related divestitures}} = 1.38.$$

$$\frac{\text{Unrelated acquisitions}}{\text{Unrelated divestitures}} = 0.97.$$

$$\frac{\text{Related acquisitions}}{\text{Related divestitures}} = 1.90.$$

For conglomerates,

$$\frac{\text{Related acquisitions} + \text{Unrelated divestitures}}{\text{Unrelated acquisitions} + \text{Related divestitures}} = 1.027.$$

The aggregate results are shown in table 4.13. Overall, there were 699 acquisitions and 522 divestitures. Of these, 393, or 56 percent, of the acquisitions were related in nature, while 315, or 60 percent, of the divestitures were unrelated. Since, by definition, the "refocusing ratio" is related acquisitions plus unrelated divestitures as a percent of unrelated acquisitions plus related divestitures, then for the whole sample this ratio equals 1.38, which implies that indeed firms were refocusing by the logic described above. The same ratio for conglomerates is 1.027, which means that the conglomerates were following a similar logic despite undertaking a disproportionally large number of unrelated acquisitions.

A Closer Look at the Conglomerates

As a final exercise for this section, a group of twelve conglomerates is compared to a group of fourteen refocusers along several dimensions. The twelve conglomerates come from the 1989 *Forbes* list. The fourteen refocusers come from my sample and are firms that displayed a decrease in diversification in all three measures of diversification that we have used so far in this study (i.e., DT, SICs, and Rumelt classification).

One of the justifications of conglomerate diversification is risk reduction through the pooling together of unrelated businesses. Table 4.14 investigates whether the conglomerates achieved such risk reduction. Risk is measured in two ways:

1. First, the equity beta of each firm was calculated using the market model. Thus, for each firm, information was collected from the CRSP tapes, and the following model was estimated:

$$R_{it} = \alpha_i + \beta_i R_{mt} + e_{it},$$

where R_{it} are the firm's returns and R_{mt} are the market returns. The model was estimated for the period $(-270, -90)$, where December 30 was day zero.

2. Second, the variation in each firm's ROS (operating income before depreciation and interest as a percent of sales) was estimated with data coming from Compustat. The variation in 1981 is taken as the standard deviation of ROS over the years 1979, 1980, and 1981. The variation in 1987 is taken as the standard deviation of ROS in the years 1985, 1986, and 1987.

In 1981, 7 of the 12 conglomerates had beta values below 1.0 which is where common stocks of average risk tend to cluster. The average beta

Table 4.14
Conglomerates versus refocusers, 1981 to 1987

	1981				1987			
	β	Debt/Equity	Risk[a]	DT	β	Debt/Equity	Risk[a]	DT
Conglomerates[b]								
American Brands Inc.	0.832	—	—	—	1.437	—	—	—
DWG Corp.	1.170	—	—	—	1.369	—	—	—
Dover Corp.	0.726	8.57	0.849	2.66	1.479	3.96	0.725	2.90
Emhart Corp.	0.607	5.32	1.468	2.77	0.901	63.97	0.749	3.02
GATX Corp.	0.924	—	—	—	0.662	—	—	—
IC Industries	1.393	—	—	—	1.428	—	—	—
IT&T Corp.	1.128	54.54	0.226	3.39	1.355	31.69	1.23	2.21
Minnesota Mining & Manufacturing	0.931	9.48	1.409	2.76	0.982	8.60	0.751	2.65
Raytheon Co.	1.135	4.90	0.334	2.93	1.082	2.42	0.077	2.92
Teledyne Inc.	1.232	34.92	0.586	3.52	0.718	27.73	0.793	3.81
Tenneco Inc.	0.781	—	—	—	1.003	—	—	—
Textron Inc.	0.989	23.37	0.572	3.17	0.852	64.4	0.318	3.16
Average	0.987	20.15	0.777	3.03	1.106	28.96	0.663	2.95
Refocusers[c]								
American Standard	1.152	40.93	0.994	2.86	1.609	32.86	0.670	1.81
B. F. Goodrich	1.243	66.79	0.898	2.24	1.430	33.90	2.016	2.09
Brunswick	1.591	47.47	1.200	2.53	1.629	46.58	0.802	2.13
Cameron Iron Works	1.078	41.69	0.285	1.71	1.516	35.43	2.618	1.25
Fleetwood Enterprises	1.685	0.00	2.325	1.44	1.859	0.00	0.262	1.38

GAF	1.105	143.79	2.077	2.41	10.53	96.78	1.269	2.28
Koppers	1.489	40.18	0.912	3.37	1.953	38.67	2.801	2.47
Mattel	1.513	62.44	2.305	1.38	1.955	235.89	2.010	0.13
Martin Marietta	1.013	29.98	2.744	2.59	1.412	31.05	0.656	1.75
Norton	0.639	32.80	0.944	2.12	0.972	30.01	1.009	1.46
PepsiCo	0.850	49.75	0.185	2.19	1.632	102.81	0.432	1.89
Rockwell International	0.978	15.13	0.520	3.18	1.744	23.01	0.818	2.94
TRW	1.043	26.69	0.130	3.16	1.323	61.40	0.559	3.13
Warner-Lambert	1.172	37.46	0.801	2.27	1.567	33.60	0.346	1.06
Average	1.182	45.22	1.165	2.39	1.547	57.28	1.162	1.84

a. Measured as the standard deviation of ROS over the preceding three years.
b. As classified by Forbes in 1989.
c. Firms whose DT decreased and SIC count decreased, and they reduced diversification according to Rumelt classification.

for the 12 conglomerates was 0.987, suggesting that the conglomerates carried the same risk as the "normal" common stock. Thus, despite their conglomerate diversification, the conglomerates only achieved an average beta.

Over the period 1981–87 the conglomerates' beta rose to 1.106, which implies a higher risk. Given the small decrease in their diversification, the increase in risk can be explained by the higher debt load that the conglomerates are now carrying, implying that their asset beta probably remained unchanged. The numbers also show that the conglomerates achieved a reduction in the variability of their profits, further reinforcing the interpretation that their higher beta is a reflection of their higher debt load.

A different story emerges for the 14 refocusers. Their average 1981 beta is 1.182 implying a higher-than-average risk. This beta jumps to 1.547 in 1987, reflecting a higher debt load but also a much less-diversified asset base (their DT falls from 2.39 to 1.84). On the other hand, there is virtually no change in the variability of their profits.

How did the stock market treat these conglomerates? Not very well, if one looks at their stock prices. For each conglomerate, closing stock price quotations were compiled for June 30 of each year in the period 1980–88. These numbers are then compared to the Standard & Poor's 500 *Composite Index*. The conglomerates underperformed the market in every year in the period, especially in 1987 and 1988.

Summary

The results of this chapter show that refocusing is primarily a 1980s phenomenon whose effect has been to reverse the trend toward unrelated diversification that characterized U.S. business in the period 1945 to 1980. Consistent with the theory of chapter 2, the overdiversified firms were found to be refocusing while the underdiversified firms were increasing their diversification. The net effect of these opposing changes has been a relatively small change in average diversification levels. Firms refocused primarily by divesting unrelated businesses and acquiring related ones.

The Characteristics of
Refocusing Firms

Although it is often assumed that only the conglomerates engaged in refocusing (e.g., *The Economist*, November 3, 1989, p. 78; Lee and Cooperman 1989; Lichtenberg 1990; Williams et al. 1988), the evidence presented in the previous chapter (and recent research by Hoskisson and Johnson, 1992) suggest that this is not the case. For one, the refocusing firms in our sample were distributed quite evenly in the Fortune 500 list—for example, there were as many firms refocusing in the Fortune 100 as there were in the Fortune 400–500. In addition the majority of the firms that were refocusing in the 1981–87 period were not conglomerates but other diversified firms. It is therefore still unclear who these refocusing firms are and what characteristics distinguished them from those that did not refocus.

In this chapter I identify the characteristics that distinguish the companies that refocused from those that did not. The goal is to test proposition 2, which argues that relative to their industry counterparts, the refocusing firms will be characterized by high diversification and poor performance. The main argument advanced here is that a firm will refocus in response to a performance crisis (probably brought about by excessive diversification), and this decision will be affected by the nature of the firm's core business. The full sample of 219 firms is used to test this proposition.

Theoretical Considerations

Consider a diversified firm in 1981. The firm is competing in several industries that differ along several dimensions. For example, some are concentrated industries, some are capital intensive, some are small, and some are profitable. This firm has a certain profitability level in 1981 that is a function of the structural characteristics of the industries the firm is competing in, the strategic actions of the firm, and the riskiness of its cash flows.

Since one of the major objectives of every firm is growth (e.g., Guth 1980), one would expect that a firm will continue to invest for growth unless a major crisis forces management to rethink its whole strategy (e.g., Wiersema 1985). A performance crisis can arise for several reasons, but as argued in chapter 2 and by Hoskisson and Turk (1990, p. 469), overinvestment in diversification will be one of these reasons: If a firm is overdiversified, either because it has overinvested in diversification or because the optimal level of diversification[1] for firms has decreased in the 1980s, its performance will suffer, reflecting the high costs of disequilibrium. The seriousness of the situation will be even more pressing for management if there exists a real threat of takeover should the performance of the firm remain subnormal for some time (e.g., Shleifer and Vishny 1988).

A performance crisis can take several meanings (Wiersema 1985). For example, the firm may be losing money. Alternatively a firm may continue to be profitable, but its performance may be subnormal relative to its past performance, or relative to its competitors. Any one of these reasons could act as a catalyst in the firm's decision to change its strategic orientation. However, research has found that it is subnormal performance relative to the competition rather than relative to past performance that prompts firms to act (e.g., Duhaime and Grant 1984; Ravenscraft and Scherer 1987).

Given a performance crisis, the firm decides to refocus (e.g., Hoskisson and Turk 1990). This decision is taken exactly because management has realized that the firm is overdiversified, and this causes diseconomies that hurt the firm's profitability (e.g., see Mueller 1987, pp. 26–29; Williamson, 1967). Comments such as "We cannot manage everything," or "We cannot be successful with the strategy of being all things to all people," are now common in the business press (e.g., *The Harbus News*, March 12, 1990, p. 5; *New York Times*, June 7, 1984, p. D1; *Wall Street Journal*, October 2, 1984: sec. 2, p. 1). They merely reflect the realization on the part of management that they have overstretched their resources in too many areas and that some consolidation is necessary.

The above discussion suggests that one of the major factors that influences the decision to refocus will be the firm's *poor* profitability relative to its competitors, which is a function of the firm's overdiversification. Thus

---

1. As argued in chapter 2, the optimal point of diversification for a particular firm is the point at which the marginal benefits (*MB*) of an additional diversification move equal its marginal costs (*MC*). Every firm has a different optimal point depending on its resources, its external environment, the type of diversification it is following (related versus unrelated), the caliber of its management team, its capacity to learn from past diversification moves, and so on.

we would expect that relative to their industry counterparts, the refocusing firms will be characterized by high diversification and poor performance. In other words, the higher the firm's diversification and the lower its profitability, the higher the likelihood that the firm will refocus.

However, we should not expect a firm to refocus on its core industry if this core is a stagnating and unprofitable business. Many firms have diversified into unrelated areas exactly because their base industry was "unattractive" (e.g., Bettis and Mahajan 1985; Montgomery 1979). We should not expect these firms to refocus unless during their diversification moves they happened upon an attractive industry that now becomes the firm's new core business. American Can's 1986 decision to get out of the paper and packaging industries so as to concentrate on financial services is a case in point. In fact this is exactly what is happening with most conglomerates (e.g., IT&T, GE): The conglomerates are now concentrating on their core businesses, but in most cases this core is a business that was not part of the conglomerate's portfolio ten years ago. The new core is usually an "acquired" core. Similar considerations apply to firms that have an attractive base industry but diversified anyway: The higher the attractiveness of the core business, the bigger the likelihood that the firm will refocus.

Trying to determine what constitutes an attractive industry can prove an elusive exercise (e.g., see Wernerfelt and Montgomery 1986). An industry is usually considered attractive if it is protected from competition and contestability by high barriers to entry. Such an industry is usually (but not always) economically profitable. On the other hand, a high-growth industry can be considered attractive even if it has low barriers to entry. In this research we will use three variables to capture the attractiveness of the core business of every firm: the industry's seller concentration ratio, its profitability, and its advertising intensity.

Another important characteristic of the firm's core business is its R&D intensity. Several researchers (e.g., Gort 1962; Hassid 1975; Lemelin 1982; MacDonald 1985; Rumelt 1974) have found that firms in science-based industries tend to diversify into other science-based industries in order to exploit their technological know-how and expertise. Technological know-how is one of the most valuable firm-specific assets that a firm can exploit by transferring it in other industries (e.g., Prahalad and Hamel 1990). This implies that a firm that is coming from a science-based core will have incentives to diversify. As a result the higher the R&D intensity of the firm's core business, the lower the likelihood that the firm will forgo the profits it can reap by transferring its science skills in other industries. Hence the lower the likelihood that it will refocus. On the other hand, however, the industry's R&D intensity can act as a barrier to entry, and this may make the core industry more attractive to its members. Hence the higher the likelihood that firms already in R&D intensive core industries will refocus to such industries. This means that R&D intensity has two quite opposite effects on the likelihood that a firm will refocus. Which of these two effects is dominant cannot be determined ex ante, so the relationship between refocusing and R&D intensity is ambiguous.

A firm's decision to refocus may also be influenced by how important the core business is to the firm. For example, Wiersema (1985) found that the relative importance of the core business (as measured by its size in the total sales of the firm) had an important effect on the firm's decision to change its strategic direction. We would expect that a firm that is over-diversified and has a big core business will be more inclined to return to its core, than a firm that does not have a big core. A case in point is Goodyear, which divested its aerospace unit and its oil and gas subsidiary to return to its core business—tires. At the time tires and related products accounted for 75 percent of Goodyear's sales.

The firm's relative position in its core industry could also affect the decision to return to it. If the firm is a major player in this industry (as measured by the firm's market share), it will be more inclined to abandon its peripheral businesses and return to this core. A positive relationship is therefore expected.

A radical change in the strategic direction of a firm is usually undertaken when a new top management team arrives (e.g., Gabarro 1985). For example, Ravenscraft and Scherer (1987, p. 170) argue that a change in the top management of the firm could act as a catalyst in the decision to refocus because new managers are "... more likely to sweep house through sell-offs, presumably because they [have] less emotional commitment to prior acquisition decisions."

Finally, the firm's ability to change its industry mix will be constrained by its debt burden: A firm enters or leaves industries more easily if entry and exit barriers to these industries are low. Since entry/exit is achieved through buying and selling units (rather than through extension of product markets), the biggest barrier that a firm faces is availability of capital. Thus the lower the debt burden of the firm, the easier it is for it to obtain financing in order to undertake refocusing. On the other hand, a high debt burden may force the company to sell units to repay its debt (Ravenscraft and Scherer 1987). Hence the sign of the relationship between refocusing and debt load is ambiguous.

Table 5.1
Summary of explanatory variables

Symbol	Definition	Mean	Standard deviation	Expected sign
$DT81$	Firm diversification	1.984	0.752	+
$DROS81$	Firm profitability	0.794%	4.504	−
$PROF(c)$	Core industry profitability	12.59%	3.28	+
$C4(c)$	Core industry concentration	0.0109	0.0172	+
$XAD(c)$	Core industry advertising intensity	3.138%	2.429	+
$XRD(c)$	Core industry R&D intensity	16.938%	23.458	?
$SIZE(c)$	Size of core industry	60.01%	22.68	+
$SHARE(c)$	Market share in core industry	1.139%	2.574	+
$DMGMT$	Change in CEO in 1981−85	0.447	0.497	+
DSE	Debt-to-equity ratio	41.02%	56.93	?

Table 5.1 provides a summary of the explanatory variables and their predicted coefficient signs. To avoid omitted variable biases and multicollinearity problems, different combinations of these variables will be used in the analysis (see "results" section).

Data and Methodology

The basic sample of 219 firms will be used for the analysis. Details on the sampling procedure were given in chapter 3. Because of missing information on the Trinet and Compustat tapes, 18 firms had to be dropped (all were spread evenly over the five Fortune groups). The final sample consists of 201 firms.

The phenomenon to be explained is refocusing. We take as our dependent variable a dummy variable with a value of one if the firm has refocused in the period 1981−85, and zero otherwise. With a dichotomous dependent variable of this sort, ordinary least squares (OLS) regression is inefficient—namely OLS assumes normally distributed errors, but it is more likely that our error structure is bimodal (Ravenscraft and Scherer 1987, p. 175). We therefore use a logit model to estimate how the refocused firms differ from those that did not refocus.

A logit model estimates the probability that the dependent variable will have a value of one (that the firm has refocused) as a function of the explanatory variables whose coefficients are estimated nonlinearly. A positive coefficient implies that the variable increases the probability that the firm will refocus. Given the discussion above on the factors that influence the decision to refocus, the exact model is formulated as follows:

Probability (refocused) $= f(DROS81, DSE81, DMGMT(85-81), DT81,$
$$SHARE81(c), XAD81(c), C4(81)(c), PROF81(c),$$
$$XRD81(c), SIZE81(c)). \qquad (5.1)$$

In the model the "refocused" variable is a dummy variable that takes the value of one if the firm refocused in the period 1981–85, zero otherwise. Firms were classified as refocused in the following manner: First, each firm's entropy index of diversification (DT) was calculated in the manner demonstrated in chapter 3. The index was calculated for the years 1981, 1983, and 1985 using data from the TRINET tapes. The 201 sample firms were then ranked according to the change in their entropy index in the period 1981–83. Those firms whose DT decreased by more than -0.05 and whose $DT(85-83)$ was smaller than $+0.05$ were classified as refocused. In addition those firms whose $DT(83-81)$ was between -0.05 and $+0.05$, and whose $DT(85-83)$ decreased by more than -0.08 were also classified as refocused. This exercise was necessary to remove from the "refocused" group any accidental or inconsistent refocusers. Of the 201 firms in the sample, 84 were classified as refocused.

Even though each firm's diversification level could be measured by a continuous index, I decided to use a dichotomous dependent variable for three reasons. First, even though the index does a good job in telling us if firm A is more diversified than firm B, the actual numerical difference between the two firms' indexes has little specific meaning (see Palepu 1985). If, for example, firm A has $DT = 3$ and firm B has $DT = 2$, we know that firm A is more diversified than firm B but the difference in their diversification $(= 1)$ can only be used as a rough indication of how much more diversified firm A is.

Second, the index is constructed by taking into account the number of industries a firm is competing in and the sales of the firm in each of these industries. As a result the index can change from year to year not only with the diversification moves of the firm but also when the firm invests or disinvests in particular industries. Thus simply looking at the change of this index over time may not be the most accurate way to decide if a firm has refocused or not. It is preferable to use instead large changes in DT as accurate enough indicators of diversifying (or refocusing) activities.

Finally, with the index calculated for each firm for the years 1981, 1983, and 1985, I could do a better job of classifying firms as refocused by studying the direction of movement of the index as well as its magnitude

Table 5.2
Frequency distribution of changes in diversification (DT)

$DT85 - DT81$	Number of firms
$\Delta DT \leq -1.00$	1
$-1.00 < \Delta DT \leq -0.50$	9
$-0.50 < \Delta DT \leq -0.40$	6
$-0.40 < \Delta DT \leq -0.30$	17
$-0.30 < \Delta DT \leq -0.20$	27
$-0.20 < \Delta DT \leq -0.10$	32
$-0.10 < \Delta DT \leq -0.05$	14
$-0.05 < \Delta DT \leq -0.00$	15
$0.00 < \Delta DT \leq +0.05$	11
$+0.05 < \Delta DT \leq +0.10$	8
$+0.10 < \Delta DT \leq +0.20$	21
$+0.20 < \Delta DT \leq +0.30$	11
$+0.30 < \Delta DT \leq +0.40$	7
$+0.40 < \Delta DT \leq +0.50$	5
$+0.50 < \Delta DT \leq +0.60$	5
$+0.60 < \Delta DT \leq +1.00$	12
$+1.00 < \Delta DT$	0
Total	201[a]

Note: Minimum $= -1.24$, maximum $= 0.99$, median $= -0.06$, mean $= -0.019$, and standard deviation $= 0.333$.
a. Of this total number of firms, 121 firms refocused and 80 firms diversified.

rather than just looking at how much the index changed. For example, a firm whose DT decreased between 1981 and 1983 by -0.20 but whose DT increased between 1983 and 1985 by $+0.15$ would not be classified as a refocused firm, even though its index over the 1981–85 period had decreased.[2] The distribution of changes in DT in 1981–85 is shown in table 5.2. Note that even though 121 firms have reduced their DT during the period, only 84 of these are classified as refocused using the above methodology.

The $DROS81$ variable in equation (5.1) is the firm's ROS (return on sales) minus its industry-weighted ROS. Return on sales is measured from Compustat as operating income before depreciation and interest as a percent of total sales. As explained in chapter 3, to calculate the industry-weighted ROS of every firm, the following procedure is followed: First, a

---

2. It turns out that our results do not significantly change when a continuous dependent variable and OLS methodology are used instead (see note 3).

Compustat program is used to identify all the firms assigned to each SIC and to calculate their *ROS*. Then, using the firms' sales as weights, the average *ROS* of every SIC is estimated. Next, a breakdown of each sample firm's sales by SIC is obtained from the TRINET tapes. The percentage of the firm's sales in each SIC is then calculated. The industry-weighted *ROS* for each firm is then estimated by multiplying the share of the firm's sales in each SIC by the corresponding *ROS* of that SIC and adding the results.

Adjusting each firm's *ROS* by its industry-weighted *ROS* is essential, given the multi-industry nature of the sample firms. A firm's *ROS* is a function of not only its operational efficiency, but also of the underlying profitability of the industries it is competing in. By adjusting for industry participation, we are making the *ROS* figure comparable across industries.

The other variables in equation (5.1) are defined as follows:

1. *DSE81* represents the firm's debt to equity ratio in 1981, estimated from Compustat.

2. *DMGMT*(85–81) is a dummy variable that takes the value of one if the CEO of the firm changed in the period 1981–85; zero otherwise (data from Moody's Industrial Manuals).

3. *DT81* is the firm's entropy index of diversification in 1981. It was estimated using data from the TRINET tapes.

4. *SHARE81*(c) is the firm's market share in its core business in 1981. The core business is taken as the 2-digit SIC in which the company has the largest percentage of its sales. Firm sales by SIC, as well as total sales in each SIC (both of which are needed to calculate this variable), were derived from the TRINET tapes.

5. *XAD81*(c) is the advertising intensity of the firm's core business, a proxy for the "attractiveness" of the core business. This was calculated as follows: A Compustat program was used to identify all the firms assigned to each SIC and to calculate their advertising intensity. Using the firms' sales as weights, the average advertising intensity of every SIC was then estimated.

6. *C4*(81)(c) is the concentration ratio of the firm's core business in 1981. It was calculated with the standard Herfindahl index, which is the sum of the squared market shares of the four largest firms in every industry (data from TRINET). In some cases this variable was replaced by the variable (*C4 − SHARE*) which measures the tightness of oligopoly in the core industry.

7. *PROF*81(c) represents the average profitability (*ROS*) of the firm's core industry in 1981. This was calculated from Compustat in the same way as the variable *XAD*.

8. *XRD*81(c) is the average R&D intensity of the firm's core industry in 1981. It was calculated from Compustat in the same way as *XAD*.

9. *SIZE*81(c) measures the relative importance of the firm's core industry, in the total business of the firm. It was measured by the sales of the firm's core industry as a percent of the total sales of the firm (data from TRINET).

Results

The results of the full model are shown as equation 1 in table 5.3. Five of the ten explanatory variables come out significant (three of them at the 1 percent level and two at the 10 percent level), and all have the predicted sign: A firm is more likely to refocus the lower its profitability and the higher its diversification relative to its industry competitors. In addition the positive and significant coefficients of *XAD* and *C4* (which act as proxies for core industry attractiveness) suggest that a firm is more likely to refocus if it has an attractive core business. It is also more likely to refocus on its core when this core is a big portion of the total business of the firm. On the other hand, firms in science-based core industries are less likely to refocus, a result that in general agreement with the academic literature on diversification (e.g., Lemelin 1982). It is interesting to note that a change in the top management of the firm has no effect on the decision to refocus. Overall these results suggest that overdiversified firms undertake refocusing in response to a performance crisis, and they are more likely to refocus if their core business is relatively big and attractive.

To account for the riskiness of the firm's cash flows, the variable *RISK* is introduced as a regressor in equation 2. Each firm's *RISK* is measured by the standard deviation of the firm's *ROS* in the five years prior to 1981. The results remain the same as in equation 1. At the same time, it can be argued from the basic industrial organisation (IO) paradigm (e.g., Shepherd 1972) that the variable core industry profitability (*PROF*) is just a function of two other variables that have been included in the model—namely core industry advertising intensity (*XAD*) and core industry concentration ratio (*C4*). To account for this, the model is run again without these two variables (equation 3). The results do not change much, the only difference being that the variables market share in the core industry (*SHARE*) and the size of the core industry (*SIZE*) become more significant.

Table 5.3
Characteristics of refocusing firms

	Intercept	DMGMT (85–81)	DSE 81	DT 81	DROS 81	XAD 81(c)	C4(81)(c)	PROF 81(c)	XRD 81(c)	SHARE 81(c)	SIZE 81(c)	RISK 81
Equation 1	−4.974	−0.169	0.004	0.985	−0.065	0.267	20.472	0.091	−0.035	0.064	0.0148	—
	$(-3.37)^{***}$	(0.52)	(1.04)	$(3.18)^{***}$	$(-1.71)^{*}$	$(2.72)^{***}$	$(1.69)^{*}$	(1.51)	$(-3.12)^{***}$	(0.76)	(1.56)	
Equation 2	−5.362	−0.190	0.004	1.050	−0.061	0.284	21.22	0.096	−0.036	0.053	0.0148	0.134
	$(-3.47)^{***}$	(−0.59)	(1.01)	$(3.29)^{***}$	(−1.58)	$(2.82)^{***}$	$(1.76)^{*}$	(1.59)	$(-3.18)^{***}$	(0.63)	(1.55)	(0.94)
Equation 3	−4.108	−0.219	0.004	0.981	−0.067	—	—	0.070	−0.014	0.103	0.0163	—
	$(-3.01)^{***}$	(0.70)	(1.10)	$(3.25)^{***}$	$(-1.81)^{*}$			(1.34)	$(-1.89)^{*}$	(1.39)	$(1.76)^{*}$	
Equation 4	−3.374	−0.185	0.004	0.930	−0.071	0.235	—	—	−0.028	0.104	0.0123	—
	$(-3.11)^{***}$	(−0.58)	(0.96)	$(3.08)^{***}$	$(-1.88)^{*}$	$(2.57)^{***}$			$(-2.77)^{***}$	(1.34)	(1.33)	
Equation 5	−3.035	−0.295	0.004	0.899	−0.070	—	4.797	—	−0.010	0.093	0.0153	—
	$(-2.87)^{***}$	(−0.94)	(0.99)	$(3.07)^{***}$	$(-1.89)^{*}$		(0.47)		(−1.48)	(1.13)	$(1.66)^{*}$	
Equation 6	−3.478	−0.134	0.004	0.971	−0.067	0.238	—	—	−0.029	—	0.0141	—
	$(-3.21)^{***}$	(−0.43)	(0.97)	$(3.23)^{***}$	$(-1.79)^{*}$	$(2.64)^{***}$			$(-2.85)^{***}$	(1.54)		
Equation 7	−2.991	−0.279	0.004	0.904	−0.071	—	—	—	−0.010	0.107	0.0149	—
	$(-2.84)^{***}$	(−0.89)	(1.00)	$(3.09)^{***}$	$(-1.91)^{*}$				(−1.51)	(1.43)	$(1.64)^{*}$	

Note: $N = 201$; t-statistics appear in parentheses: $^{***} = p < 0.01$ (two-tail test), $^{**} = p < 0.05$ (two-tail test), $^{*} = p < 0.1$ (two-tail test).

This means that *SHARE* and *SIZE* are capturing some of the effect of the two excluded variables.

When the variable ($C4 - SHARE$) is introduced to replace C4, all of the relationships remain unchanged and the new variable comes out negative and significant. If we assume that this variable measures the tightness of oligopoly in the firm's core industry and that there is a positive relationship between this and profit variation in the industry (e.g., Caves and Yamey 1971), then the negative coefficient of the variable suggests that firms will be unwilling to refocus to core industries that are characterized by profit variability.

Because the variables core industry advertising intensity (*XAD*), core industry concentration ratio (*C4*) and core industry profitability (*PROF*) all attempt to capture the same phenomenon (but not the same dimension of the phenomenon)—namely core industry attractiveness—the model is run again, but this time these variables are introduced separately rather than together (see Ravenscraft and Scherer 1987, p. 170). The results are shown in equations 3, 4, and 5. There is no basic change to the relationships discovered above. To account for the possibility that the variable market share in the core industry (*SHARE*) may be capturing the same phenomenon as the above three variables—namely core industry attractiveness—we try equations 6 and 7. The results remain robust.

The variable firm diversification level (*DT*) comes out positive and highly significant in all regressions. What this means is that the more diversified a firm is, the higher the probability that it will refocus. However, we would expect this relationship to hold only for the overdiversified firms. To see this, consider the following example: Assume that we know that all firms have an optimal diversification level equal to $DT = 2$. Then a firm with a diversification level of 3 will be more likely to refocus than a firm whose diversification is only 2.5. On the other hand, a firm with a diversification level of 1.5 should not be a more likely candidate to refocus than a firm whose diversification is 1. To test this, we run the model only on those firms that are likely to be below their optimal diversification level: We take these firms to be those that have a diversification level lower than the sample median ($N = 101$). The results are shown in table 5.4.

The most prominent result to emerge from this table is the total absence of significance in the variable firm diversification level (*DT*), which is exactly what we predicted above. This implies that it is only within the overdiversified group of firms that the positive relationship between refocusing and diversification applies. It is also interesting to note that the

Table 5.4
Logit regression on low-diversity group

	Coefficient
Intercept	−4.29
	(−1.64)*
DMGMT (85−81)	−0.866
	(−1.56)
DSE81	0.004
	(1.09)
DT81	−0.032
	(−0.04)
DROS81	0.003
	(0.06)
XAD81(c)	0.252
	(1.34)
C4 81(c)	50.42
	(2.39)**
PROF81(c)	0.214
	(2.30)**
XRD81(c)	−0.0498
	(−2.19)**
SHARE81(c)	0.0748
	(0.70)
SIZE81(c)	0.0018
	(0.10)

Note: The firms whose 1981 DT is less than the sample median DT ($N = 101$); t-statistics appear in parentheses: *** $= p < 0.01$ (two-tail test), ** $= p < 0.05$ (two-tail test), * $= p < 0.1$ (two-tail test).

variable firm profitability ($DROS$) also comes out insignificant. This implies that the refocusing decision of the underdiversified firms is not affected by their profitability. The only factor that seems to affect their refocusing decision is the attractiveness of their core industry (as captured by its profitability $PROF$ and concentration $C4$). Note also that within this group a firm is more likely to refocus if there is no change in its top management ($DMGMT$).

The above regression-to-the-mean problem was also attacked from another angle, using the following method: Firms were first assigned to their core industry, and within each industry they were ranked according to

Table 5.5
Logit regression with diversification as a dummy variable

	Coefficient
Intercept	−1.771
	(−2.02)**
Over-*DT*	1.062
	(2.94)***
*DROS*81	−0.075
	(−2.11)**
*XAD*81(c)	0.224
	(2.47)**
*XRD*81(c)	−0.024
	(−2.40)**
*PROF*81(c)	0.0201
	(0.40)
*SIZE*81(c)	0.006
	(0.75)

Note: $N = 201$; *t*-statistics appear in parentheses: *** = $p < 0.01$ (two-tail test), ** = $p < 0.05$ (two-tail test), * = $p < 0.1$ (two-tail test).

the value of their diversification index (*DT*). Those firms whose *DT* was bigger than their corresponding industry-median *DT* were classified as overdiversified, while those firms whose *DT* was smaller than their industry-median *DT* were classified as underdiversified. The above regressions were then repeated with diversification being measured as a (0, 1) dummy variable that took the value of 1 if the firm was overdiversified, and zero if the firm was underdiversified. The results are shown in table 5.5.

As expected, the diversification variable comes out positive and highly significant, implying that the refocusing firms are characterized by high diversification relative to their industry counterparts. The variable firm profitability (*DROS*) is again negative and significant, suggesting that the unprofitable firms are more likely to refocus than the profitable ones.[3]

---

3. To test the sensitivity of these results to the exact specification of the dependent variable, I repeated the analysis. But instead of using a dichotomous dependent variable, I used the actual change in the diversification index over the period 1981–85 [*DT*85 − *DT*81] as my dependent variable. I also used the percentage change in this index [(*DT*85 − *DT*81)/ *DT*81] as the dependent variable. The results reported above do not change fundamentally. The only major difference to emerge is that the variable firm profitability (*DROS*81) does not come out significant while the variable *RISK* does.

Summary

This chapter sought to identify the characteristics that distinguish the companies that refocused in 1981–85 from those that did not. Relative to their industry counterparts, the refocusing firms were characterized by high diversification and poor performance. In addition a firm was more likely to refocus the higher the size, concentration ratio, and advertising intensity of its core industry—that is, the higher the attractiveness of its core business. On the other hand, the higher the R&D intensity of the firm's core business, the lower was the likelihood that the firm would refocus. A change in the top management of the firm; as well as the firm's debt-to-equity ratio, had no effect on the refocusing decision.

These results are consistent with the notion that every firm has an intrinsic limit to how much it can diversify. The firms that diversify beyond this limit run into some form of diseconomies—probably managerial diseconomies to scale (e.g., Hoskisson and Turk 1990; Penrose 1959). As a result their profitability suffers, and the managers of the firms come under pressure to either rectify the situation or face the discipline of the external market for corporate control. Refocusing can therefore be viewed as an effort by these overdiversified firms to reduce the spectrum of their activities and thus improve their profitability.

This implies that the prevailing belief that only the conglomerates are "de-diversifying" is incorrect: Along with the conglomerates every overdiversified firm will be refocusing. Although the conglomerates are the most likely candidates to be overdiversified, there is no theoretical reason to believe that no other firm is overdiversified. In fact recent research by Hoskisson and Johnson (1992) has found that it is the Related-linked firms (the firms that have a mixture of related and unrelated business units) that have restructured. This finding is in general agreement with the results of this chapter.

6

The Consequences of Corporate Refocusing: Ex ante Evidence

Our task in this chapter is to determine whether the market value of firms that refocus increases, as the theory predicts. A sample of forty-five firms is examined using the event-study methodology to assess the stock-market reaction surrounding their refocusing announcement. In an efficient capital market (in the semistrong form) the announcement effect reflects the long-term consequences of refocusing. This effect may not prove to be accurate, but it will be unbiased (neither too high nor too low on average). According to proposition 4 this effect should be positive and statistically significant.

The Sample

A search through the business press literature produced 870 announcements of restructuring in the period 1980 to 1988. Each of these announcements was then screened to isolate those involving refocusing. To be classified as a refocusing announcement, the announcement had to meet one of the following criteria:

1. The terms "refocusing" or "concentrate on the core" were explicitly stated in the announcement (e.g., "Baton Broadcasting Inc. said it plans to get out of printing and packaging industry ... to concentrate on its core broadcasting business"—*Wall Street Journal*, October 12, 1988, sec. B, p. 6).

2. The business press evaluated the action as a refocusing program, and described it as such (e.g., "Eli Lilly & Co, in an effort to focus its resources on its core pharmaceuticals business, put its Elizabeth Arden cosmetics unit on the block ..."—*Wall Street Journal*, April 3, 1987, p. 7).

3. The action announced amounts to a return to the firm's core business (e.g., "Ametek plans to spin off several of its divisions into a separate com-

pany, allowing it to concentrate on its precision-technology businesses"—
Wall Street Journal, March 28, 1988, p. 4).

This screening process produced eighty-one refocusing announcements. This is a very conservative estimate of the number of refocusing announcements in the original sample because the screening criteria are very strict. Strict criteria were set so that no value judgment was required on my part to decide if the announcement was refocusing or not. I also wanted to make sure that I captured only the initial announcement of the firm's decision to embark on a refocusing program rather than the individual divestiture announcements following this announcement of intent (see Schipper and Thompson 1983). In this way I am confident that all of the announcements are true refocusing actions (and are perceived by the market as such) rather than major divestitures.

To be included in the final sample, each of these refocusing announcements had to meet the following additional criteria:

4. The date of the refocusing announcement could be identified in the *Wall Street Journal Index*.

5. No major confounding announcements (earnings, dividends, share repurchases) were made within $+/-5$ days of the announcement day.

6. The refocusing firm's stock price returns were available on the Center for Research in Security Prices (CRSP) tapes.

In addition the *Wall Street Journal Index* was screened for three years prior to the announcement to make sure that no other refocusing announcements were made in previous years. In all, thirty-six announcements were eliminated. The final sample consists of forty-five "clean" refocusing announcements that met all of the above criteria.

Methodology

Standard event-study methodology is used to assess the impact of refocusing announcements on shareholder wealth. This methodology is based on the capital asset pricing model (CAPM) and has been extensively used to analyze individual firm events such as earnings, dividends, stock splits, share repurchases, mergers, and divestiture announcements (see Copeland and Weston 1988 for a review of the various applications of the CAPM). The most crucial assumption of the methodology is that capital markets are efficient (in the semistrong form), which implies that the price of any security incorporates all currently available public information and adjusts to the public release of new information instantaneously.

The most commonly used event-study methodology is based on a market model described by Fama (1976). The model predicts a firm's "normal" or expected return given the market return (a control for exogenous events) and the firm's historical relationship to the market. Thus, for each firm the following model is calculated:

$$R_{it} = \alpha_i + \beta_i R_{mt} + e_{it},$$

where R_{it} is the return on the security of firm i at time t. R_{mt} is the return on the market portfolio at time t. In this study, we use the equally-weighted market return on New York Stock Exchange (NYSE) and American Stock Exchange (ASE) stocks from the CRSP tapes. α_i and β_i are the parameters of the relationship between the return on the individual security and that of the market, and e_{it} is the residual of the relationship at time t, assumed to be distributed normally with mean equal to zero, a constant variance over the control and prediction periods, and zero correlation between residuals over time ($e_{it} \sim N(0, s^2)$). The parameters alpha (α_i) and beta (β_i) are estimated for each security i over a period -270 to -90 days prior to the announcement of the event under study (refocusing). These parameters are then used to calculate the expected returns over the test period. The difference between the actual returns and the expected returns for each day and for each firm are called "abnormal returns" (AR_{it}) and are computed as follows:

$$AR_{it} = R_{it} - (\hat{\alpha}_i + \hat{\beta}_i R_{mt}).$$

A two-day abnormal return is calculated for each refocusing announcement. A two-day abnormal return is necessary to capture the full impact of the refocusing announcement: Day $t = 0$ is the day the news of refocusing is published in the *Wall Street Journal*. In many cases, however, the news is announced on the previous day, $t = -1$, and reported the next day. If the refocusing is announced before the market closes, then the market's response to the news actually predates the announcement day by one. If the news is announced after the market closes, the market will respond on the next day and the announcement day is indeed $t = 0$. Thus, in reality, there is a two-day announcement "day," $t = -1$ and $t = 0$. This two-day return is called the cumulative abnormal return (CAR) and is calculated as

$$CAR_{i(-1,0)} = \sum_{t=-1}^{0} AR_{it}.$$

For a sample of N securities, the average cumulative abnormal return is calculated by

$$\overline{CAR}_{(-1,0)} = \left(\frac{1}{N}\right) \sum_{i=1}^{N} CAR_{i(-1,0)}.$$

Finally, a t-statistic is computed for the average CAR as

$$t = \frac{\overline{CAR}_{(-1,0)}}{s_{CAR(-1,0)}/\sqrt{N}},$$

where $s_{CAR(-1,0)}$ equals the standard deviation of the two-day excess returns; and N equals the number of firms in the sample.

The cumulative abnormal returns ($CARs$) are used to determine whether the decision taken by the firm had a material effect on its stock value. Positive $CARs$ indicate that the equity market expects the event (refocusing) to create value for the shareholders involved. Negative $CARs$, on the other hand, imply that refocusing will actually destroy value.

The logic behind an event-study is the following (Linn and Roseff 1984, p. 432):

Assuming that the current price of a company's stock reflects the market's assessment of its prospective cash flows, and that the market reacts quickly and unbiasedly to news, immediate stock price reactions to [a refocusing] announcement can be seen as conveying the market's perception of the *long-run* cash flow consequences of the [refocusing]. That perception may not prove to be accurate, but it will be "unbiased"—that is, neither too high, nor too low on average.

Who Are the Overdiversified Firms?

As noted earlier, proposition 4 can only be tested if we can identify ex ante who the overdiversified firms are in the sample. This would require us to identify every firm's optimal diversification level. While theoretically feasible, such a task is practically impossible. Every firm has a different limit depending on its resources, its external environment, the type of diversification it is following (related versus unrelated), the caliber of its management team, its capacity to learn from past diversification moves, and so on. The optimal diversification limit for a particular firm is really a theoretical concept, much like the utility concept in economics; it cannot be measured precisely. To identify the overdiversified firms in the sample, we will therefore need to take an indirect route and to use proxies.

For this study, six different strategies were used to classify the sample firms into under- and overdiversified groupings. The six classification strategies used are the following:

1. It was assumed that any firm that decides to refocus must be doing so for a good reason—that it perceives itself as overdiversified and suffering as a result. Therefore the whole sample of 45 firms is classified as over-diversified. This implies that we should get a positive abnormal return for the whole sample.

2. For each sample firm I calculate its entropy index of total diversification (DT) and its entropy index of unrelated diversification (DU) in the manner demonstrated by Palepu (1985). The index is calculated for the year prior to the refocusing year. If this is unavailable, the index from the previous year is used. The data come from the TRINET tapes. Because of missing information on TRINET, the index can only be calculated for 33 of the sample firms. Those firms whose DT is above the sample median ($N = 17$) are classified as overdiversified, while those firms whose DT is below the sample median ($N = 16$) are classified as underdiversified. (The analysis is repeated using DU as the index of diversification.) Since it is very likely that most, if not all, of the sample firms are refocusing because they con-sider themselves overdiversified, this subdivision increases our chances of selecting the truly overdiversified firms.

3. To improve even further the chances of correctly selecting the over-diversified firms (but at the cost of smaller subsample sizes), the sample is subdivided into quartiles (according to DT as well as DU). The first quartile ($N = 8$) contains the firms with the smallest diversification levels in the sample and is designated the underdiversified group. The fourth quartile ($N = 9$) contains the firms with the highest diversification levels in the sample and is designated the overdiversified group.

4. Even though every firm has a different optimal diversification level, it is likely that within a given industry (if we control for industry effects) the optimal diversification levels for most firms in that industry would lie within a narrow range. I therefore assume that within each industry the most likely firms to be overdiversified are firms whose diversification level is higher than their industry median diversification level. To carry out this classification I proceeded as follows: First, I define each firm's core industry as the 2-digit SIC in which the company had the largest percentage of its sales. This is arguably a crude measure given the multi-industry nature of the sample firms, but it is the only practical alternative. Next, to estimate every industry's median DT, I use our original sample of the 250 Fortune 500 firms. For each of these firms I estimate its diversification level DT, but because of missing information on the TRINET tapes, 40 firms were lost (all were spread evenly over the 5 Fortune groups). Each of the remaining 210 firms is sorted by core industry, and in each industry, firms are ranked

according to their diversification level DT. Next, I place each of the 33 refocusing firms in their respective core industries. Those firms whose DT is higher than their industry's median DT are classified as overdiversified ($N = 21$); the rest are classified as underdiversified ($N = 12$). (The same exercise is repeated using DU to classify firms.[1])

5. The median DT for the 210 Fortune 500 firms is 1.99. Since the Fortune 500 firms are the most diversified firms in the U.S. economy, this number is probably on the high side of the diversification scale. I therefore use it as a reasonable cutoff point[2]: Refocusing firms whose DT is higher than 1.99 ($N = 20$) are classified as overdiversified; the rest ($N = 13$) are classified as underdiversified.

6. As argued before, the overdiversified companies are likely to be characterized not only by excessive diversification but also by poor profitability. I therefore classify as overdiversified those firms whose DT is bigger than the sample median and whose profitability is lower than the sample median[3] ($N = 10$). Profitability is measured as the firm's return on sales (ROS) minus its industry-weighted ROS. To calculate the industry-weighted ROS, I used the procedure[4] described in chapter 3.

To double-check the results, I use the same criteria to reclassify the firms, but instead of using the index of total diversification DT to separate the overdiversified firms, I use the index of unrelated diversification DU. I expect little difference in the results since the two indexes are highly collinear ($r = 0.85$).

---

1. The Fortune 500 list is selected for this exercise for two reasons: (1) The majority of the 33 refocusing firms in our sample (88 percent) comes from the Fortune 500. For comparison reasons, the average DT of the 33 sample firms is 2.15, versus 1.98 for the 210 Fortune 500 firms; and the average size (1985 sales) of the 33 sample firms is $3.1 billion, versus $4.5 billion for the Fortune 500 firms. (2) The Fortune 500 list contains the most diversified firms in America. By using these firms to calculate industry median diversification levels, I am increasing the likelihood that those firms we classify as overdiversified have truly gone beyond their limits of diversification.

2. Also, since most of the refocusing firms in the sample come from the Fortune 500, a convenient cutoff point can be the median diversification level of these firms.

3. I also subdivide the sample according to core industry DT and core industry profitability. The analysis is then repeated on this subsample of overdiversified firms ($N = 12$).

4. First, a Compustat program was used to identify all the firms assigned to each 2-digit SIC and to calculate their ROS. Then, using their sales as weights, the average ROS of every SIC was estimated. Next, a breakdown of each refocusing firm's sales by 2-digit SIC was obtained from the TRINET tapes. The percentage of the firm's sales in each SIC was then calculated. The industry-weighted ROS for each firm was estimated by multiplying the share of the firm's sales in each SIC by the corresponding ROS of that SIC and adding the results. This adjustment accounts for the multi-industry nature of the sample firms and makes the ROS figure comparable across industries.

Results

Of the 45 two-day CARs calculated, 15 are negative and 30 are positive (see table 6.1). They range in value from -12.7 to $+18.9$ percent. The average two-day CAR for the whole sample is $+1.73\%$ and has a t-statistic of 2.03, which is statistically significant at the 5 percent level (two-tail test). This means that on average, refocusing creates shareholder value, a result that is consistent with proposition 4 of this study.

The majority of the abnormal returns fall within the narrow range -10 to $+10$ percent. There is, however, one relatively big positive outlier ($+18.9$ percent) and a smaller negative outlier (-12.7 percent). To determine if the above result is being driven by these outliers, the positive outlier is first dropped from the sample. The CAR falls to 1.34 percent but remains statistically significant at $t = 1.73$. When both outliers are dropped from the sample, the CAR jumps to 1.67 percent and becomes highly significant at $t = 2.31$. For the rest of the analysis I report results for both the whole sample and the subsample, which excludes the two outliers.

A more detailed breakdown of the daily abnormal returns surrounding the refocusing announcements is shown in table 6.2. The movement and level of average and cumulative residuals before and after $t = 0$ are consistent with those found in earlier research on divestitures (e.g., Linn and Rozeff 1985; Markides and Berg 1988 for a survey). The biggest abnormal return (1.61 percent) occurs on day $t = -1$, a result that is consistent with an efficient capital market. From $t = -10$ through the refocusing

Table 6.1
Distribution of abnormal returns

CAR $(-1, 0)$	Number of companies
$-9--15\%$	1
$-5--9$	5
$0--5$	9
Total negative	15
$0-5\%$	20
$5-10$	6
$10-15$	3
$15-20$	1
Total positive	30

Note: Total number of companies $= 45$. Mean CAR $(-1, 0) = +1.73$ percent ($t = 2.03$). Minimum CAR $= -12.7$ percent. Maximum CAR $= +18.9$ percent. Median CAR $= +1.40$ percent.

Table 6.2
Daily average abnormal returns ($N = 45$)

Day	Daily average residual	t-statistic	CAR	Percent positive
−10	−0.00051	−0.16	−0.00051	46.6
−5	−0.001118	−0.29	0.00652	48.9
−4	0.001931	0.57	0.00845	44.4
−3	0.001267	0.29	0.00972	44.4
−2	0.006926	1.73*	0.01665	51.1
−1	0.016107	2.45***	0.03275	71.1
0	0.001238	0.25	0.03399	51.1
1	−0.004104	−1.55	0.02989	42.2
2	−0.00562	−1.99**	0.02426	33.3
3	0.002002	0.51	0.02626	40.0
4	−0.001953	−0.81	0.02431	42.2
5	0.006189	2.65****	0.03050	62.2
10	0.005879	1.97**	0.03431	53.3

Note: All tests are two-tail tests: **** = $p < 0.01$, *** = $p < 0.02$, ** = $p < 0.05$, * = $p < 0.1$.

announcement, the CARs total 3.39 percent (statistically significant at the 2 percent level). For the ten days following the announcement, the abnormal returns appear to follow a random walk and they cancel each other out, so no real value change occurs during this period. Again this is consistent with an efficient capital market in that all new information is quickly incorporated in the stock price of the firm.

To test the robustness of the main finding of this study that refocusing creates market value, I also calculate CARs for longer-time windows. Some of these are shown in table 6.3. For the period −10 to +10 the CAR is 3.43 percent and significant. About 99 percent of this value creation occurs in the period (−10, 0), during which the CAR is 3.39 percent and highly significant. It is interesting to note that more than 75 percent of the total CAR is created in the relatively short period of five days immediately before the refocusing announcement. It is also important to note that in the period (0, +10) no value is created. Again these are results consistent with an efficient capital market. None of these basic findings changes when the two outliers are removed from the analysis.

As argued before, it is likely that these firms are refocusing exactly because they perceive themselves as overdiversified. Therefore one way of identifying the overdiversified firms is to assume that anybody who is refocusing is overdiversified. The above result that the whole sample

Table 6.3
Cumulative abnormal returns for various time windows

Time window	CAR (%)	t-statistic
A. Full sample ($N = 45$)		
$(-10, 10)$	3.43	2.10**
$(-5, 5)$	2.28	2.09**
$(-3, 3)$	1.78	1.51
$(-2, 2)$	1.45	1.41
$(-1, 0)$	1.73	2.03**
$(-10, 0)$	3.39	2.36***
$(-5, 0)$	2.63	2.81****
$(-5, -1)$	2.51	3.06****
$(1, 5)$	-0.35	-0.72
$(0, 10)$	0.15	0.17
B. Excluding the two outliers ($N = 43$)		
$(-10, 10)$	2.71	1.67*
$(-5, 5)$	1.89	1.87*
$(-1, 0)$	1.67	2.31**
$(-10, 0)$	2.73	1.91*
$(-5, -1)$	2.16	2.69****
$(-5, 0)$	2.26	2.62****
$(0, 10)$	0.07	0.08
C. Excluding the positive outlier ($N = 44$)		
$(-10, 10)$	3.08	1.89*
$(-5, 5)$	1.79	1.79*
$(-1, 0)$	1.34	1.73*
$(-10, 0)$	3.04	2.13**
$(-5, -1)$	2.22	2.82****
$(-5, 0)$	2.18	2.59****
$(0, 10)$	0.00	0.00

Note: All tests are two-tail tests: **** $= p < 0.01$, *** $= p < 0.02$, ** $= p < 0.05$, * $= p < 0.1$.

creates a positive significant CAR is consistent with this assumption. As described above, several other strategies were used to identify the over-diversified firms. The results from these strategies are shown in table 6.4. The main result to emerge from this sensitivity analysis is that no matter what classification strategy is used, the group of firms classified as over-diversified consistently create statistically significant abnormal returns while the group of firms classified as underdiversified create no abnormal returns. This result does not change when the two outliers are removed from the sample.

Table 6.4
Abnormal returns for overdiversified firms, classified as such according to DT

Classification criterion	Full sample			Excluding two outliers		
	N	CAR $(-1, 0)$	t-statistic	N	CAR $(-1, 0)$	t-statistic
Anybody who refocuses	45	1.73%	2.03**	43	1.67%	2.31**
According to sample median DT						
Underdiversified firms	16	0.84	0.64	15	0.89	0.63
Overdiversified firms	17	3.64	2.28**	16	3.50	3.58****
According to quartiles						
First quartile	8	−2.41	−1.44	8	−2.41	−1.44
Second quartile	8	4.09	3.38****	8	4.09	3.38****
Third quartile	8	4.32	2.01*	7	2.25	2.14*
Fourth quartile	9	3.03	1.31	8	5.00	3.26***
According to core industry median DT						
Underdiversified firms	12	0.79	0.37	11	−0.86	−0.58
Overdiversified firms	21	3.14	2.79***	20	3.94	4.61****
According to full 210 sample median DT						
Underdiversified firms	13	0.46	0.29	13	0.46	0.29
Overdiversified firms	20	3.47	2.55***	18	3.51	4.04****
According to sample median DT and sample median profitability						
Underdiversified firms	23	1.14	0.91	22	1.77	1.54
Overdiversified firms	10	4.91	2.81***	9	3.36	3.21***

Note: All tests are two-tail tests: **** $= p < 0.01$, *** $= p < 0.02$, ** $= p < 0.05$, * $= p < 0.1$.

Of the 6 strategies used to identify the overdiversified firms, the most likely to correctly do so is the sixth one: the truly overdiversified firms should be characterized not only by "high" diversification but also by poor profitability. As shown in table 6.4, this group of firms ($N = 10$) creates the biggest CAR (4.91 percent) of all groups, and this is highly significant. To double-check this result, I use the same criterion to identify the overdiversified firms, but instead of using the sample median DT and the sample median profitability as our cutoff points, I use the core industry median DT and the core industry median profitability as the cutoff points. (The full sample of 210 Fortune 500 firms is used for this exercise as explained before.) Again the overdiversified group ($N = 12$) creates a highly significant ($t = 3.25$) CAR (4.23 percent); while the underdiversified group creates an insignificant CAR.

Table 6.5
Abnormal returns for overdiversified firms, classified as such according to *DU*

Classification criterion	Full sample			Excluding two outliers		
	N	CAR (−1, 0)	t-statistic	N	CAR (−1, 0)	t-statistic
According to sample median *DU*						
Underdiversified firms	16	0.10%	0.09	16	0.10%	0.09
Overdiversified firms	17	4.33	2.66***	15	4.51	4.13****
According to quartiles						
First quartile	8	−2.30	−1.34	8	−2.30	−1.34
Second quartile	8	2.49	2.87**	8	2.49	2.87**
Third quartile	8	4.42	2.62**	8	4.42	2.62**
Fourth quartile	9	4.26	1.58	7	4.61	3.48***
According to core industry median *DU*						
Underdiversified firms	15	1.21	0.78	15	1.21	0.78
Overdiversified firms	18	3.18	2.21**	16	3.19	3.87****
According to full 210 sample median *DU*						
Underdiversified firms	7	−1.79	−0.96	7	−1.79	−0.96
Overdiversified firms	26	3.38	2.89****	24	3.41	3.98****

Note: All tests are two-tail tests: **** $= p < 0.01$, *** $= p < 0.02$, ** $= p < 0.05$, * $= p < 0.1$.

As a final exercise, the sensitivity of these results is tested by using the same criteria to classify firms, but instead of using the index of total diversification *DT* to separate the overdiversified firms, we use the index of unrelated diversification *DU*. Some of these results are shown in table 6.5. Again the main result to emerge is that no matter what criterion is used, the group of firms classified as overdiversified consistently create significant positive abnormal returns, while the group of firms classified as underdiversified create no value. This result remains unchanged when the outliers are removed from the sample. As in the previous table these results have to be approached with some hesitancy, given the small size of the different subsamples.

It would be interesting to examine if, at least in the short term, the capital market's expectation (that refocusing creates value) is actually met. This is not a pointless exercise. For example, we know from numerous event studies on divestitures that divestitures on average create value. Yet Montgomery and Thomas (1988) have found that divesting firms do not (on average) perform better than a control group of nondivesting firms—in the short term. Similarly with mergers: Event studies on mergers generally conclude that mergers are value-creating transactions, at least for the targets. Yet Caves (1989) has shown that this result does not receive support from IO studies that examine ex post performance.

From the list of 45 refocusing announcements in the sample, those made in the period 1981–86 were selected—a total of 12. Eight of these announcements created positive CARs and 4 created negative CARs. The average two-day CAR for the twelve firms is +2.09 percent. For these 12 firms their DROS was calculated (ROS minus industry-weighted ROS), starting with the year immediately prior to their refocusing announcement and ending with 1988. (For 1988, the firm's 1987 industry participation was used to calculate the industry-weighted ROS. For 1980, the 1981 weights were used.) The results are shown in table 6.6.

For all 12 firms, their average DROS goes from −0.0021 in 1980 to −2.64 in 1988—hardly a confirmation of the stock market's expectation. Of the 12 firms, 6 have improved their performance after the announcement of refocusing, 5 have done much worse, and one firm was taken over in 1988. Of the 8 firms for which the market expected an improved performance (i.e., positive CAR), 4 have done better and 4 have done worse. Of the 4 firms for which the market expected worse performance after refocusing, 2 have done better and 2 have done worse.

The only conclusion that I can draw from these results is that the stock market's expectation for improved performance after refocusing is not fulfilled in the short term. (Could it be that the market expects improved stock performance?)

The Determinants of Market Valuation

It is clear from table 6.1 that there is quite a lot of variation in the distribution of CARs. The interesting question that arises is therefore What can explain this variation? I seek in particular to determine whether the firm's profitability and diversification level in the year it announces its refocusing affect how its refocusing announcement is valued by the market.

The market's valuation of a refocusing announcement will depend on two main factors: (1) the position that the firm is in when it decides to refocus and (2) the nature (or "attractiveness") of the core industry the firm is returning to.

If a firm starts out close to its optimal diversification level, any refocusing on its part will not affect its operations by much, and so the market should not value its refocusing highly. If, however, the firm is overdiversified, refocusing will allow it to remove the diseconomies associated with excessive diversification and thus improve its operational efficiency. Its

Table 6.6
Actual performance of refocused firms

Company[a]	CAR (−1, 0)	DROS80	DROS81	DROS85	DROS87	DROS88	Better = √
Average for 12 companies[b]	+	−0.0021	−1.27	−4.49	−2.64	−2.64	×
Coastal Corp. (1981)	−	0.177	−4.39	−1.74	−10.28	−10.54	×
Beatrice (1983)	+		−0.739	−2.004	−1.514	−1.005	×
Paramount (1983)	+		−4.11	−9.038	11.118	9.83	√
Ashland Oil (1984)	+		−7.18	−6.57	−5.069	−4.474	√
Colgate-Palm. (1985)	+			−4.79	−7.209	−6.008	×
Control Data (1985)	−			−19.37	−17.51	−17.99	√
General Mills (1985)	+			−0.529	1.089	0.413	√
IU Intl. (1985)	+			−3.55	−2.418	Taken over	×
Beneficial Corp (1986)	−			9.71	20.34	18.26	√
CBS Inc. (1986)	−			−10.15	−15.40	−15.67	×
B.F. Goodrich (1986)	+			−4.58	−3.56	0.56	√
Sherwin Williams (1986)	+			−1.27	−1.32	−2.39	×
ROS for 12 companies		12.02	10.76	10.66	15.29	15.99	

a. Refocusing announcement year in parentheses.
b. Average $CAR(-1, 0)$ for 12 companies = +0.0209.

refocusing should therefore be valued highly by the market. I therefore expect a positive relationship between the firm's diversification level and the market's valuation of its refocusing.

Similar arguments could be made with respect to the firm's profitability in the year it decides to refocus. If the firm is doing poorly, then by announcing its decision to refocus it may be sending a signal to the market that it is ready and willing to do something about it. At the same time, if its poor performance is a direct result of excessive diversification, then by refocusing it sets the preconditions for improved performance in the future. Its refocusing should therefore be valued highly by the market. On the other hand, if a profitable firm decides to refocus, its profitability should not be affected much, so the market will not value its action highly. This means that the relationship between a firm's profitability and the market's valuation of its refocusing will be negative.

The "attractiveness" of the firm's core business should also affect the valuation of its refocusing. A firm that is returning to an attractive industry should receive a higher valuation than a firm that is returning to an unattractive core. Hence I expect a positive relationship.

To test these propositions, I use the sample of forty-five refocusing announcements from above. Because of missing information on the Compustat and TRINET tapes, data could only be collected for thirty-three of the firms. For each firm the following variables were estimated: (1) The firm's entropy index of diversification (DT) in the year it announced its refocusing. If this was unavailable for the refocusing year, the index from the previous year is used; (2) The firm's operating income as a percent of sales (ROS) in the year it announced its refocusing; (3) The firm's $DROS$ (firm ROS minus its industry-weighted ROS) in the year it announced its refocusing. If this could not be calculated for the refocusing year, the $DROS$ from the previous year is used; (4) The profitability (ROS), seller concentration ratio ($C4$), and advertising intensity (XAD) of the firm's core business in the refocusing year. These three variables proxy for the attractiveness of the core industry. The results of the regressions attempted are shown in table 6.7.

In regression A the two-day CAR is regressed against DT, $DROS$, and core ROS. As expected, DT and $DROS$ come out significant and with the "correct" sign. The core industry's profitability does not appear to affect the market's valuation, but this result may be due to the fact that this variable's effect is already captured by $DROS$. In regression B I use the same variables as before, plus the two variables that proxy for core attractiveness. The results remain unchanged, with DT and $DROS$ coming out

Table 6.7
Determinants of market valuation

	Dependent variable = $CAR(-1, 0)$		
	(A)	(B)	(C)
Intercept	−0.0383	−0.0397	−0.0203
	(−1.07)	(−1.07)	(−0.36)
$DT(t)$	0.0176	0.0215	0.0177
	(1.35)*	(1.52)*	(1.41)*
$DROS(t)$	−0.0042	−0.0041	—
	(−2.02)**	(−1.88)**	
Core $ROS(t)$	0.0011	0.0008	0.0032
	(0.88)	(0.66)	(1.98)**
Core $C4(t)$	—	0.0569	—
		(0.09)	
Core $XAD(t)$	—	−0.0004	—
		(−0.89)	
$ROS(t)$	—	—	−0.0036
			(−2.32)**

$N = 33$; t-statistics are in parentheses: ** = $p < 0.05$ (one-tail test). * = $p < 0.1$ (one-tail test).

significant again. To allow core ROS to show its true effect, I use ROS instead of $DROS$ in regression C. All three variables come out significant as expected. It is interesting to note that whereas the variable $DROS$ comes out hardly significant, ROS emerges highly significant. This implies that the market responds to a firm's apparent profitability rather than its more relevant industry-adjusted profitability. Overall these results confirm my expectations that a firm's refocusing announcement is valued higher the bigger its diversification level and the lower its profitability level in the refocusing year.[5]

Four Case Studies

In an effort to go beyond central tendencies, I now look in more detail at the events that preceded and followed the refocusing announcement of four firms. Each of the four firms has been selected so as to highlight a unique aspect of its refocusing. Thus Gulf & Western is selected because it

---

5. The results remain unchanged when interaction effects between DT and $DROS$ are included in the model.

is one of the "pioneers" of refocusing; American Can is a company "in search of a focus"; Goodyear Tire refocused after a takeover threat; and Continental Group refocused (or, as some people believe, was dismembered) after it was taken over.

For each firm I try to identify the market's reaction to events leading to and following the announcement of refocusing. For this purpose I again use the event study methodology to calculate two-day cumulative abnormal returns around the different events. Since I follow a company over several years, a new beta is calculated for each year using the first event we study in each year as day zero. In certain cases where it was judged that a major divestiture or acquisition in the middle of the year would most likely affect the firm's asset beta, the beta was calculated again using smaller subperiods of relative stability for the firm.[6]

The selection of "major events" to study was somewhat arbitrary. Some of them are not "clean" events, so the market's reaction incorporates any interaction effects—and there is nothing I could do about this. Furthermore measured abnormal returns reflect unanticipated events. If the market anticipated any of the events studied, the size of the abnormal return will be underestimated. The sign of the abnormal return, however, can be unambiguously interpreted (Ruback 1983).

Gulf & Western

Gulf & Western (now Paramount) represents one of the pioneers of refocusing. As its CEO, Martin Davis, boasted in *Fortune* in 1985:

... before restructuring (selling operations that no longer fit a company's strategy and buying ones that do) exploded into vogue, G&W announced [in 1983] a far-reaching realignment to reflect changing conditions ... G&W's metamorphosis into a much more narrowly focused company with operations in entertainment, publishing and financial services presaged most of the restructurings we see today. (*Fortune*, December 9, 1985. p. 171)

The company ended 1982 with declining earnings and a large portfolio of equity investments in numerous well-known companies such as Libbey-Owens-Ford, J.P. Stevens and Co, Clark Equipment, and Amfac. In February 1983 the firm's CEO Charles Bluhdorn died. Upon the announcement of his replacement (Martin Davis), the company's stock produced an abnormal return of 12.4 percent (see table 6.8). Four days later it was reported in the press that the new leadership will try to cast the company in

---

6. The biggest problems—unstable beta—emerged in the case of the Continental Group.

Table 6.8
Gulf & Western: Abnormal returns

Event date	Announcement	$CAR(-1, 0)$
2/24/83	Named Martin Davis as new CEO	0.12374
2/28/83	New leader to sell firms's stock portfolio	0.04788
3/16/83	Revised firms's structure and acts to sell portfolio	−0.04048
8/15/83	Directors approve a massive divestiture plan	0.013152
8/26/83	Sells inventory assets of Sega Enterprises	0.01847
9/09/83	Sells building-product operations	−0.011062
11/14/83	Sells Crown Textile Co.	−0.01292
11/16/83	Sells E. W. Bliss Manufacturing	−0.016091
12/05/83	Completes the liquidation of its stock portfolio	0.008318
12/14/83	Sells Advanced Fuels Technology	−0.004675
	Average β in 1983 = 1.106	
2/24/84	Sells Roosevelt Raceway	−0.00977
3/20/84	Buys MTI Teleprograms Inc.	−0.00058
6/13/84	Sells sugar and resort businesses	−0.03929
8/21/84	Sells seven units	0.024036
8/28/84	Buys Calvin Klein's women's underwear unit	−0.014556
9/10/84	Sells Morse cutting tools unit	−0.0006572
11/06/84	Proposes to buy Prentice-Hall	−0.005797
11/27/84	Buys Prentice-Hall	−0.005143
	Average β in 1984 = 1.260	
3/26/85	Sells Belwin-Mills Publishing Corp.	0.013952
4/23/85	Buys Xerox's Ginn & Co. unit	0.02903
6/10/85	To sell its consumer and industrial products groups	0.071866
9/13/85	Completes $1 billion sale of consumer/industrial units	0.031266
	Average β in 1985 = 1.839	
	Total	0.2206

its own image and that it is considering selling most of the firm's stock portfolio. This announcement produced an abnormal return of 4.8 percent. When the first actions were taken to implement this decision (on March 16), a negative 4.1 percent abnormal return was created, reflecting perhaps disappointment on the part of the market on the "limited" actions taken.

Between March and December 1983 the company proceeded to slowly get rid of its portfolio investments. For example, in April it sold its holdings in Fieldcrest Mills, Bank of New York, Amoskeag Co., J.P. Stevens, and Central Soya; in May it got out of Hayes-Albion and Hammermill Paper; and in June it sold its holdings in Mohasco and General Tire and

Rubber Co. The liquidation of the stock portfolio was finally completed in December 1983 with the sale of its 24 percent interest in Amfac. This announcement was accompanied by a relatively "small" abnormal return of (about) 1 percent implying that the effect of this action had already been incorporated into the firm's stock price over the period.

In the meantime rumors had begun circulating that the company was considering a major change in strategy. As early as July 1, 1983, the press reported that "the firm is expected to take more than $200 million in write-offs as part of a broad restructuring plan." Finally, on August 16, 1983, it was reported in the press that "Directors approved a massive divestiture plan that would result in write-offs of about $470 million and a net loss of about $215 million; the plan is the result of efforts to streamline G&W by getting rid of low-margin industrial businesses and focusing on consumer products, entertainment, and financial services." The announcement of the plan created an abnormal return of 1.3 percent. This return clearly underestimates the "true" impact of the action since the event had been anticipated by the market for a long time before the announcement.

Over the next two years the company proceeded with the implementation of its restructuring, by buying and divesting units. The first unit to be sold was Sega Enterprises, and the announcement produced an abnormal return of 1.8%. The firm's other transactions are listed in table 6.8. Most of the transactions in 1984 created small but negative abnormal returns (surprising). By contrast, all the transactions in 1985 created relatively big positive returns. Overall, the twelve events listed in 1984–85 created a net positive return of 9.4 percent. On June 10, 1985, the company completed its restructuring plan by selling its consumer and industrial products group. The *Wall Street Journal* reported that "... the sale [of the group] shrinks G&W in half; the $1 billion cash sale completes Martin Davis' transformation of G&W from a volatile giant into a streamlined entertainment, communications and financial firm." The announcement was accompanied by an abnormal return of 7.2 percent. When the sale was finalized on September 13, an additional 3.1 percent abnormal return was created.

Overall Gulf & Western's restructuring moves in the period 1983–85 appear to have created a net positive abnormal return of about 22 percent. Assuming an efficient capital market, this implies that the refocusing strategy has allowed the company to create market value and to improve its competitive position. When we look at G&W's performance over the period, this is indeed the picture that emerges (see tables 6.9 and 6.10).

By any count, the strategy appears to be a success. In the period 1981–88, the company's profitability nearly doubled, while its stock price in-

Table 6.9
Gulf & Western's business structure

Business segment	Revenues as a % of total sales			
	1979	1982	1986	1988
Natural resources	7.6	0.0	0.0	0.0
Consumer and agricultural products	7.4	0.0	0.0	0.0
Apparel and hosiery	18.5	20.1	0.0	0.0
Bedding and home furnishings	18.5	11.7	0.0	0.0
Manufacturing	21.2	13.0	0.0	0.0
Auto parts distribution	8.6	6.4	0.0	0.0
Entertainment	15.6	15.3	30.4	36.4
Publishing/information	15.6	3.7	25.1	23.3
Consumer/commercial finance	20.9	23.2	44.5	40.2
Other	—	6.3	0.0	0.0

Source: Company annual reports.

Table 6.10
Selected financial statistics for Gulf & Western

	1981	1983	1985	1987	1988
Revenues ($ million)	7,409	2,522	3,321	4,701	5,107
Total assets ($ million)	5,893	4,554	4,064	4,929	5,378
Net earnings ($ million)	290.9	(191.7)	247.8	356.1	384.7
ROS (%)	3.9	(7.6)	7.4	7.6	7.5
ROA (%)	4.9	(4.2)	6.1	7.2	7.1
Stock price—close	$15\frac{7}{8}$	$30\frac{1}{8}$	$49\frac{6}{8}$	$71\frac{1}{8}$	$81\frac{2}{8}$
Book value per share	27.5	24.5	29.15	35.05	39.0
S&P 500 composite—close	122.55	164.93	211.28	247.08	277.72

creased by more than five times. Shareholders who owned G&W stock over the period 1983–88 have earned a 239 percent return on their investment. By contrast, the Standard & Poor's Composite Index of 500 stocks showed only a 96 percent return over the same period.

American Can

American Can (now Primerica) is the prime example of a company that decided to refocus by moving out of its core—paper and packaging—and into a new core—financial services and health care. It did this over a relatively short period of time (1981–86), exclusively through divestitures and acquisitions. Why the management of this firm felt that they can transfer their packaging skills into financial services overnight, is unclear. The fate of American Can makes clear how wise this decision was.

After a disappointing 1980—net income fell 33 percent to $85.7 million—the company announced on April 2, 1981, that it will undertake a restructuring of its operations. The paper and forest-products operations (sales = $1.1 billion) were targeted for sale. The announcement was received favorably by the market, and a positive 8.5 percent abnormal return was created (see table 6.11). Some of this gain was later lost when the implementation of the decision was undertaken. Thus, when on January 5, 1982, it was reported in the press that: "American Can reached a 'preliminary understanding' to sell certain of its domestic paper businesses to James River Corp. for $420 million in cash and stock; discussions are continuing with interested parties regarding the sale of the balance of American Can's paper and forest-based assets," the announcement was accompanied by a negative abnormal return of 2.1 percent (disappointing price?) Similarly the sale of the firm's Canadian timber rights and pulp mill operations to James River in February 1983, also created a negative return (−3.3 percent). Overall, it appears that the sale of one of the firm's core businesses had a small but positive net effect.

The first announcement that the company was planning to enter the financial services field came in October 1981, shortly after the decision to sell the paper business. On October 28, 1981, American Can acquired Associated Madison Co., its first acquisition in a new field. A negative abnormal return of 0.7 percent was created. Over the next few years the company made several acquisitions in this new field—including the acquisition of Smith Barney in 1987. Some of these acquisitions created positive returns, while others created negative returns. The net effect of moving into this field appears to be negative (about −1.1 percent).

The firm's decision to enter another new field—health care—was also received unfavorably by the market. In November 1985 it was announced that American Can would try to enter the health care field through an acquisition, and that it was interested in making a separate acquisition that could cost as much as $1 billion, in an unspecified field. The announcement created a negative abnormal return of 3 percent.

With hindsight, it appears that the company's decision to get out of its major business—packaging—had been made as early as 1984, two full years before the actual sale of the business. In February 1984 the firm's Canadian and British packaging operations were sold, an event that created a small negative abnormal return. In the next two years the company actually proceeded to build its domestic packaging business. Thus in

Table 6.11
American Can: Abnormal returns

Event date	Announcement	$CAR(-1, 0)$
4/02/81	Sells forest products operations	0.08476
10/28/81	Plans to enter the financial services field	−0.00727
11/25/81	Sells Inolex Chemical Division	−0.01991
1/05/82	To sell its domestic paper business to James River	−0.02071
4/26/82	Sells MRI Corp.	−0.012326
5/27/82	To acquire Transport Life Insurance Co.	0.01057
9/02/82	Unit to merge with PennCorp Financial Inc.	−0.008949
2/08/83	To sell Canadian timber rights and pulp mill	−0.03292
5/26/83	To buy American General's mutual fund and services	−0.005326
6/01/83	To buy Voyager Group Inc., insurance company	−0.008205
10/03/83	To buy insurance unit	0.00762
0/28/83	To buy brokerage house	0.006192
2/01/83	To buy Michigan Bulb Co.	0.009736
2/02/84	To spin off 20% of Fingerhut Corp.	−0.01337
2/03/84	To sell Canadian and British packaging operations	−0.00713
9/28/84	Sells Alabama timberland	0.00669
10/30/84	To sell its Canadian operations	−0.00957
11/23/84	Sells ACC Chemical Co.	−0.009568
12/07/84	To buy Reliable Corp.	0.01518
2/28/85	Buys two financial services units	−0.011487
3/12/85	Buys certain packaging operations	0.008638
11/08/85	To enter the health care field through acquisitions	−0.03018
7/18/86	Sells its packaging operations	0.09663
11/06/86	To buy Looart Press Inc.	−0.018529
5/27/87	To buy Smith Barney	0.00893
8/06/87	To get out of the mail-order business	0.0549
12/01/87	Sells Looart Press Inc.	0.000868
	Total	0.09526

March 1985 it bought certain packaging operations of Champion International, and in January 1986 it reorganized its packaging sector into three business groups. Then on July 18, 1986, it was announced that the company had agreed to sell its packaging operations to Triangle Industries for about $570 million, ending eighty-five years in the business. The sale completed American Can's move out of the paper and packaging industries into financial services and specialty retailing. The announcement created a positive abnormal return of 9.7 percent.

The final strategic move by the company took place in August 1987, when it was announced that it was selling its mail-order businesses. The transactions were expected to fetch "well in excess of $1 billion," and the proceeds were to be used to repay debt from the firm's recent acquisition of Smith Barney. The announcement was accompanied by a positive abnormal return of 5.5 percent. Overall it seems that every exit from a core business produced positive returns, while every entry into a new business created negative returns. Thus more shareholder wealth would have been created if the company sold off all its operations and ceased to exist!

Table 6.12
American Can's business structure

| | Revenues as a % of total sales | | | | |
Business segment	1982	1984	1985	1986	1987
Investment banking	0.0	0.0	0.0	0.0	10.6
Financial services	5.5	44.4	51.7	50.7	42.2
Specialty retailing	38.5	42.3	46.7	47.8	45.1
Other businesses	56.0	13.3	1.6	1.4	2.1

Source: Company annual reports.

Table 6.13
Selected financial statistics for American Can

	1982	1984	1985	1986	1987
Revenues ($ million)	1,959	2,353	2,475	2,887	3,762
Total assets ($ million)	2,406	3,810	4,750	5,350	13,217
Operating income ($ million)	(142)	230	290	409	393
Net income before tax ($ million)	(133)	136	88	229	198
ROE (%)	—	11.1	5.7	15.8	13.1
ROS (%)	(7.2)	9.8	11.7	14.1	10.4
Stock price—close	$30\frac{7}{8}$	$50\frac{4}{8}$	$59\frac{6}{8}$	$84\frac{1}{8}$	$96\frac{4}{8}$
S&P 500 composite—close	140.64	167.24	211.28	242.17	247.08

The longer-term effects of American Can's strategy on its business structure and financial position are shown in tables 6.12 and 6.13 below. It appears that the strategy allowed American Can to improve its performance and to strengthen its stock price. Apparently this was not enough. In August 1988 Primerica was acquired by Commercial Credit Group Corp. for $1.7 billion in stock and each.

Continental Group

Continental Group (now a private company called Continental Can) represents a company that returned to its original core after it was taken over. The company started out making cans, then diversified into insurance, paper and energy, but finally returned to cans after its takeover in 1984. The story of Continental Group is best told by its former president, Richard Hofmann (*Directors and Boards*, winter 1989, p. 13):

In the early 1970s, Continental Can's management became disenchanted with the pedestrian returns from the container business. This was a period of time before Peters and Waterman of *In Search of Excellence* fame when there was a lot of talk about cash cows, dogs, and stars. Packaging was not, in the minds of management, a good place to be. Projected returns in insurance and energy were deemed to be much better.

Slowly, strategically, but surely, cash was taken from the core business. The first acquisition was Richmond Corp., basically made up of Life of Virginia, Lawyers Title, and a casualty company. In 1976 we changed our name to the Continental Group Inc instead of the Continental Can Co. in an attempt to convince the world that we were no longer dependent on packaging. In 1980 the purchase of Florida Gas completed the vision as Continental Group acquired a major pipeline, an exploration company, and gas producing properties.

The following four years for the corporate managers of Continental Group were spent trying to develop a new management process, struggling with corporate identity in financial markets, and, internally, trying to determine whether we

Table 6.14
Continential Group's business structure

Business segment	Revenues as a % of total sales			
	1979	1981	1982	1983
Packaging	65.8	62.8	61.4	58.6
Forest products	20.6	10.9	9.9	10.5
Insurance	10.7	12.4	12.2	14.2
Energy	2.8	13.8	16.4	16.5

Source: Company annual reports.

were a holding company or an operating company [see table 6.14]. The confusion as to whether we were a portfolio company with divisions to be bought or sold, or an operating company serving customers and markets, defocused divisions and corporate management alike.

In May 1984, Sir James Goldsmith brought considerable focus to all with a $50-a-share cash offer for all of Continental Group's shares. Our stock was at the time trading in the high 30s, roughly at its book value. It is amazing how "focusing" survival can be for a management team! Without going into the details, history records that by November 1 of that year, the Continental Group was owned by Kiewit Co. and by David Murdock at $58.50 a share. Both private organizations had incurred a great deal of debt to swing the deal. Over the next three years the Continental Group was dismantled--the insurance, paper, and energy interests sold off. Today, essentially all that is left is the original Continental Can Co.

The stock market's reaction to some of the events described above is shown in table 6.15. Two interesting results stand out:

1. The firm's June 26, 1984, announcement that it will oppose the takeover by selling all or part of its assets, created a positive abnormal return of 8.3 percent. In another study (Ittner and Markides 1990) we have found that defensive divestitures whose primary goal is to help a firm avoid an unfriendly takeover, on average create no value. The only defensive divestitures that seem to create any value are those aimed to appease bidders or dissident shareholders by implementing some of the changes

Table 6.15
Continental Group: Abnormal returns

Event date	Announcement	$CAR(-1, 0)$
6/02/83	Sells its Canadian packaging business	0.01822
7/12/83	Sells six PET bottle plants	0.01472
8/19/83	To sell its forest-products business	0.06228
6/06/84	Receives unsolicited offer to merge with Diamond Land, which is controlled by Sir James Goldsmith	0.05128
6/07/84	Company plans to oppose any takeover	0.00921
6/11/84	Hires Morgan Stanley to mount a defense against Goldsmith	−0.0369
6/26/84	Considering ways of selling all or part of its assets	0.08329
6/28/84	Arranged a $2 billion credit line; may go private	0.02037
7/02/84	Taken over by Peter Kiewit Sons Inc. for $2.75 billion	0.0723
8/30/84	Kiewit to sell $1 billion of assets to finance acquisition	−0.0015
9/04/84	Sells two Continental group units	−0.00246
	Total	0.29081

that the hostile bidder or the dissidents view as desirable. The case of Continental seems to support this general finding.

2. The two announcements that follow the takeover are concerned with the firm's dismantling. It is interesting to note that both of them create negative returns. This may be an indication of how the market views forced dismantling. Unfortunately, we do not have any data to follow up the dismantling of the company after 1984 (since it was taken private.)

Some statistics on the performance of Continental Group prior to its acquisition are shown in table 6.16. According to reports in the business press, Continental's takeover "has been a bonanza" for its employees and shareholders (*Forbes*, August 12, 1985, p. 40). Prior to the takeover the company's stock was trading at about $35, or approximately the book value of the company. Kiewit paid $58.50 per share, and despite this huge premium the company was expected to make a huge profit in the transaction. For example, *Forbes* reported that in 1985 "the can company alone will this year have pretax cash flow of $190 million, and conservative calculations suggest such a manufacturing firm should sell for at least five times cash flow—or, in Continental's case, nearly $1 billion. Acquiring a $1 billion company for $200 million is not bad." (*Forbes*, August 12, 1985, p. 40).

In addition few of Continental's 40,000 employees lost their jobs during the company's dismantling. Corporate staff, on the other hand, has been reduced from 500 to 40. Thus Continental's "forced refocusing" can be termed a success. According to *Forbes*, "In its takeover of Continental, Kiewit has embarked on what corporate takeovers should really be about —realizing a company's untapped resources. With Continental's sleepy-head management now out of the way, Kiewit has a good chance of succeeding."

Table 6.16
Selected financial statistics for Continental Group

	1981	1982	1983
Total sales ($ million)	4,643	4,694	4,916
Net earnings ($ million)	234	180	199
Total assets ($ million)	4,135	4,199	3,653
ROS (%)	5.0	3.8	4.0
ROA (%)	5.6	4.3	5.4
Stock price—close	$32\frac{6}{8}$	34	54
S&P 500—close	122.55	140.64	164.93

Goodyear Tire and Rubber Co.

Goodyear had begun a major diversification drive in 1983, in an effort to become less dependent on the auto industry. This effort had to be abandoned in late 1986 following the firm's successful repulse of a takeover attempt by Sir James Goldsmith.

In October 1986, following rumors of a possible takeover, Goodyear announced that it is considering a restructuring, and retained two investment banks to assist it in "developing a program for maximizing shareholder value over the near term." This announcement produced a positive abnormal return of 14 percent, but it is unclear if the return was created in response to the takeover rumors or the restructuring announcement (see table 6.17).

Six days later it was announced that a group led by Goldsmith had acquired an 11.5 percent stake in the firm. This created a negative return of 3.3 percent. The negative return is very atypical of what usually happens when a takeover is announced. What could explain the negative return are the following two facts: (1) The market expected that Goldsmith would

Table 6.17
Goodyear Tire & Rubber Co.: Abnormal returns

Event date	Announcement	$CAR(-1, 0)$
10/27/86	Following rumors of takeover, will restructure	0.14028
11/03/86	Sir J. Goldsmith acquired 11.5% stake in Goodyear	−0.03309
11/04/86	In response to threat, sells its oil and gas subsidiary	−0.01045
11/07/86	Goldsmith bids $4.71 billion for Goodyear; company unveils ambitious restructuring plan	−0.02451
11/14/86	To sell Goodyear Aerospace Corp. to Martin Marietta	−0.00658
11/21/86	Buys back Goldsmith's 11.5% stake, ending takeover threat	−0.00938
11/24/86	Agrees to abandon diversification and return to its roots: tires	−0.03627
12/12/86	Begins repurchase of 40 million of its shares	−0.000972
	Average β in 1986 = 1.088	
1/02/87	Acquires land properties	0.004399
1/13/87	Sells its aerospace unit	−0.003876
6/05/87	Sells part of its oil and gas reserves	0.036613
8/11/87	Sells Celeron Oil & Gas Co.	0.02114
	Average β in 1987 = 1.105	
	Total	0.0773

acquire 15 percent instead of the 11.5 percent it acquired, and (2) along with the above announcement, Goldsmith also announced that he won't immediately make a tender offer because the firm's stock price was too high. Both of these facts showed lack of commitment on the part of Goldsmith, which decreased the probability that the takeover will be carried out. Hence the negative return.

On November 4, 1984, in response to the takeover threat, Goodyear announced that it will sell its oil and gas subsidiary (Celeron Corp.). This announcement also created a negative abnormal return (about 1 percent), possibly reflecting the lowered probability that the takeover will succeed. The same explanation could account for the fact that when Goldsmith finally bid $4.71 billion for the company on November 7, a negative 2.4 percent return was created: The same day Goodyear had countered to the bid by unveiling an ambitious restructuring plan that included repurchasing as many as 20 million of its common shares outstanding and selling as many as three major units. This action probably made the takeover highly unlikely.

Table 6.18
Goodyear's business structure

Business segment	Revenues as a % of total sales			
	1981	1983	1987	1988
Tires and related transportation products	73.3%	75.0%	86.5%	86.0%
Gas and oil	11.4	7.8	0.0	0.0
Industrial rubber, chemical, and plastic products	10.3	10.0	12.5	13.4
Other products and services	5.1	7.2	0.9	0.7

Source: Company annual reports.

Table 6.19
Selected financial statistics for Goodyear

	1981	1983	1985	1987	1988
Net sales ($ million)	10,323	9,736	8,341	9,905	10,810
Total assets ($ million)	5,973	5,985	7,537	8,396	8,618
Operating income ($ million)	942	766	549	1,077	1,003
ROS (%)	9.1	7.8	6.6	10.8	9.3
ROA (%)	15.7	12.8	7.3	12.8	11.6
Stock price—low	$15\frac{7}{8}$	27	$25\frac{1}{8}$	35	47
Book value per share	27.27	28.61	32.44	32.19	35.30

On November 21, Goodyear ended the takeover threat by buying back Goldsmith's 11.5 percent stake. The announcement created only a 1 percent negative return, implying that the takeover's limited chances of success had already been factored into the firm's stock price by the market. Three days later the details of Goodyear's settlement with Goldsmith were made public: The company agreed to sell about 25 percent of its assets and abandon its long-term diversification plan so as to focus on its roots—tires and related products. The announcement produced a negative abnormal return of 3.6 percent. The net effect of the month-long events was a positive 2 percent return.

During 1987 the company proceeded with the implementation of its refocusing. With the exception of the sale of its aerospace unit (which created a small negative return), the sale of its oil and gas units produced positive abnormal returns.

The effects of Goodyear's refocusing strategy on the company's business structure and financial position are shown in tables 6.18 and 6.19. Overall it appears that the strategy had a small but beneficial effect on the company's operations: Compared to Goodyear's performance in the year before the takeover attempt (1985), the company is now more profitable, and its 1988 stock price was three times its 1981 value.

Summary

This chapter examined the ex ante valuation consequences of refocusing. Refocusing announcements were generally associated with statistically significant positive abnormal returns, which implies that reductions in diversification create market value. As expected from the theory, value creation was found to be concentrated in the overdiversified group of firms. In addition a firm's refocusing announcement was valued higher the bigger the firm's diversification level and the lower its profitability level in the refocusing year. The market's expectation for improved operating performance after refocusing was not fulfilled in the short term, and this implies that it may take some time before refocusing's beneficial effects materialize.

These results lend support to the proposition that there is a limit to how much a firm can diversify, and that some firms have gone beyond their limits. Refocusing can be viewed as an adjustment process that brings these overdiversified firms back closer to their optimal limit.

The Consequences of Refocusing: Ex post Evidence

So far we have found that (1) a significant proportion of major diversified firms in the United States have reduced their diversification in the 1980s by refocusing on their core businesses, (2) this refocusing is primarily a 1980s phenomenon, (3) the refocusing firms are characterized by high diversification and poor profitability relative to their industry counterparts, and (4) refocusing is associated ex ante with improved stock-market value.

I now turn to a major objective of this study which is to learn what actually happens after a firm refocuses its strategic configuration. I seek in particular to determine whether, on average, the explicit strategy of re-focusing is followed by profitability improvements as suggested by stock-market event study interpretations. As argued by Shleifer and Vishny (1991, p. 54), there is very little ex post evidence that refocusing is associated with profitability improvements.

The specific goal of this chapter is to test proposition 3, which argues that for the overdiversified firms reductions in diversification will lead to profitability improvements, and proposition 6, which argues that at low levels of diversity there exists a positive relationship between diversification and changes in profitability, while at high levels of diversity the relationship is negative. The whole sample of 219 firms will be used for these tests. Because of missing information, 19 firms had to be dropped; hence a final sample of 200 firms is used in this chapter.

Generally there are two ways in which to determine the effect of a particular strategic action on firm performance: (1) by comparing the performance of a select group of firms that has undertaken the strategic action with a control group of firms that has not taken such action, or (2) by comparing the performance of a firm before and after the action and then isolating the change in performance directly attributable to the action. Since the firms in our sample are widely diversified companies competing in several industries, it would be impossible to develop an appropriate control group of firms. We will therefore follow the second approach.

The Model

To determine the effect of refocusing on firm profitability, I will use the model:

Firm profitability $= f$(refocusing, industry structure, strategy, risk).

For this study I will specifically try to determine the relationship between changes in diversification and changes in profitability in the period 1981–87. The model will be tested on the high-diversity group of firms (as defined below). As argued in proposition 3, a positive relationship is expected.

The inclusion of variables in the above model is based on economic theory. For example, the inclusion of industry structure variables is based on the basic industrial organization (IO) paradigm, which states that differences in profitability across firms can be explained by differences in what Williamson (1975, p. 8) calls the "outer environment"—market structure, variables including concentration, barriers to entry, and elasticity of demand. There is now ample evidence from a rich body of research that shows these market structure variables to indeed affect firm performance (e.g., Scherer 1980; Shepherd 1972, 1979). Despite some strong criticism of the structuralist hypothesis (e.g., see Bothwell, Cooley, and Hall 1984; Donsimoni, Geroski, and Jacquemin 1984), I will follow standard practice.

Similarly the inclusion of strategy variables in the model is based on the belief that firms within the same industry can use different assets and pursue different strategies (even in the long run) to improve their performance (Porter 1979). For example, short-run differences in profitability may well reflect returns (i.e., rents) to unique firm assets (e.g., a superior management team or an effective R&D laboratory). Evidence for this has been provided by Buzzell and Gale (1987). These strategy variables are what Williamson (1970, p.180) calls the "inner environment" of the firm.

The inclusion of the variable risk is really a recent development. For example, out of forty-seven profitability studies from the IO literature reviewed by Weiss (1974), only one included a measure of risk. Recently, however, researchers have begun considering the potential trade-off between risk and return (e.g., Bettis 1981; Christofides and Tapon 1979; Edwards and Haggestad 1979), and an increasing number of studies has explicitly studied the relationship between risk and performance. Some have found a positive relationship—as expected from finance theory (e.g., Bettis and Hall 1982)—while others have—surprisingly—found a negative relationship (e.g., Bowman 1980, 1982).

The above model has come to be considered as "complete." That is, it is believed that it captures most of the systematic structural determinants of profitability (even though some of the included variables may be proxying for other unobserved variables). The model, however, has been criticized for being misspecified—especially because it assumes unidirectional causality between the variables (i.e., it assumes only random departures from long-run equilibrium). Several researchers (e.g., Aaker and Jacobson 1987; Bettis 1981, 1982; Clark 1986; Hurdle 1974) have pointed out that the model can be better estimated as part of a simultaneous equations system, where variables such as profitability, risk, and refocusing are treated as endogenous variables. Such a complication becomes unnecessary if I assume that the system is recursive rather than endogenous. That is, if I assume that the feedbacks in the system occur at sufficiently long lags, then I can pull out individual equations for separate treatment (e.g., see Cowling 1972; Sawyer 1982).

It is important to stress that the goal is not to estimate all the determinants of a firm's performance. Rather, I want to isolate the effect of the refocusing variable on performance. This implies that in choosing which strategy and industry variables to include in the equation, I should be guided by the question: How many influences on refocusing and performance should be controlled to make sure that the relation between them is not due to other variables affecting both? (Caves 1981). For a diversified firm the included variables must be industry weighted (Carter 1977).

A rich body of IO research has identified several industry structure variables that affect firm profitability (e.g., see Ravenscraft 1983; Scherer 1980; Shepherd 1972). In this analysis I will use three of the most important ones: seller concentration, R&D intensity, and advertising intensity. The effect of these variables on firm profitability has been found to be positive (e.g., Scherer 1980).

Given that the goal is to isolate the effect of refocusing on profitability (and not to estimate the determinants of profitability), the rationale for including these industry-structure variables in the equation should be made more explicit: Through refocusing, a firm can exit unattractive industries and enter attractive ones—that is, enter industries that have structural characteristics, such as high industry concentration, that allow a firm to earn above-normal profits. If I assume that a firm changes its industry structure solely because of refocusing, then I don't have to control for industry structure changes; refocusing will be proxying for their effects, and this will be appropriate since it is refocusing that has brought about these industry-structure changes.

However, it is more likely that we find firms in attractive industries in 1987, not only because they moved there during 1981–87 but also because our firms happened to be in these industries long before they undertook any refocusing. Furthermore a firm may not have changed its industry participation at all during the study period, but the structure of its industries may have changed for the better over the period, anyway. This implies that I should not let refocusing take all the credit for these beneficial industry-structure changes. I could do this by controlling for these industry variables (i.e., including them in the equation). Note, however, that by controlling for these variables I am preventing refocusing from taking any credit for their effect, even though it may be responsible for some of it. Hence the coefficient of refocusing will be underestimating the true effect of refocusing.

Similar considerations apply for the strategy variables included in the equation: The theoretical discussion suggests that refocusing helps firms return to their optimal diversification level, and this should improve overall efficiency. However, many other factors may have also affected the efficiency of firms during the study period, and their effect should be controlled by including these variables in the equation. It is impossible to control for everything; of the numerous strategy variables that could be included in the model, the following were chosen:

1. *Change in top management.* There is evidence from the business literature (e.g., Gabarro 1985) that a change of CEO could result in a dramatic increase in efficiency. This effect should be controlled.[1]

2. *Debt burden.* A high debt level implies that management has little discretion in the allocation of the free cash flow of a company. The discipline imposed by the debt burden forces management to invest wisely and thus be more efficient (Jensen 1986).

3. *Foreign sales.* The literature on international diversification suggests a positive relationship between profitability and foreign operations (e.g., Caves 1971). I should control for the fact that a firm's profitability may be

---

1. It is possible that the change in top management has been entirely brought about by refocusing. This implies that I should not control for this variable but let refocusing take all the credit for any change in performance. As shown later, removing this variable from the equations does not affect the results.

higher now, not because of improvements in efficiency (resulting from refocusing) but because the firm has diversified abroad.

4. *Employee productivity.* Labor productivity could have increased during the study period as a result of renegotiated labor contracts, or new investments in technology, as well as better monitoring from the refocused firm's managers; this effect should be controlled.

5. *Capital investments.* Increased capital investment during the period could result in higher total factor productivity, that may not be attributable to refocusing; this effect should therefore be controlled.

It is very likely that some strategy variables affecting both refocusing and profitability have been omitted from the model. This implies that refocusing will be proxying for part of the effect of these omitted variables; hence refocusing's effect will be overstated. However, as explained below, the problem with omitted variables may not be as serious with the model being used in this study.

With respect to the specification of the model, several concerns should be aired at this point. To begin with, the model omits several important variables such as elasticity of demand (e.g., Cowling 1976; Phillips 1976), minimum efficient scale (e.g., Comanor and Wilson 1967), and measures of countervailing power such as buyer concentration (e.g., Cowling 1976). Many researchers have argued that omitting these variables from the model introduces serious bias that clouds many relationships (e.g., Clarke and Davies 1982; Cowling 1976).

These problems with omitted variables are not so serious in my model because I am studying changes in, rather than levels of firm profitability (e.g., Cowling and Waterson 1976; Geroski 1982a). That is, the basic IO model tells us that

$$\frac{PR + F}{R} = \frac{-H(1 + q)}{e},$$

where PR is profits, F is fixed costs, R is revenue, H is the index of concentration, e is the price elasticity of demand, and q is the conjectural variation term. Assuming that all elasticities of demand (e) as well as the conjectural variation terms (q) are constant over the relevant period of analysis (which is likely given the short period we are examining), then

$$\frac{(PR/R)_t}{(PR/R)_{t-1}} = \frac{H_t}{H_{t-1}}.$$

Thus I need not concern myself with variables such as e and q because they cancel out when I look at changes in profitability.

Another problem facing the model involves lagged effects and the model's failure to account for them. Singh (1972) and Cowling (1976) suggest that changes in industry structure affect profitability, but this effect is not fully realized until a five-year period has elapsed. For example, a change in concentration in 1983 may not show its effect on profitability until 1988. I will try to account for this in the model by taking the changes in the industry variables in the period 1981–85, rather than 1981–87.

The same problem arises with respect to refocusing's effect on profitability: As shown in the previous chapter, it may take some time before this effect is fully realized. Thus the firms that undertook most of their refocusing at the beginning of the study period will show a bigger profitability change than those firms that undertook most of their refocusing at the end of the period. To account for this, I will measure the refocusing activity of each firm in three distinct time periods[2]: 1981–83, 1983–85, and 1985–87. I expect that refocusing in the period 1981–83 will have the biggest effect on profitability changes.

The model to be tested is therefore specified as follows:

$$\text{Change in profitability } 1987{-}81 = f(Refoc(83 - 81), Refoc(85 - 83),$$
$$Refoc(87 - 85), WXAD(85 - 81),$$
$$WXRD(85 - 81), WC4(85 - 81),$$
$$DMGMT(86 - 81), DSE(87 - 81),$$
$$Foreign(87 - 82), Employee(87 - 81),$$
$$CAPX(87 - 81), RISK(87 - 81)).$$

The variables in the model are defined as follows:

Profitability (DROS). The firm's *ROS* minus its industry-weighted *ROS*.[3] To calculate the industry-weighted *ROS*, I used the procedure described in chapter three.[4] To test the sensitivity of the results to the exact specification of the dependent variable, I also run our regressions using industry-weighted return on equity (*ROE*) and return on assets (*ROA*) as the dependent variable (see the results section).

---

2. It may be interesting to note that about 54 percent of the firms that refocused in periods 2 or 3 also refocused in period 1.

3. *ROS* is measured from Compustat as operating income before depreciation and interest as a percent of sales.

4. As shown later, using *ROS* instead of *DROS* as the dependent variable does not alter the results.

Refocusing. Defined in the next subsection.

WXAD. The firm's industry-weighted industry advertising intensity (advertising outlays as a percent of sales). This was calculated as follows: First, a Compustat program was used to identify all the firms assigned to each two-digit SIC, and to calculate their advertising intensity. Then, using their sales as weights, the average advertising intensity of every SIC was estimated. Next, each firm's sales by SIC were obtained from TRINET, and the percentage of the firm's sales in each SIC was calculated. The firm's industry-weighted industry advertising intensity was then calculated by multiplying the share of the firm's sales in each SIC by the corresponding advertising intensity of that SIC, and adding the results. The procedure was repeated for 1985.

WXRD. The firm's industry-weighted industry R&D intensity. This was calculated in a similar manner as *WXAD*.

WC4. The firm's industry weighted industry four-firm concentration ratio. This was measured with the Herfindahl index using data from TRINET. It was calculated in the same way as *WXAD*.

DMGMT. A dummy variable that takes the value of 1 if the CEO of the firm changed in the period 1981–86; zero otherwise (data from *Moody's Industrial Manuals*).

DSE. The firm's debt to shareholder equity ratio (from Compustat).

Foreign. The firm's foreign sales as a percent of total sales. The year 1982 is used because 1981 data could not be obtained from Compustat.

Employee. Sales per employee (from Compustat).

CAPX. Capital expenditures as a percent of sales (from Compustat).

RISK. The firm's total risk, as measured by the standard deviation of its *ROS* in the five years prior to the year under study (from Compustat).

It is important to stress again that our model tries to identify the relationship between changes in profitability in 1981–87 and changes in the values of all these variables during the study period.[5]

How to Measure Refocusing

As argued in chapter 3, a critical issue for this study is how to identify those firms that are refocusing. Since there is no precise way of measuring

---

5. A few of the regressions were tried using not only changes in the industry-structure variables but also their absolute levels. Again the basic results were not affected.

refocusing, I use five different methods to measure each firm's refocusing during the study period. Multiple measurements of refocusing, coming from different sources, allow me to test the sensitivity of the results to the exact specification of the refocusing variable. The five methods used are the following:

1. Similar to Hoskisson and Johnson (1992) I take as refocusing those firms that publicly announced in the *Wall Street Journal* their intention to refocus and actually divested at least 10 percent of their asset base. The number and size of the divestitures undertaken by the sample firms was collected from a variety of sources such as the SDC Database on Mergers and Acquisitions; the journal *Mergers & Acquisitions*; Predicast's *Index of Corporate Change*; Quality Services Co, *Merger and Acquisition Sourcebook*; W.T. Grimm & Co, *Mergerstat Review*; and Cambridge Corp., *The Merger Yearbook*. Multiple sources were used because during the course of this research no single source was found to be reliable or complete.

2. The 200 sample firms were classified according to Rumelt's (1974) strategic categories using data from Trinet as well as annual reports.[6] The firms were placed in their strategic category in both 1981 and 1987. Those firms that moved from a broad strategic category in 1981 to a more narrow one in 1987, were classified as refocused. Specifically the refocused firms were those that moved from Unrelated to Single, Dominant or Related; from Related to Single or Dominant; and from Dominant to Single.

3. For each firm I calculated its entropy index of diversification (DT) in the manner shown by Palepu (1985), using data from the TRINET tapes. The index was calculated for all four years 1981, 1983, 1985, and 1987. If a firm's index of diversification decreased in the relevant period, then that firm was classified as refocused.

4. For each firm, I identified (from TRINET) the number of industries (2-digit SICs) that the firm was competing in for both 1981 and 1987. Firms were classified as refocused if during the study period they reduced the number of their competing industries by more than two.

5. Hoskisson and Johnson (1992) found that restructuring firms were of two types: Unrelated-business firms that were increasing their diversification (i.e., DU/DT increasing, DR/DT decreasing) to exploit internal capital

---

6. To test the validity of this classification, forty firms were picked at random and were reclassified using information from their annual reports only. Thirty-four firms were placed in the same categories as before. For the other six there was disagreement as to whether they were Dominant- or Related-business firms. The classification of all Dominant and Related firms in the sample was therefore reexamined.

market economies, and Related-linked firms that were decreasing their diversification (i.e., DU/DT decreasing, DR/DT increasing) to improve their control systems. For our sample firms, I calculate the Related (DR) and Unrelated (DU) components of their entropy index of diversification (DT) for 1981 and 1987. I then take as restructuring the Unrelated-business firms that increased their DU/DT and decreased their DR/DT, or decreased their DU/DT and increased their DR/DT; and the Related- or Dominant-business firms that reduced their DU/DT and increased their DR/DT. Hence restructuring firms are not only those decreasing their diversification but also those that are increasing their diversification to exploit capital market economies. However, since I am only concerned with refocusing firms, out of this subsample of restructuring firms, I take as refocusing those that decreased their DU/DT and increased their DR/DT. In addition, to avoid accidental refocusers being selected, only firms that changed the above diversification ratios by more than 0.1 are selected.

Who Are the Overdiversified Firms?

To test proposition 3, I need to identify ex ante who the overdiversified firms are in the sample. Similarly, to test proposition 6, I need to separate the low-diversified firms from the high-diversified ones. A priori I don't really know which of the sample firms are overdiversified. Ideally, to identify the overdiversified firms, I will need to find each firm's optimal diversification level. This is practically impossible. Every firm has a different optimal limit depending on its resources, its external environment, the type of diversification it is following (i.e., related versus unrelated), the caliber of its management team, and so on. To identify the overdiversified firms in the sample, I will therefore need to take an indirect route, and use proxies. Five different strategies were used to assign firms to the overdiversified group.

Strategy 1. The 200 sample firms were ranked according to their 1981 diversification level (DT) and the 70 most-diversified firms were picked to represent the high-diversity group. The dividing point was equal to (mean $DT + 1/2$ s.d.). To make sure that the results are not sensitive to this cutoff point, sensitivity analysis was also performed by altering the dividing point and repeating the analysis.

Strategy 2. Each firm was sorted by core industry[7] and in each industry

---

7. On average, the core industry accounted for about 60 percent of the total sales of a firm. The second-largest industry accounted for about 16 percent of sales.

firms were ranked according to their diversification level *DT*. Those firms whose *DT* was bigger than their industry's median *DT* were placed in the high-diversification group.[8] Since firms belonging to the same core industry are likely to have similar optimal diversification levels, I believe that classifying firms as overdiversified by comparing their diversification to their industry's median diversification is a more accurate way of identifying the overdiversified firms. It should also be noted that the Fortune 500 firms are presumably the most diversified firms in the U.S. economy. By using these firms to calculate industry median diversification levels, I increase the likelihood that the firms classified as overdiversified are truly so.[9]

Strategy 3. According to the Rumelt (1974) classifications, 42 sample firms belonged to the Unrelated-business category in 1981. These unrelated-business firms were picked to represent the overdiversified firms.[10]

Strategy 4. Whether a firm is overdiversified depends on the diversification strategy it is following. The 200 sample firms are therefore grouped by diversification strategy. Within the group of Unrelated-business firms, those firms whose *DT* is greater than the group median are classified as overdiversified. Similarly within the group of Related-business firms, those firms whose *DT* is greater than the group median are classified as overdiversified. Finally, within the group of Dominant-business firms, those firms whose *DT* is greater than the group median are classified as overdiversified.

Strategy 5. Following the findings of Hoskisson and Johnson (1992), I take the Related-linked firms as the most likely to have inconsistent control systems and to be in need of refocusing. These firms are therefore selected to represent the high-diversity group. I take as related-linked those firms

---

8. Unavoidably a few firms belonged to core industries for which I did not have enough firms to estimate a meaningful industry median diversification level. These firms were therefore classified by comparing their diversification to the median diversification level for the whole sample: The firms whose diversification level was bigger than the sample median diversification ($DT = 1.97$) were classified as overdiversified; all others as underdiversified. This classification exercise produced 103 overdiversified firms and 97 underdiversified ones.
9. At the same time, however, it should be noted that the Fortune 500 are primarily manufacturing firms, so the results of this study may not be representative of other types of firms coming from the mining and service sectors.
10. It is interesting to note that the unrelated-business firms start the period with a much lower profitability level than the single-business firms. In fact the unrelated-business firms have a negative *DROS*, which suggests that these firms are doing worse than their industry counterparts. The lower profitability of the overdiversified firms is also evident when the other two strategies are used to identify the overdiversified firms.

that have above-median *DR* and above-median *DU* (Hoskisson and Johnson, 1992).

Results

Table 7.1 presents descriptive statistics and correlations for all the variables in the study. The low intercorrelations among these variables suggest no problems with multicollinearity. The same finding emerges when I look at the correlations among the variables in the different subsamples used. For example, in the subsample of overdiversified firms, classified as such using strategy 1, the highest correlation is that between $DSE(87-81)$ and *Employee*$(87-81)$ and stands at only 0.309. The low correlations imply that there is sufficient independent variation among the variables used in this study to allow discrete effects to be estimated.

The results of the regression runs when refocusing is measured using the *Wall Street Journal* announcements are reported in table 7.2. Throughout, the dependent variable is the increase in each firm's industry-weighted profitability from 1981 to 1987. Five regressions are reported, one for each strategy used to identify the overdiversified firms. Thus, for example, column A reports the regression results on the subsample of firms classified as overdiversified using strategy 1, column B reports the regression results on the subsample of firms classified as overdiversified using strategy 2, and so on. The adjusted R^2, F-statistic, and Durbin-Watson statistic for each regression run are also reported.

The first regression reports the results when the model was run on the high-diversity group classified as such using the first strategy.[11] The equation is statistically significant at the 99 percent level. The most striking result is the positive and statistically significant coefficient of the Refocusing variable. This implies that refocusing by the overdiversified firms is associated with profitability improvements—a strong confirmation of proposition 3. This basic finding appears robust and as shown by the results in columns B, D, and E, it is not sensitive to the exact definition of the overdiversified firms.

The validity of these results was further reinforced by the supporting results that emerged when refocusing was measured using the Rumelt

---

11. The sensitivity of these results to the exact specification of the dividing point between high- and low-diversity groups was tested by repeating the analysis numerous times and altering the dividing point by as much as $+/-10$ percent. The basic relationships discovered above do not change.

Table 7.1
Means, standard deviations, and intercorrelations

Variables	Mean	Standard deviation	1	2	3	4	5	6	7	8	9	10	11	12	13
$DROS(87-81)$	−1.018	5.886													
$Refoc(83-81)$	0.515	0.501	0.068												
$Refoc(85-83)$	0.585	0.494	0.056	−0.066											
$Refoc(87-85)$	0.385	0.487	−0.022	0.089	−0.021										
$WXADI(85-81)$	1.791	3.884	−0.049	0.014	−0.049	0.044									
$WXRD(85-81)$	107.4	696.5	−0.027	−0.084	0.057	0.081	0.054								
$WC_4(85-81)$	0.0001	0.0064	0.010	0.036	−0.006	−0.060	0.044	−0.041							
$DMGMT(86-81)$	0.450	0.498	−0.011	0.033	−0.013	0.007	0.142	0.145	0.107						
$DSE(87-81)$	9.106	180.8	−0.120	−0.146	−0.0006	−0.001	0.080	0.012	−0.038	−0.006					
$Foreign(87-82)$	1.885	8.584	−0.173	−0.052	−0.032	−0.080	−0.004	−0.071	−0.017	0.095	−0.043				
$Employee(87-81)$	26.958	60.895	0.079	0.104	0.076	0.062	−0.066	0.007	−0.039	0.005	−0.031	0.242			
$CAPX(87-81)$	−1.302	3.613	0.320	−0.001	−0.024	−0.031	−0.139	−0.275	−0.100	−0.177	−0.106	−0.093	0.053		
$RISK(87-81)$	0.461	1.982	−0.143	−0.040	−0.023	−0.053	−0.144	0.016	0.055	0.068	0.007	0.242	0.060	−0.041	

Note: $N = 200$. Correlation coefficients greater than 0.19 are significant at $p < 0.05$, those greater than 0.25 are significant at $p < 0.01$, and those greater than 0.32 are significant at $p < 0.001$.

Table 7.2
Regression results when refocusing is measured using the WSJ announcements

Independent variables	A	B	C	D	E
Constant	−3.892***	−3.235***	−1.915	−3.423***	−3.629***
	(−4.50)	(−4.42)	(−1.42)	(−4.32)	(−3.59)
$Refoc(87 − 81)$	2.460**	2.167**	−0.2573	2.714***	2.383*
	(2.34)	(2.44)	(−0.16)	(2.73)	(1.97)
$WXAD(85 − 81)$	−0.221*	−0.166	−0.0897	−0.1553	−0.1921
	(−1.85)	(−1.46)	(−0.62)	(−1.36)	(−1.14)
$WXRD(85 − 81)$	−0.0004	−0.0002	−0.0031	−0.0005	−0.0023
	(−0.94)	(−0.46)	(−1.02)	(−1.09)	(−0.33)
$WC4(85 − 81)$	34.019	158.62**	119.27	74.883	7.201
	(0.34)	(2.26)	(0.98)	(0.78)	(0.06)
$Share(85 − 81)$	3.676*	0.0382	1.595	0.5235	3.714*
	(1.84)	(0.04)	(0.74)	(0.36)	(1.68)
$DMGMT(86 − 81)$	0.944	0.965	1.898	0.0329	1.304
	(1.00)	(1.19)	(1.42)	(0.03)	(1.23)
$DSE(87 − 81)$	−0.0069**	−0.0031*	−0.0109	−0.0029	−0.0087*
	(−2.34)	(−1.78)	(−1.67)	(−1.64)	(−1.74)
$Foreign(87 − 82)$	−0.0587	0.0008	−0.1624	−0.0156	−0.0342
	(−0.69)	(0.02)	(−1.19)	(−0.21)	(−0.38)
$Employee(87 − 81)$	0.1002***	0.0702***	0.0478	0.0761***	0.0834***
	(5.21)	(5.01)	(1.61)	(4.38)	(3.38)
$CAPX(87 − 81)$	0.1267	0.1959	0.5087*	0.0703	0.2491
	(0.76)	(1.39)	(1.89)	(0.43)	(1.29)
$RISK(87 − 81)$	0.547	0.282	0.8787	0.8423*	0.9261*
	(1.07)	(0.65)	(1.40)	(1.70)	(1.71)
N	70	103	42	77	58
Adjusted R^2	0.354	0.250	0.244	0.251	0.255
F-statistic	4.44	4.09	2.20	3.31	2.78
Durbin-Watson	1.95	1.88	1.92	2.19	2.10

Note: Dependent variable is $(DROS87 − DROS81)$. The t-statistics are reported in parentheses: * = $p < 0.1$, ** = $p < 0.05$, *** = $p < 0.01$ (all are two-tail tests).

Table 7.3
Regression results when refocusing is measured using the Rumelt categories

Independent variables	A	B	C	D	E
Constant	−4.402*	−7.369***	−2.523*	−5.798**	−5.754**
	(−1.81)	(−3.86)	(−1.96)	(−2.43)	(−2.32)
$Refoc(87 − 81)$	5.032**	5.296***	2.306*	5.745**	4.429*
	(2.12)	(2.93)	(1.84)	(2.51)	(2.20)
$WXAD(85 − 81)$	−2.468**	−0.8281	−0.0777	−1.069	0.0963
	(−2.39)	(−1.18)	(−0.57)	(−1.17)	(0.10)
$WXRD(85 − 81)$	0.0002	−0.0005	−0.0029	−0.0005	−0.0823**
	(0.28)	(−0.80)	(−1.02)	(−0.63)	(−3.06)
$WC4(85 − 81)$	192.28	251.51***	87.915	288.38	−371.59
	(0.79)	(2.69)	(0.83)	(1.33)	(−1.72)
$Share(85 − 81)$	−1.813	−2.909**	0.3666	−2.707	13.852**
	(−0.32)	(−2.15)	(0.17)	(−0.85)	(2.38)
$DMGMT(86 − 81)$	1.669	2.840*	1.840	0.6084	0.4765
	(0.74)	(1.77)	(1.46)	(0.26)	(0.22)
$DSE(87 − 81)$	−0.0007	−0.0038	−0.0128**	−0.0034	−0.0129
	(−0.13)	(−1.00)	(−2.05)	(−0.61)	(−1.56)
$Foreign(87 − 82)$	0.1690	−0.1463	−0.1462	−0.0902	−0.1856
	(0.73)	(−0.80)	(−1.15)	(−0.38)	(−0.87)
$Employee(87 − 81)$	0.1021**	0.0834***	0.0388	0.0872**	0.1225**
	(2.82)	(3.42)	(1.41)	(2.45)	(2.77)
$CAPX(87 − 81)$	0.5119	0.1901	0.5399**	0.1634	−0.7099
	(1.41)	(0.64)	(2.12)	(0.40)	(−1.52)
$RISK(87 − 81)$	−0.7359	0.7541	0.6881	0.8409	0.2650
	(−0.56)	(0.96)	(1.14)	(0.74)	(0.29)
N	23	36	42	28	21
Adjusted R^2	0.569	0.435	0.34	0.369	0.621
F-statistic	3.64	3.45	3.12	2.44	3.97
Durbin-Watson	2.96	1.55	1.93	2.54	2.97

Note: Dependent variable is $(DROS87 − DROS81)$. The t-statistics are reported in parentheses: * = $p < 0.1$, ** = $p < 0.05$, *** = $p < 0.01$ (all are two-tail tests).

categories. The results are shown in table 7.3: No matter what strategy is used to identify the overdiversified firms, refocusing by these firms is associated with profitability improvements—again a result consistent with proposition 3.

The sensitivity of the above results to the exact measurement of the refocusing variable was further tested by using the remaining three indexes of refocusing that I have developed: Table 7.4 reports the regression results when refocusing is measured using the SIC codes, table 7.5 reports the regression results when refocusing is measured using the Hoskisson and Johnson (1992) restructuring index, and table 7.6 reports the regression results when refocusing is measured using the entropy index (DT). In all three cases the central finding that refocusing by the overdiversified firms is associated with profitability improvements remains unchanged.

Altogether, using the 5 indexes of refocusing along with the 5 strategies defining the overdiversified firms, I have developed 25 different regression equations to examine whether refocusing is associated with profitability improvements. As shown in tables 7.2 through 7.6, 24 of these equations have provided support for the central thesis of this chapter. This I take as strong support for proposition 3.

Further Sensitivity Analysis

So far I have tested the sensitivity of the results to the exact definition of refocusing as well as the exact measurement of overdiversification. I have not yet tested whether the results are sensitive to the exact definition of the dependent variable, profitability. To correct for this, I calculate for every firm its industry-weighted return on assets (ROA) and return on equity (ROE) for 1981 and 1987. The three profitability variables are also calculated for 1991. The intercorrelations among the profitability variables are reported in table 7.7.

All twenty-five regressions reported above are then repeated using the new profitability variables. Some of the results obtained are reported in table 7.8. This table reports the regression results when refocusing is measured using the Wall Street Journal announcements and the overdiversified firms are classified using strategies A and D. These results are very representative of the results obtained when the other strategies were used to classify the overdiversified firms and when refocusing is measured with the other indexes I developed: Throughout, the refocusing variable comes out positive and statistically significant, but not as statistically significant as in

Table 7.4
Regression results when refocusing is measured using the SIC codes

Independent variables	A	B	C	D	E
Constant	−3.707***	−3.427***	−3.587***	−3.361***	−3.359***
	(−4.15)	(−4.54)	(−2.90)	(−4.01)	(−3.41)
$Refoc(87 − 81)$	1.588*	1.981**	3.849***	1.591*	2.148*
	(1.76)	(2.44)	(3.31)	(1.68)	(1.84)
$WXAD(85 − 81)$	−0.2310*	−0.1860	−0.1402	−0.1697	−0.1551
	(−1.95)	(−1.63)	(−1.13)	(−1.43)	(−0.93)
$WXRD(85 − 81)$	−0.0002	−0.00001	−0.002	−0.0002	−0.0034
	(−0.49)	(−0.003)	(−0.79)	(−0.54)	(−0.48)
$WC4(85 − 81)$	67.873	181.85***	118.63	121.87	31.772
	(0.77)	(2.63)	(1.25)	(1.24)	(0.30)
$Share(85 − 81)$	2.776	−0.5391	3.206*	−0.7314	2.909
	(1.47)	(−0.64)	(1.70)	(−0.50)	(1.36)
$DMGMT(86 − 81)$	1.5615*	1.168	2.416**	0.4843	1.3455
	(1.69)	(1.46)	(2.11)	(0.50)	(1.27)
$DSE(87 − 81)$	−0.0078**	−0.0027	−0.0072	−0.0023	−0.0079
	(−2.73)	(−1.55)	(−1.27)	(−1.28)	(−1.56)
$Foreign(87 − 82)$	−0.1132	−0.0188	−0.2602**	−0.0254	−0.0688
	(−1.36)	(−0.26)	(−2.19)	(−0.33)	(−0.79)
$Employee(87 − 81)$	0.0993***	0.0708***	0.0438*	0.0761***	0.0710***
	(5.18)	(5.06)	(1.78)	(4.18)	(2.74)
$CAPX(87 − 81)$	0.1282	0.1706	0.5935**	0.0618	0.2413
	(0.80)	(1.21)	(2.57)	(0.37)	(1.24)
$RISK(87 − 81)$	0.2029	0.2455	0.4615	0.6741	0.8248
	(0.40)	(0.56)	(0.84)	(1.32)	(1.51)
N	70	103	42	77	58
Adjusted R^2	0.315	0.250	0.446	0.199	0.248
F-statistic	3.89	4.09	4.00	2.72	2.71
Durbin-Watson	1.97	1.93	2.10	2.21	2.30

Note: Dependent variable is $(DROS87 − DROS81)$. The t-statistics are reported in parentheses: * = $p < 0.1$, ** = $p < 0.05$, *** = $p < 0.01$ (all are two-tail tests).

Table 7.5
Regression results when refocusing is measured using the restructuring index

Independent variables	A	B	C	D	E
Constant	−3.952***	−3.551***	−3.849***	−3.704***	−3.7603***
	(−4.76)	(4.82)	(−3.03)	(−4.54)	(−3.97)
Refoc(87 − 81)	2.857***	2.530***	3.948***	2.540***	3.032***
	(3.13)	(3.13)	(3.32)	(2.83)	(3.03)
WXAD(85 − 81)	−0.225*	−0.1848*	−0.1402	−0.1588	−0.1008
	(−1.95)	(−1.66)	(−1.13)	(−1.40)	(−0.64)
WXRD(85 − 81)	−0.0001	−0.00002	−0.0049*	−0.0001	−0.0019
	(−0.40)	(−0.05)	(−1.88)	(−0.36)	(−0.28)
WC4(85 − 81)	98.965	195.141***	43.553	145.18	39.058
	(1.06)	(2.88)	(0.45)	(1.53)	(0.39)
Share(85 − 81)	1.772	−0.6147	1.904	−0.8015	1.629
	(0.94)	(−0.74)	(1.04)	(−0.57)	(0.81)
DMGMT(86 − 81)	0.6727	1.1523	1.255	0.2132	0.9336
	(0.73)	(1.46)	(1.08)	(0.23)	(0.93)
DSE(87 − 81)	−0.0062**	−0.0023	−0.0150**	−0.0019	−0.0090*
	(−2.18)	(−1.35)	(−2.63)	(−1.09)	(−1.91)
Foreign(87 − 82)	−0.0963	−0.0264	−0.1999*	−0.0396	−0.1061
	(−1.18)	(−0.37)	(−1.73)	(−0.54)	(−1.29)
Employee(87 − 81)	0.0935***	0.0619***	0.0597**	0.0816***	0.0712***
	(4.95)	(4.38)	(2.39)	(4.75)	(2.98)
CAPX(87 − 81)	0.0957	0.1235	0.2272	0.0732	0.1875
	(0.59)	(0.88)	(0.93)	(0.45)	(1.02)
RISK(87 − 81)	−0.0284	0.0891	0.6007	0.3998	0.5877
	(−0.05)	(0.20)	(1.11)	(0.80)	(1.11)
N	70	103	42	77	58
Adjusted R^2	0.395	0.278	0.447	0.256	0.327
F-statistic	5.11	4.58	4.01	3.38	3.52
Durbin-Watson	2.03	1.81	1.98	2.04	2.50

Note: Dependent variable is ($DROS87 − DROS81$). The t-statistics are reported in parentheses: * = $p < 0.1$, ** = $p < 0.05$, *** = $p < 0.01$ (all are two-tail tests).

Table 7.6
Regression results when refocusing is measured using the entropy index (DT)

Independent variables	A	B	C	D	E
Constant	-4.231^{***}	-4.194^{***}	-6.064^{**}	-3.573^{***}	-3.667^{**}
	(-3.30)	(-3.82)	(-2.42)	(-3.01)	(-2.48)
$Refoc(83-81)$	2.246^{**}	2.132^{**}	3.799^{**}	1.912^{**}	2.317^{*}
	(2.23)	(2.49)	(2.46)	(2.01)	(1.98)
$Refoc(85-83)$	0.2073	0.6056	1.5970	-0.0516	-0.6299
	(0.21)	(0.69)	(1.10)	(-0.05)	(-0.53)
$Refoc(87-85)$	-0.4972	0.1099	-0.6467	-0.3804	0.4262
	(-0.54)	(0.14)	(-0.54)	(-0.42)	(0.41)
$WXAD(85-81)$	-0.1816	-0.1457	-0.1039	-0.1139	-0.0467
	(-1.47)	(-1.26)	(-0.76)	(-0.95)	(-0.26)
$WXRD(85-81)$	-0.0001	0.00004	-0.0034	-0.0002	0.0036
	(-0.20)	(0.08)	(-1.21)	(-0.39)	(0.50)
$WC4(85-81)$	54.243	175.71^{**}	-48.983	86.034	13.865
	(0.54)	(2.49)	(-0.40)	(0.86)	(0.13)
$Share(85-81)$	1.597	-0.9109	3.294	-1.0372	1.417
	(0.80)	(-1.05)	(1.55)	(-0.71)	(0.64)
$DMGMT(86-81)$	0.9228	1.028	2.884^{**}	0.1738	0.9045
	(0.96)	(1.27)	(2.12)	(0.17)	(0.83)
$DSE(87-81)$	-0.0060^{*}	-0.0021	-0.0105^{*}	-0.0018	-0.0072
	(-1.985)	(-1.16)	(-1.66)	(-0.93)	(-1.37)
$Foreign(87-82)$	-0.0980	-0.0078	-0.2710^{**}	-0.0441	-0.1103
	(-1.11)	(-0.10)	(-2.04)	(-0.56)	(-1.23)
$Employee(87-81)$	0.0983^{***}	0.0642^{***}	0.0647^{**}	0.0777^{***}	0.0686^{**}
	(4.94)	(4.35)	(2.29)	(4.29)	(2.62)
$CAPX(87-81)$	0.1651	0.1874	0.1504	0.0811	0.2679
	(0.97)	(1.31)	(0.51)	(0.47)	(1.33)
$RISK(87-81)$	0.1670	0.1705	1.0635^{*}	0.6028	0.7826
	(0.32)	(0.38)	(1.79)	(1.16)	(1.35)
N	70	103	42	77	58
Adjusted R^2	0.330	0.239	0.344	0.192	0.235
F-statistic	3.62	3.46	2.65	2.39	2.35
Durbin-Watson	2.14	1.96	2.21	2.12	2.32

Note: Dependent variable is ($DROS87 - DROS81$). The t-statistics are reported in parentheses: $^{*} = p < 0.1$, $^{**} = p < 0.05$, $^{***} = p < 0.01$ (all are two-tail tests).

Table 7.7
Means, standard deviations, and intercorrelations among profitability variables

Variable	Mean	Standard deviation	(1)	(2)	(3)	(4)	(5)	(6)	(7)	(8)	(9)
(1) ROA87	0.1592	0.0633	—								
(2) ROA91	0.1402	0.0652	0.528	—							
(3) ROS87	0.1339	0.0594	0.652	0.418	—						
(4) ROS91	0.1257	0.0617	0.342	0.698	0.682	—					
(5) ROE87	0.3536	0.4275	0.324	0.125	0.104	0.006	—				
(6) ROE91	0.3873	0.6481	0.141	0.203	0.136	0.193	−0.121	—			
(7) ROA(87 − 81)	−0.0168	0.0732	0.551	0.088	0.448	0.109	0.215	−0.013	—		
(8) ROS(87 − 81)	0.0081	0.0603	0.474	0.169	0.672	0.323	0.155	0.012	0.779	—	
(9) ROE(87 − 81)	0.0001	0.4413	0.267	0.054	0.122	0.004	0.937	−0.121	0.374	0.269	—

Note: $N = 200$. Correlation coefficients greater than 0.19 are significant at $p < 0.05$, those greater than 0.25 are significant at $p < 0.01$, and those greater than 0.32 are significant at $p < 0.001$.

Table 7.8
Regression results with different measures of profitability

	Strategy A			Strategy D		
	DROS (87 − 81)	DROA (87 − 81)	DROE (87 − 81)	DROS (87 − 81)	DROA (87 − 81)	DROE (87 − 81)
Constant	−3.892*** (−4.50)	−2.091*** (−3.158)	−2.239*** (−3.42)	−3.423*** (−4.32)	−1.967*** (−3.31)	−2.106*** (−3.63)
Refoc(87 − 81)	2.460** (2.34)	1.384* (1.72)	1.405* (1.77)	2.714*** (2.73)	1.310* (1.76)	1.186* (1.64)
WXAD(85 − 81)	−0.221* (−1.85)	−0.1930** (−2.10)	−0.188** (−2.08)	−0.1553 (−1.36)	−0.1760** (−2.06)	−0.1733** (−2.08)
WXRD(85 − 81)	−0.0004 (−0.94)	−0.000004 (−0.01)	−0.00005 (−0.14)	−0.0005 (−1.09)	−0.00002 (−0.07)	3.38×10^{-5} (0.09)
WC4(85 − 81)	34.019 (0.34)	−28.448 (−0.37)	−40.207 (−0.53)	74.883 (0.78)	−10.693 (−0.14)	−20.499 (−0.29)
Share(85 − 81)	3.670* (1.84)	0.769 (0.50)	1.117 (0.74)	0.5235 (0.36)	0.0803 (0.07)	0.1488 (0.14)
DMGMT(86 − 81)	0.944 (1.00)	−0.1052 (−0.14)	0.1528 (0.21)	0.0329 (0.03)	0.1796 (0.25)	0.3406 (0.49)
DSE(87 − 81)	−0.0069** (−2.34)	−0.0033 (−1.47)	−0.0035 (−1.58)	−0.0029 (−1.64)	0.000014 (0.01)	−0.0014 (−1.09)

Foreign(87 − 82)	−0.0587	0.0253	0.0056	−0.0156	0.0548	0.0322
	(−0.69)	(0.38)	(0.08)	(−0.21)	(0.99)	(0.59)
Employee(87 − 81)	0.1002***	0.0149	0.0183	0.0761***	0.0025	0.0065
	(5.21)	(1.01)	(1.26)	(4.38)	(0.19)	(0.51)
CAPX(87 − 81)	0.1267	0.0098	0.0485	0.0703	0.0010	0.0377
	(0.76)	(0.07)	(0.38)	(0.43)	(0.00)	(0.32)
RISK(87 − 81)	0.547	−0.0774	−0.1157	0.8423*	−0.2324	−0.2381
	(1.07)	(−0.19)	(−0.30)	(1.70)	(−0.62)	(−0.66)

Note: Refocusing is measured using the WSJ announcements. The t-statistics are in parentheses: $* = p < 0.1$, $** = p < 0.05$, $*** = p < 0.01$ (all are two-tail tests).

the original regressions when profitability was measured as return on sales. Out of the regression, sixteen equations come out with a statistically significant refocusing variable when profitability is measured as return on assets, and fifteen equations have a statistically significant refocusing variable when profitability is measured as return on equity. Again I take this evidence as strong support of proposition 3.

These same regressions were also tried using changes in *ROS* (rather than *DROS*) as the dependent variable: The basic relationships uncovered above remain the same. Similar results were also obtained when the variable *DMGMT* was removed from the regressions, as well as when the absolute levels of the industry-structure variables were used along with the changes in these variables.

As was shown in table 7.6, of the three refocusing variables, only refocusing early on in the period (in 1981–83) comes out significant. One possible reason for this is that refocusing's beneficial effect on profitability takes some time to materialize: It may be that the sudden change in strategic direction, together with the major divestitures and/or acquisitions accompanying refocusing, may put the company in some turmoil and uncertainty, and it may take a few years before the company is able to exploit the economies of refocusing. On the other hand, it is possible that refocusing later in the decade may not have had a substantial effect on performance due to an innovation effect (e.g., Armour and Teece 1978).

To examine these possible explanations, I subdivide all the refocusing firms in the sample into three groups: The early-refocusers who did most (i.e., more than 50 percent) of their refocusing in 1981–83, the middle-refocusers who did most of their refocusing in 1983–85, and the late-refocusers who did most of their refocusing in 1985–87. Of the three groups of firms, only the early-refocusers are doing better than their industry average in 1987. Both the middle- and the late-refocusers are doing worse than their industry average, with the late-refocusers doing the worst of all three groups. These results seem to suggest that it takes some time for refocusing's beneficial effects to materialize.

To double-check this, I repeat the regressions, but now I use as the dependent variable the change in profitability between 1987 and 1991. No matter which of the three profitability variables are used, the result remains unchanged: the refocusing variables for 1983–85 and 1985–87 do not come out statistically significant. Contrary to the conclusion above, this evidence points towards an innovation effect.

So far, proposition 6 has not been tested explicitly; the results provide indirect support for this proposition (in that they show that the relation-

Table 7.9
The curvilinear relationship between diversification and profitability

	Dependent variable		
	ROS87	ROA87	ROE87
Constant	0.1533	0.0986***	0.1975**
	(0.05)	(3.14)	(2.01)
DT(87)	5.128**	0.0471*	0.0610
	(2.18)	(1.69)	(0.70)
$(DT87)^2$	−0.982*	−0.0118*	−0.0133
	(−1.71)	(−1.74)	(−0.62)
WXAD87	0.2476	0.0065***	0.0216***
	(1.17)	(2.65)	(2.79)
WXRD87	0.0206**	−0.0002	−0.0007*
	(1.95)	(−1.55)	(−1.76)
WC4(87)	−2.620	−0.0368	−1.0116
	(−0.09)	(−0.11)	(−1.04)
Share87	0.1364	0.0006	0.0063
	(0.93)	(0.39)	(1.19)
DSE87	0.0005	-1.84×10^{-5}	0.0013***
	(0.25)	(−0.74)	(17.04)
Foreign87	−0.0304	−0.0005*	−0.0004
	(−1.31)	(−1.93)	(−0.46)
Employee87	0.0057	-1.90×10^{-5}	4.04×10^{-6}
	(1.54)	(−0.43)	(0.03)
CAPX87	0.9119***	0.0053***	0.0054
	(8.44)	(4.11)	(1.33)
RISK87	−0.273	−0.0109***	−0.0229***
	(−1.52)	(−4.75)	(−3.20)
N	200	190	189
Adjusted R^2	0.322	0.179	0.639
F	9.59	4.76	31.28

Note: The t-statistics are in parentheses. $* = p < 0.1$, $** = p < 0.05$, $*** = p < 0.01$ (all are two-tail tests).

ship between diversification and profitability is not monotonic) but a direct test is called for. A direct way to test the validity of a curvilinear relationship between diversification and profitability will be to actually fit a curvilinear relationship to the whole sample.

The simple model $ROS87 = b_0 + b_1(DT87) + b_2(DT87)^2$ gives the estimated coefficients: $b_1 = 7.338$ ($t = 2.66$), and $b_2 = -1.741$ ($t = -2.57$), both of which are statistically significant at the 1 percent level. The negative coefficient of the squared diversification variable suggests that there exists an inverse-U relationship between diversification levels and profitability. This result is further examined using the more complete model:

$$ROS87 = f(DT87, (DT87)^2, \text{control variables}).$$

The results of this regression are shown in the first column of table 7.9. The coefficient of the (squared) diversification variable is again negative and statistically significant. This implies that an inverse-U curve fits the data well. Hence the existence of a curvilinear relationship appears to be confirmed by the data.[12] The same result emerges when profitability is measured as return on assets (as shown in the second column of the table). However, when profitability is measured as return on equity, no curvilinear relationship is uncovered.

Discussion

Perhaps the most important contributions of this chapter are the findings that (1) refocusing in the 1980s by the overdiversified firms is associated with profitability improvements, and (2) a curvilinear relationship appears to exist between diversification and profitability. The first finding is consistent with the ex ante evidence from chapter 6, which shows that refocusing is associated with market value improvements. The second finding is consistent with a growing consensus in the strategy literature that the relationship between diversification and performance is not monotonic (e.g., Grant and Thomas 1988; Hoskisson and Hitt 1990). For example, in their survey of the existing literature on diversification, Hoskisson and Hitt (1990, p. 474) argue that "... research and theory ... suggest an overall curvilinear relationship between performance and diversification." These results also support those who argue that there is a limit to how much a

---

12. Similar results are obtained when the model is run on the 1981 data. For example, the coefficient of $(DT81)^2$ comes out equal to -0.24, with a t-statistic of -2.59 (significant at the 1 percent level).

firm can grow (e.g., Prahalad and Bettis 1986; Williamson 1967) and are in conformity with the propositions of transaction-cost economists (e.g., Montgomery and Wernerfelt 1988) who argue that firms diversify to exploit their excess specific assets. But as they diversify away from their core, their assets lose some of their efficiency and earn declining rents.

The existence of a curvilinear relationship could help explain the conflicting results that emerged in the literature regarding the relationship between diversification and profitability. For example, studies by Carter (1977), Miller (1969), and Rhoades (1973) have found a positive correlation between diversification and profitability, while studies by Arnould (1969), Berry (1974), and Markham (1973) have failed to find a positive relationship. If the "true" relationship is curvilinear—as this study has argued—then some studies will find a positive relationship if their sample is predominantly made up of underdiversified firms, while other studies will find a negative relationship if their sample is made up of overdiversified firms, and on average no relationship will be discovered. In fact, when the model of this study is run on the whole sample of 200 firms, the relationship between changes in profitability and refocusing comes out insignificant.

The results of this study also lend support to the claim by Wernerfelt and Montgomery (1988, p. 246) that the existence of a negative relationship between diversification and the firm's average profitability "... does not [necessarily] imply that diversifying firms are not maximizing profits, only that their marginal returns decrease as they diversify farther afield." This suggests that future research projects on diversification should be examining the marginal contribution of an additional diversification move on the firm's profitability rather than the effect of diversification on average profitability (for illustrative examples, see Baumol et al. 1970; Friend and Husic 1973; Hiller 1978). On the other hand, it is still unclear whether the existence of overdiversified firms can be explained as non-profit-maximizing behavior by the managers of these firms (e.g., Jensen 1986; Mueller 1972), or whether these firms were profit maximizing but found themselves in this position now that their optimal level of diversification has been lowered by external events.

Specifically the existing literature and the theoretical discussion in chapter 2 have identified several possible reasons why firms may have overdiversified in the past twenty years. These include, among others, agency reasons, stock market inefficiencies, tax incentives, changes in the capital market, and increased globalization. This chapter has not explicitly tested which of these reasons is valid: My focus has not been to explain why firms overdiversified but to determine if refocusing by these overdiversified firms is associated with ex post profitability improvements. However, recent empirical work has begun to address this question. For example, Hoskisson, Johnson, and Moesel (1993) have found that restructuring intensity is directly related to firm performance and strategy which in turn are preceded by weak corporate governance. This points to an agency explanation of overdiversification. On the other hand, Liebeskind and Opler (1992) have found that refocusing during the 1980s was primarily a response to changing competitive forces in the U.S. economy; this points to a downward-shifting optimal diversification level as the primary cause of overdiversification. Finally, Morck et al. (1990) have found that in the 1960s, the stock market reacted positively to diversifying acquisitions which, with hindsight, appears to have been a mistake (i.e., many of these diversifying acquisitions turned out to be business failures in the 1970s); this suggests that capital market inefficiencies may also have had a role to play in overdiversification.

The main model of this chapter is also tried on the group of firms classified (using a variety of strategies) as underdiversified. Given our theoretical propositions, I expected a negative relationship between refocusing and profitability for this group of firms (i.e., these firms still need to diversify toward their optimal level). The empirical results did not consistently support this prediction: For some regression runs I obtained the predicted negative sign, but for many other regression runs the refocusing coefficient was not statistically significant. This result is in conformity with Reed's (1991) theory of bimodality in diversification. He argues that some firms are good at focus while others are good at managing diversification. Thus the analysis of this chapter is valid only for those firms that have diversified beyond a certain level; the curvilinear relationship is applicable for the group of firms that have diversified beyond the first diversification mode (single- or dominant-business firms).

Future research efforts could try to identify the exact reasons why firms have overdiversified over the past twenty years. I have proposed several possible reasons for overdiversification but have not tested any of them. Similarly a future research project could try to explain why firms are refocusing now. Even though this chapter has hinted that the threat of takeover may have prompted managers to act, this is by no means certain and additional studies are needed to examine the issue. Finally, additional research is needed to examine whether the benefits of refocusing are slow to materialize and whether these benefits are sustained in the long term.

8 Organization Structure, Refocusing, and Profitability

So far I have argued that many firms have overinvested in diversification and that, by refocusing, they can improve their efficiency and profitability. In this chapter I go one step further and propose that in addition to refocusing, firms must also adopt a new organizational structure that better suits their new strategy, if they are to fully realize the benefits of reduced diversification (see also Hoskisson, Hill, and Kim 1993). More specifically I propose that, on average, the most appropriate structure for the refocused firms is the centralized M-form structure, whereas the most appropriate structure for the very diversified firms is the M-form structure. In this chapter I build the theoretical arguments behind this proposition and then offer empirical evidence that provides tentative support for the proposition.

Theory and Hypotheses

The organizational structure of a firm must be designed in such a way as to facilitate the firm's chosen strategy. This idea is neither new nor novel. It was Chandler (1962) who first pointed out that structure must follow strategy to facilitate realization of the strategy's objectives. This implies that control arrangements within the basic firm structure must fit with the firm's strategy if the firm is to realize the economic benefits associated with that strategy (Hill and Hoskisson 1987). Unfortunately, this idea—while correct in its basic premises—has received some unwarranted simplification in the academic literature.

Williamson (1970, 1975) used Chandler's findings to develop a theory of internal organization. His basic proposition is that diversified firms must follow a multidivisional structure (the M-form structure) in order to achieve the best performance (Williamson 1970, p. 134). However, as argued by Hill (1988), this hypothesis suffers from one serious simplification: It treats diversification as a single homogeneous strategy. Hill (1988) proposes that at the very least, we have to differentiate between two major types of diversification: related and unrelated diversification. The benefits sought through the strategy of related diversification (i.e., synergistic economies) are clearly different from the benefits sought through the strategy of unrelated diversification (i.e., financial economies); see also Hill, Hitt, and Hoskisson (1992). This implies that the internal structure of a related diversifier must be different from the internal structure of an unrelated diversifier, if the benefits sought by each strategy are to materialize.

It is not surprising therefore that the research that empirically tested Williamson's hypothesis has produced ambiguous results: Four studies (Hill 1985a; Hoskisson and Galbraith 1985; Steer and Cable 1978; Teece 1981) have found evidence of superior M-form performance, three studies (Armour and Teece 1978; Harris 1983; Thompson 1984) have found ambiguous results, and three studies (Cable and Dirrheimer 1983; Cable and Yasuki 1984; Holl 1983) have found no evidence of superior M-form performance. On the other hand, the hypothesis that unrelated and related diversifiers must adopt different structures to pursue their respective strategies has received tentative support from Hill (1988) and Hoskisson (1987a).

Consider now a diversified firm that decides to refocus. As long as the firm is widely diversified, its primary goal is to reap the benefits of high diversification, which are primarily financial in nature (i.e., reduced portfolio risk and the benefits of the internal capital market). These benefits can be better exploited if the firm adopts control systems that are consistent with an internal capital market (Williamson 1975). Hence the firm must adopt an M-form structure that is characterized by a separation of strategic and operating functions, among other things, and that represents the optimal internal capital market (Williamson 1975).

However, once the firm refocuses, it is changing its strategy in one fundamental way: It is now seeking to exploit interrelationships and synergies among fewer and more related units. It is also seeking to reduce the control loss associated with excessive diversification (Hill and Hoskisson 1987). To achieve this, the firm must exercise more central control over its units, and the head office has to become more involved in operating decisions (Hill 1988; Hill et al. 1992). As Hill and Hoskisson (1987, p. 334) argue:

Realizing synergistic economies ... requires interdivisional coordination and/or resource sharing. Linkages must be established between divisions. In addition, the head office must acquire detailed knowledge of operational affairs if it is to identify possibilities for exchange or joint actions.

As proposed by Hill (1988) and Hill et al. (1992), the organizational structure that best fits these requirements is the centralized M-form (CM-form) structure.[1]

The same argument can be formulated in terms of the costs of diversification: A firm that is very diversified has achieved a significant portfolio risk reduction but has also sacrificed a lot of operating control over its units. Its large and detached corporate staff knows very little about the actual business of the operating units and can only intervene at a cost. The principal function of the staff will be to act as an "internal" banker to the units (M-form structure) so that the firm operates more like a holding company than an operating company.

Suppose, now, that conditions have changed and the firm is forced to refocus (e.g., the capital market no longer accepts the reduced portfolio risk as a valid justification of diversification). By reducing its diversification, the firm is willing to allow some increase in its portfolio risk (something which is empirically supported by the data in chapter 4), but in return it is now in a better position to exercise more central control over its units and thus decrease its operating risk (CM-form structure).

The above discussion points to several hypotheses. Specifically:

Hypothesis 1 (H_1)   In the 1980s, along with refocusing, there should be a shift away from the M-form structure toward the centralized M-form structure.

Hypothesis 2 (H_2)   M-form firms will not outperform other firms that have adopted a different structure.

Hypothesis 3 (H_3)   On average, the most appropriate structure for the refocused firms is the centralized M-form structure, whereas the most appropriate structure for the very diversified firms is the M-form structure.

Alternatively:

Hypothesis 3' (H_3'):   Firms that are very diversified should follow an M-form structure; firms that are not very diversified should follow a centralized M-form structure; undiversified firms should follow a functional structure (U-form).

The difference between H_3 and H_3' is the following: H_3 is concerned with changes in diversification, whereas H_3' looks at levels of diversification.

---

1. Williamson (1975) originally called this organization structure the "corrupted" M-form structure. Hill (1988) renamed it "centralized" M-form to emphasize the difference in interpretations.

That is, H_3 looks at firms that have reduced their diversification in the study period, but a firm may have refocused and still be very diversified (e.g., ITT). Therefore H_3' should do a better job in capturing the relationship between diversification and structure.

Research Design

To test the above hypotheses, I need to collect information that would allow me to classify firms according to the organizational structure they have adopted. For this purpose I will use a classification scheme developed by Williamson and Bhargava (1972). This scheme recognizes four preconditions of an efficient internal capital market. The four conditions are listed by Hill (1988, p. 72) as follows:

1. Cash flows are reallocated by the head office between competing claims and are not returned to source divisions.

2. Operating functions are decentralized so that the head office does not get involved in the daily operating decisions of the divisions.

3. The head office is profit oriented and evaluates divisional performance according to abstract profit criteria.

4. The head office exercises central strategic and financial controls.

The classification scheme is summarized in table 8.1.

Williamson's theory predicts that the M-form firms will outperform the CM-form and H-form types (Williamson 1975) because only the M-form structure represents an optimal internal capital market. The discussion above, however, suggests that the M-form structure is only appropriate for the very diversified firms. For firms that have refocused to moderate levels of diversity, the CM-form is a more appropriate structure.

The information to undertake the above classification exercise was collected by a questionnaire (see appendix at the end of this chapter). A questionnaire was sent to the CEO of all the companies that met the following criteria: The company was incorporated in the United States, belonged to SIC 0-40 (i.e., no service firms), was not taken over in 1988, and had 1988 sales in, excess of $400 million. A total of 457 questionnaires were sent, addressed personally to the CEO of the company with the instruction that he/she completes it or pass it along to the most appropriate manager in the organization. A total of 136 valid responses were received—a response rate of 30 percent—which is considered very satisfactory for this type of research.

Table 8.1
Classification scheme

Form	Main characteristics
M-form	Multidivisional firms, characterized by a separation of strategic and operating functions, centralized strategic and financial control systems built around abstract profit criteria, and the reallocation of cash flows between competing claims. Optimal internal capital market.
CM-form	Centralized multidivisionals, characterized by head office involvement in operating decisions. Internal capital market difficult to operate due to equivocality.
H-form	Holding companies, these are decentralized multidivisionals which lack the requisite internal control apparatus of the M-form. Cash flows are not exposed to an internal competition but returned to source divisions. Hence no internal capital market. No strategic controls.
T-form	Transitional firms undergoing a process of organizational adjustment. Due to changes and learning, it is unlikely that internal capital market is optimal.
U-form	Functionally centralized firms with no divisional structure. Optimal organization for small single product enterprises. No internal capital market.
X-form	Firms which are a mixture of U-form and multidivisional types. May be particularly appropriate for vertically integrated enterprises.

Source: Reprinted by permission of Basil Blackwell Ltd. from C. W. L. Hill, *Internal capital market controls and financial performance in multidivisional firms, Journal of Industrial Economics* 37 (September 1988): 72. Copyright © Basil Blackwell 1988.

Using questionnaire data and Hill's (1988) methodology, three composite scales were constructed: operate, strategic, and financial. "Operate" measured head office involvement in the operating decisions of the divisions. It ranged in value from 1 to 4. A score of less than 2 on this scale indicated that the firm was decentralized with respect to operating functions. "Strategic" measured the extent to which strategic controls were centralized. Similarly, "financial" measured the extent to which the head office exercised centralized financial controls over divisions based upon abstract profit criteria. These scales ranged in value from 1 to 5. A score of 2 or less indicated centralized strategic and financial controls. Hence a high score on operate, along with low scores on strategic and financial indicated the major characteristics of an M-form internal capital market.

In addition, two other variables were constructed. The variable "stability" was a (0, 1) dummy that took the value of 1 if the firm did not change its structure in the past two years, and zero if it did. The variable *ICM* (internal cash management) was another (0, 1) dummy that took the value of 1 if cash was reallocated between divisions, and zero if cash was returned to source. The classification procedure is summarized in

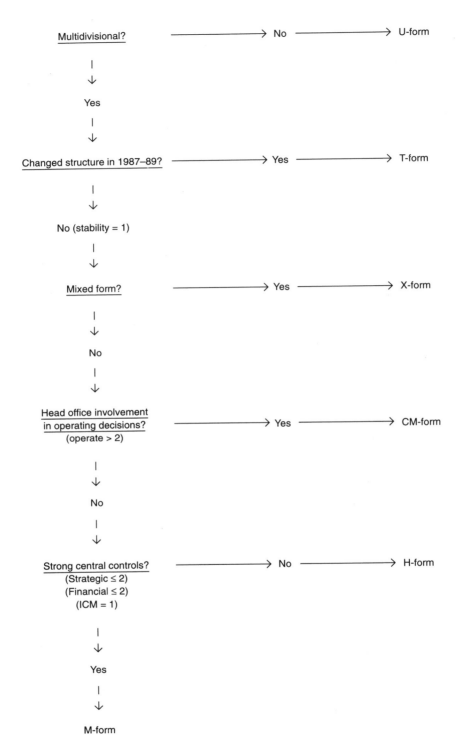

Figure 8.1
Classification exercise

Table 8.2
Distribution of U.S. companies by organizational form

Form	1970[a]		1989	
	Number of firms	Percentage	Number of firms	Percentage
M-form	81	53.3	53	41.1
CM-form	12[b]	7.9	27	20.9
H-form	12[c]	7.9	19	14.7
T-form	13	8.5	10	7.8
X-form	15	9.8	6	4.6
U-form	8	5.2	14	10.8
Uncertain	4	—	3	—
Other	11[d]	7.2	—	—
Total	156		132	

Note: M = multidivisional organization, CM = centralized multidivisional organization, H = holding company organization, T = transitional organization, X = mixed organization, U = functional organization.
a. Adapted from Bhargava (1973).
b. Bhargava classifies these firms as D_1 and $\bar{D}$.
c. Bhargava classifies these firms as D_2 and H.
d. Bhargava classifies these firms as D_1-D_2 variant.

figure 8.1. The cutoff points used to assign firms to categories were derived from the wording of the original questions.

For each firm I also calculated its entropy index of diversification (DT) for the years 1981 and 1987, using data from TRINET. The index, along with information from the questionnaires was used to identify those firms that refocused in the period. Finally, each firm's profitability for the years 1980 to 1988 was estimated from Compustat.

Results

The results of the classification are given in table 8.2. As expected, the multidivisional structure predominates. About 89 percent of the sample firms are multidivisional in nature, primarily of the M-form variety. In order to examine how organizational structures evolved over time (H_1), I need a similar classification of American firms from the past. The only other study that undertook a classification of this sort is that by Bhargava (1973) who did his study under the supervision of Williamson. Bhargava uses a slightly different classification scheme than the one used here (the main difference being terminology and semantics). To ensure comparability,

Table 8.3
Distribution of U.K. companies by organizational form

Form	1964–66[a] Number of firms	1964–66[a] Percentage	1970–72[a] Number of firms	1970–72[a] Percentage	1985[b] Number of firms	1985[b] Percentage
M-form	21	19.6	35	32.1	51	35.2
CM-form	17	15.9	7	6.4	31	21.4
H-form	37	34.6	14	12.8	34	23.4
T-form	12	11.2	40	36.7	23	15.9
X-form	6	5.6	4	3.7	—	—
U-form	14	13.1	9	8.3	6	4.1
Uncertain	13	—	11	—	11	—
Total	120		120		156	

a. Date from Steer and Cable (1978, pp. 13–30).
b. Data from Hill (1988, p. 75).

I went through Bhargava's classification and made some adjustments to his terminology as shown at the bottom of the table.

Comparing Bhargava's results with our results, I find strong confirmation of H_1: The incidence of centralized M-form (CM-form) firms increases from 7.9 percent of the sample in 1970 to 20.9 percent in 1989. I have to keep in mind, though, that some of this increase can be a function of the different population of firms under study. That is, Bhargava examined the Fortune 200 firms, whereas this study includes many more smaller firms that are likely to be less diversified (and of the CM-form variety). For comparison, table 8.3 reports the results of similar classifications from the United Kingdom. As can be seen, a very similar trend toward the CM-form structure is also evident in the U.K. data. Also evident (from both tables) is the (quite big) increase in the number of holding companies.

To test H_2, the data in table 8.4 is utilized. The analysis is carried out using both *ROS* and *DROS* as the measure of firm profitability. As can be seen, the M-form structure does not significantly outperform the CM-form and H-form types (in none of the three years studied). Thus H_2 is supported by the data—and so is, by implication, the theoretical analysis of the previous section which argues that not all diversified firms are served well by adopting the M-form structure (e.g., Hoskisson 1987; Hoskisson, Hill, and Kim 1993). The most prominent result in the table is the superior performance of the mixed-form (X-form) firms. This could be an aberration (due to the small number of X-form firms under study), or it may reflect the fact that these firms, by adopting a mixed form of organization rather

Table 8.4
Organizational form and profitability

Form	ROS86	ROS87	ROS88	DROS88
M-form ($N = 53$)	12.02%	12.51%	13.16%	−0.7877%
CM-form ($N = 27$)	11.51	11.96	12.40	−0.9968
H-form ($N = 19$)	11.10	11.74	13.16	+0.1504
T-form ($N = 10$)	8.44	11.18	12.88	+0.0595
X-form ($N = 6$)	16.82	17.90	16.60	+0.8621
U-form ($N = 14$)	13.85	13.39	13.94	−0.7655

F-statistics	1986	1987	1988
All	1.75	1.09	0.44
M-form vs. rest	0.54	0.81	0.57
CM-form vs. rest	1.00	1.41	1.39
H-form vs. rest	1.50	1.47	0.31
T-form vs. rest	5.69**	1.57	0.34
X-form vs. rest	3.55*	3.76*	1.06
U-form vs. rest	0.51	0.00	0.00

Note: The number of firms appears in parentheses. The difference in the profitability between the M-form firms and the CM-form firms is not statistically significant; ** $= p <$ 0.05, * $= p < 0.1$.

than a pure form, were able to achieve a closer fit between their control arrangements and their strategy. The inferior performance of the T-form firms is as expected, since these firms are going through a transition. Also noteworthy is the good and steady performance of the U-form firms.

To double-check Hill's (1988) contingency hypothesis, I also classified each sample firm according to Rumelt's (1974) diversification categories and carried out the analysis shown in table 8.5. In total, a significant amount of variance in profitability is explained for the first two years under study and significant interaction effects are observed for all three years. Surprisingly Hill's (1988) contingency hypothesis is not supported by the results: For Related firms, the CM-form structure is not associated with superior profitability (relative to the M-form structure); similarly for Unrelated firms, the M-form structure is not associated with superior profitability (relative to the CM-form structure). In fact the profitability of the different subgroups are exactly the opposite of what the contingency hypothesis proposes. The F-statistics of the differences in the means of various subgroups of interest are reported in table 8.6. The only statistically significant difference occurs among Related and Unrelated CM-form firms: Unrelated firms that adopt a CM-form structure do better than Related

Table 8.5
Diversification, organizational structure, and profitability

Organizational structure		Single business				Dominant business				Related business				Unrelated business		
		ROS86	ROS87	ROS88		ROS86	ROS87	ROS88		ROS86	ROS87	ROS88		ROS86	ROS87	ROS88
M-form	(11)	10.69%	11.08%	12.02%	(16)	11.52%	12.22%	12.78%	(15)	13.51%	13.68%	13.79%	(11)	12.06%	12.76%	13.97%
CM-form	(3)	13.57	13.11	12.38	(11)	11.25	12.37	13.21	(8)	11.18	10.87	10.89	(3)	16.13	14.99	16.14
H-form	(3)	15.11	15.70	13.44	(6)	13.15	15.23	17.62	(4)	5.53	3.40	4.59	(4)	10.54	12.37	12.99
T-form	(4)	7.51	8.06	16.19	(3)	14.77	15.06	14.44	(2)	4.91	13.44	12.15	(1)	6.55	7.44	−3.54
X-form	(2)	8.14	9.35	9.50	(3)	24.05	24.74	22.47	(1)	12.49	14.47	13.18	(0)	—	—	—
U-form	(8)	14.66	15.67	15.25	(4)	12.59	10.36	12.48	(2)	13.13	10.25	11.64	(0)	—	—	—

Statistics	F-Value		
	1986	1987	1988
Total variance explained	1.50*	1.51*	1.19
Organisation structure effects	1.79	1.12	0.43
Strategic category effects	0.36	0.69	0.93
Interaction effects (form/strategy)	1.62*	1.86**	1.58*

Note: Number of firms appears in parentheses; ** = $p < 0.05$, * = $p < 0.1$.

Table 8.6
Structure, strategy, and profitability

Category	F-statistics		
	1986	1987	1988
(M-form and Related) vs. (M-form and Unrelated)	0.48	0.37	−0.07
(CM-form and Related) vs. (CM-form and Unrelated)	−1.89*	−1.88*	−2.37*
(M-form and Related) vs. (CM-form and Related)	1.14	1.23	0.27
(CM-form and Unrelated) vs. (M-form and Unrelated)	−1.00	−0.60	−0.54

Note: * = $p < 0.10$.

firms that adopt the same structure. Again this finding goes against Hill's (1988) contingency proposition.[2]

To test H_3, the sample is divided into refocused and nonrefocused firms (based on their 1981 and 1987 DT as well as information from their questionnaires). I expect that in the refocused group the CM-form structure will outperform all others, while in the nonrefocused group the M-form firms will outperform all others. The results are shown in table 8.7. There is no evidence in support of this hypothesis: There is no statistical difference in the performance of the M-form and CM-form firms. The only group of firms that consistently displays superior performance is the X-form firms.

As argued before, this should not be a surprising result because it may be difficult to establish a relationship between changes in diversity and organizational structure. For example, a firm may have done a lot of refocusing in the period, but at the end of the period it may still be very diversified and would therefore be better served by adopting an M-form structure rather than a CM-form structure. A better test of the contingency hypothesis would therefore involve examining the relationship between levels of diversity and organizational structure. This is hypothesis H_3'.

To test H_3', I subdivide the sample into three groups: Those firms whose 1987 entropy index of diversification (DT) is above the sample mean are placed in the high-diversity group. Those firms whose 1987 DT is smaller than the sample mean minus one standard deviation are placed in the low-diversity group. All others are placed in the moderate-diversity group. I would expect that in the high-diversity group the M-form firms will outperform all others, whereas in the moderate-diversity group the

2. A possible explanation for this result has recently been offered by Markides and Williamson (1994b). They argue that the reason why Hill's contingency hypothesis is not supported empirically is because of the inappropriate way that relatedness among business units has traditionally been measured (i.e., relatedness has traditionally been measured at the market level rather than the strategic asset level).

Table 8.7
Organizational form, strategy, and profitability, 1981 to 1988

Form	Refocused				Nonrefocused			
	ROS86	ROS87	ROS88	DROS88	ROS86	ROS87	ROS88	DROS88
M-form	12.62%	13.16%	13.69%	-1.417% (N = 24)	11.61%	11.98%	12.72%	-0.248% (N = 27)
CM-form	10.91	12.57	12.49	-0.999 (N = 13)	12.78	12.27	13.37	-0.01453 (N = 13)
H-form	8.62	9.34	10.39	-3.179 (N = 6)	12.43	13.23	14.00	$+1.984$ (N = 11)
T-form	9.19	8.68	23.24	$+15.326$ (N = 2)	9.17	12.88	11.12	-3.375 (N = 7)
X-form	20.46	22.08	16.83	$+4.319$ (N = 2)	17.40	18.91	20.05	$+2.954$ (N = 3)
U-form	16.18	18.03	18.27	$+2.66$ (N = 3)	13.22	12.11	12.76	-1.6997 (N = 11)

Note: Number of firms appears in parentheses. The difference in the profitability between the M-form firms and the CM-form firms is not statistically significant.

CM-form firms will outperform the others. In the low-diversity group the U-form firms should do well.

The results are shown in tables 8.8(A) and 8.8(B). In the first table, profitability is measured as *ROS*; in the second table, profitability is measured as industry-adjusted *DROS*. Both tables provide strong support of the hypothesis: Within the high-diversity group the M-form firms outperform the CM-form firms, whereas within the moderate-diversity group it is the CM-form firms that outperform the M-form ones. This is by far the strictest of the four hypotheses, and the evidence seems to support it completely.

A Dynamic Model

The relationships between organization structure and profitability uncovered above may be biased if there are variables that affect both structure and profitability but whose effect is not controlled by inclusion in the analysis (e.g., firm size). To account for this as well as other possible interaction effects, the three hypotheses are tested again using a more dynamic model.

To test the hypothesis that the M-form structure is not superior to the other structural forms, the following model was attempted[3]:

$$ROS88 = \beta_0 + \beta_1(\text{M-form}) + \beta_2(\text{Restructuring}) + \beta_3(Risk88)$$
$$+ \beta_4(\text{Growth}) + \beta_5(DSE88) + \beta_6(Size88) + \sum_{i=2}^{18} \beta_i D_i,$$

where

$ROS88$ = profitability of the firm in 1988 (from Compustat),

M-form = a (0, 1) dummy variable that takes the value of 1 if the firm has an M-form structure; zero otherwise (from the questionnaire),

Restructuring = dummy variable that takes the value of 1 if the firm restructured during 1981–87; zero otherwise (from the questionnaire),

$Risk88$ = firm's risk in 1988 as measured by the standard deviation of its profitability over the past five years (from Compustat),

Growth = firm's growth rate as measured by the compound annual growth rate of its sales over the past five years (from Compustat),

---

3. To account for systematic differences in market technology across industries, the analysis is also carried out using *DROS88* as the dependent variable—that is, each firm's profitability is industry adjusted.

Table 8.8
Organizational form, diversity, and profitability, 1988

Form	High diversity[a]	Moderate diversity[b]	Low
A. Profitability (ROS88)			
M-form	14.80% ($N = 34$)	9.93% ($N = 13$)	13.59% ($N = 3$)
CM-form	11.53 ($N = 14$)	14.34 ($N = 7$)	14.07 ($N = 4$)
H-form	13.23 ($N = 7$)	13.09 ($N = 8$)	9.53 ($N = 2$)
T-form	6.81 ($N = 3$)	13.40 ($N = 3$)	17.05 ($N = 4$)
X-form	23.89 ($N = 2$)	15.34 ($N = 3$)	5.79 ($N = 1$)
U-form	14.16 ($N = 4$)	13.52 ($N = 5$)	14.20 ($N = 5$)
B. Profitability (DROS88)			
M-form	+0.05917% ($N = 35$)	−2.780 ($N = 13$)	−2.2143 ($N = 3$)
CM-form	−1.164 ($N = 14$)	−2.336 ($N = 7$)	+0.9402 ($N = 4$)
H-form	+1.326 ($N = 7$)	+0.1635 ($N = 8$)	−3.920 ($N = 2$)
T-form	−7.213 ($N = 3$)	−1.1373 ($N = 3$)	+6.4115 ($N = 4$)
X-form	+16.49 ($N = 1$)	+0.253 ($N = 4$)	−12.329 ($N = 1$)
U-form	−0.97 ($N = 4$)	−1.0022 ($N = 5$)	−0.360 ($N = 5$)

Note: Number of firms appears in parentheses.
a. Within the high-diversity group, the difference in profitability between M-form and CM-form firms is statistically significant at the 10 percent level.
b. Within the moderate-diversity group, the difference in profitability between CM-form and M-form firms is statistically significant at the 5 percent level.

$DSE88$ = firm's 1988 debt-to-equity ratio (from Compustat),

$Size88$ = firm's size in 1988 as measured by its total fixed assets (from Compustat),

D_i = industry dummies.

The results from this model are shown in table 8.9. One of the industry dummies (construction industry) has been dropped to avoid singularity in the data matrix. Thus the industry structure coefficient shows deviations from a non-M-form firm in the construction industry. As seen in the table, the coefficient for the M-form structure is statistically insignificant, as expected from H_2. This implies that either there has been an optimal diffusion of the M-form structure so that every firm that should adopt it has done so, or the M-form does not outperform the other structural forms.

To test H_3', the sample is again divided into moderate- and high-diversity groups as before, and the following model is tested on the two groups separately:[4]

---

4. The analysis is repeated using $DROS88$ as the dependent variable.

Table 8.9
Regression results for the whole sample

	Dependent variable ROS88	Dependent variable DROS88
Intercept	10.1238	−1.8642
	(2.04)**	(−2.11)**
M-form	0.9369	0.57099
	(0.73)	(0.41)
Restructuring dummy	−3.8014	−3.5396
	(−2.69)***	(−2.31)**
Risk 1988	0.7725	0.8329
	(2.71)***	(2.66)***
Sales growth	0.1469	0.1504
	(2.34)**	(2.29)**
DSE 1988	0.00037	0.00082
	(0.36)	(0.71)
Assets 1988	8.73×10^{-5}	8.8×10^{-5}
	(2.66)***	(2.38)**

Note: $N = 112$; industry dummy coefficients (17 in all) are not reported in order to save space. Numbers in parentheses are t-statistics. ** $= p < 0.05$ (two-tail test), *** $= p < 0.01$ (two-tail test). The industry dummy D_1 (SIC 15 = construction industry) is not included in the regression so as to avoid singularity in the data matrix.

$$ROS88 = \beta_0 + \beta_1(\text{M-form}) + \beta_2(\text{CM-form}) + \beta_3(\text{H-form}) + \beta_4(\text{T-form})$$
$$+ \beta_5(\text{X-form}) + \beta_6(\text{U-form}) + \text{same variables as above.}$$

The organization structure variables are all $(0, 1)$ dummies that take the value of 1 if the firm has that particular structure, and zero otherwise. In all the regressions attempted, one organization dummy and one industry dummy were excluded to avoid singularity problems.

The results for the high-diversity group are shown in table 8.10. In regression 1 the M-form dummy is excluded from the model so that β_0 represents the effect of an M-form structure on profitability. As expected, this effect is positive and statistically significant. On the other hand, the effect of the CM-form structure is not statistically significant. The same results emerge when DROS88 is used as the dependent variable.

The exact opposite result emerges for the moderate-diversity group. As shown in table 8.11 (regression 1), β_0 is positive and statistically significant; this means that for the moderate-diversity firms the CM-form structure has a positive effect on their profitability. On the other hand, the effect of the M-form structure is not statistically significant. Unfortunately,

Table 8.10
Regression results for the high-diversity group

	Dependent variable ROS88			Dependent variable DROS88[a]
	Regression 1[a]	Regression 2[b]	Regression 3[c]	
Intercept	9.654	8.405	4.746	9.0047
	(2.50)**	(1.62)	(1.77)*	(1.65)*
M-form	—	1.2488	3.534	—
		(0.35)	(1.65)*	
CM-form	−3.732	−2.483		−1.2836
	(−1.56)	(−0.60)		(−0.40)
H-form	0.562	1.811		3.1203
	(0.20)	(0.44)		(0.90)
T-form	−15.056	−13.807		−13.1795
	(−2.52)**	(−2.05)**		(−1.76)*
X-form	7.936	9.185		11.863
	(1.54)	(1.55)		(1.39)
U-form	−1.2488	—		0.8881
	(−0.35)			(0.21)
Restructuring dummy	1.551	1.551	—	0.4659
	(0.67)	(0.67)		(0.15)
Risk 1988	0.729	0.729	2.095	−0.4024
	(0.94)	(0.94)	(2.37)**	(−0.41)
Sales growth	0.3455	0.3455	0.326	0.3122
	(3.398)***	(3.398)***	(2.59)***	(2.40)**
DSE 1988	−0.0421	−0.0421	—	−0.0647
	(−2.118)**	(−2.118)**		(−2.56)***
Assets 1988	0.000106	0.000106	2.27×10^{-5}	1.78×10^{4}
	(2.66)***	(2.66)***	(0.67)	(2.38)**
Seven industry dummies	Not reported	Not reported	Not included	Not reported

Note: The 57 companies whose 1987 entropy index of diversification is bigger than the sample mean. Numbers in parentheses are t-statistics: *, **, ***, denote significance at 10, 5, and 1 percent, respectively; all tests are two-tail.
a. Excludes the organization dummy M-form and the industry dummy D_2 (food industry).
b. Excludes the organization dummy U-form and the industry dummy D_2 (food industry).
c. $N = 42$ (only those firms classified as M-form or CM-form); excludes all industry dummies.

Table 8.11
Regression results for the moderate-diversity group

	Dependent variable ROS88			Dependent variable DROS88[a]
	Regression 1[a]	Regression 2[b]	Regression 3[c]	
Intercept	17.631	7.230	5.311	0.8220
	(4.83)***	(0.86)	(1.41)	(0.22)
M-form	6.0729	0.7887		6.1849
	(1.44)	(0.20)		(1.43)
CM-form	—	−5.2841	2.738	—
		(−1.22)	(1.096)	
H-form	3.2539	−2.0302		3.6453
	(1.00)	(−0.52)		(1.09)
T-form	2.9304	−2.3537		3.8045
	(0.67)	(−0.47)		(0.39)
X-form	8.413	3.1291		7.497
	(1.88)*	(0.74)		(1.63)
U-form	5.284	—		4.851
	(1.22)			(1.09)
Restructuring dummy	−7.212	−7.2126		−7.4455
	(−2.76)**	(−2.76)**		(−2.84)***
Risk 1988	0.6951	0.6951	0.303	0.7755
	(1.86)*	(1.86)*	(0.62)	(2.01)**
Sales growth	0.1153	0.1153	0.331	0.0564
	(0.67)	(0.67)	(1.308)	(0.32)
DSE 1988	−0.00186	−0.00186	—	−0.00391
	(−0.27)	(−0.28)		(−0.56)
Assets 1988	00.000601	0.000601	0.0022	0.000108
	(1.11)	(1.11)	(1.78)*	(2.50)**
Seven industry dummies	Not reported	Not reported	Not included	Not reported

Note: For 35 firms whose 1987 DT is between the sample mean minus one standard deviation and the mean ($0.94 \leq DT \leq 1.69$). *, **, ***, denote significance at 10, 5, and 1 percent, respectively; all tests are two-tail.
a. Excludes the organization dummy CM-form and the industry dummy D_4 (chemical industry).
b. Excludes the organization dummy U-form and the industry dummy D_1 (construction industry).
c. $N = 17$ (only those firms classified as M-form or CM-form); excludes all industry dummies.

this result does not appear robust: When $DROS88$ is used as the dependent variable, β_0 comes out insignificant. Overall these results are in agreement with the static results reported above, and they provide *tentative* support for the hypotheses of this chapter.

Summary

This chapter examined the proposition that refocusing is a necessary but not sufficient condition for improved performance. More specifically it was argued that on average, the refocused firms would be better served by adopting a centralized M-form structure, while the high-diversity firms would do better by adopting an M-form structure. The results provide tentative support for this proposition. In addition it was argued that as more firms refocused in the 1980s, there would be a shift away from the M-form structure toward the CM-form structure. This proposition was also supported by the data.

Although this chapter has argued that refocused firms need to adopt a new organizational structure, it has not examined in detail the characteristics of the new structure needed. Future research needs to examine not only the overall form but also particular incentives, controls and processes that refocused firms might use to reinforce improved profitability. For example, issues examining executive compensation of refocused firms has yet to be undertaken. Similarly the role that better controls and improved information systems may have on the profitability of refocused firms needs to be explored.

Appendix: The Questionnaire

Instructions

1. Please answer questions by placing a check mark in the appropriate box or, where a scale of responses is given, by circling the appropriate response.

2. Check two or more boxes if necessary.

1. Please indicate which of the following most closely resembles the basic organizational structure of your company:

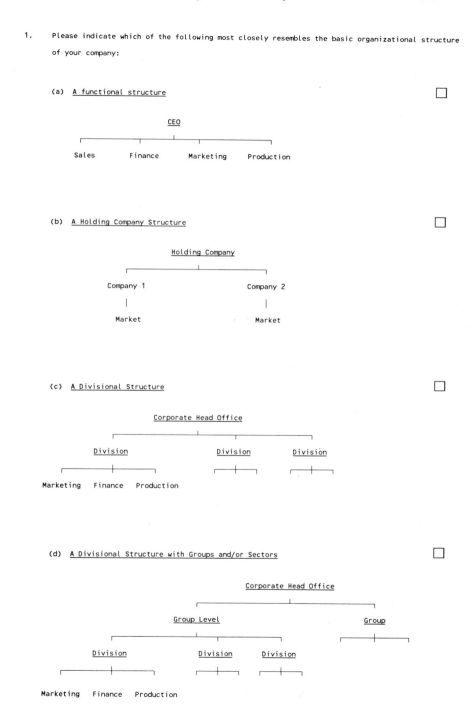

(a) A functional structure

CEO

Sales   Finance   Marketing   Production

(b) A Holding Company Structure

Holding Company

Company 1   Company 2

Market   Market

(c) A Divisional Structure

Corporate Head Office

Division   Division   Division

Marketing   Finance   Production

(d) A Divisional Structure with Groups and/or Sectors

Corporate Head Office

Group Level   Group

Division   Division   Division

Marketing   Finance   Production

(e) <u>OTHER--Please Give Details</u>   ☐

2. How long has the organizational structure you indicated been in existence?

☐ Less than a year

☐ About a year

☐ For two years

☐ For more than two years

If your organization is divisionalized (i.e., if you checked (c), (d), or (e) in Question 1), please answer all of the remaining questions. If not, please go to Question #9.

3. How many operating divisions does your company have? _____

4. Into how many groups are these divisions organized? _____

5. Which of the following factors are used by the Corporate Head Office to evaluate the performance of divisions?

    Please indicate the importance of each factor as follows:

    1 = very important
    2 = important
    3 = Of average importance
    4 = rarely used
    5 = not a factor

PLEASE CIRCLE THE APPROPRIATE RESPONSE

Gross Profit	1	2	3	4	5
Profit Growth	1	2	3	4	5
Return on Sales	1	2	3	4	5
Return on Investment	1	2	3	4	5
Sales Growth	1	2	3	4	5
Market Share	1	2	3	4	5
Cash Flow	1	2	3	4	5
Capital Investment Levels	1	2	3	4	5
Capacity Utilization	1	2	3	4	5
Labor Productivity	1	2	3	4	5
Cost Levels	1	2	3	4	5
Other--please specify	1	2	3	4	5

6. With respect to the cash generated by each division, is it:

    ☐ Left with the individual division, except for funds needed to pay dividends,

        pay central services, etc.

    ☐ Reallocated within the company as a whole by corporate headquarters

☐ Other--please specify _____

_____

_____

7. To what extent do <u>divisional</u> general managers have the authority to act on the problems described below, without corporate (or group) approval? (Assume business conditions are fairly good, and all divisions are profitable.)

Please circle the appropriate response using the following scale:

    1 = The divisional manager can take action without any contact with corporate headquarters

    2 = Divisional manager takes action--informs headquarters later

    3 = Advise headquarters in advance of action he/she intends to take

    4 = The divisional manager has to get formal approval from headquarters before taking any action

<u>Problem Requiring Action</u>:

Problem Requiring Action				
- Hire a replacement for the division manager's secretary who is retiring	1	2	3	4
- Authorize a temporary $100,000 increase in division raw material inventory, in anticipation of a possible strike	1	2	3	4
- Select the replacement for the manufacturing superintendent who will retire soon	1	2	3	4

7. (continued)

Please circle the appropriate response using the following scale:

1 = The divisional manager can take action without any contact with corporate headquarters
2 = Divisional manager takes action--informs headquarters later
3 = Advise headquarters in advance of action he/she intends to take
4 = The divisional manager has to get formal approval from headquarters before taking any action

Problem Requiring Action:

- Pass final approval on the design of a new product, and
   authorize work to start on production tooling   1   2   3   4

- Settle a minor dispute with union representatives   1   2   3   4

- Fire the manufacturing superintendent for poor
   performance   1   2   3   4

- Establish next month's manufacturing schedule for the
   division, at an increased level which will require the
   hiring of two additional people in the factory   1   2   3   4

- Establish next month's manufacturing schedule at a
   substantially higher level which will require an addition
   of 50 people in the factory   1   2   3   4

- Postpone the scheduled introduction of a new model by 45
   days and authorize a modification to the design   1   2   3   4

- Establish the list price of a major product line   1   2   3   4

- Increase the price of an existing product line by 5%, to
   attempt to recover cost increases in material and labor.
   This will place the price above the competitive level   1   2   3   4

- Make a change in the division inventory standards,
   which will reduce field shipping stocks but increase
   factory work-in-process inventory, maintaining the same
   total investment   1   2   3   4

- Increase investment in inventory on a different product by $1 million, because the sales department feels that they can get more sales if they have greater product availability	1	2	3	4
- Introduce a new system into the factory, that may lead to a strike	1	2	3	4
- Change the advertising program of the division, reducing magazine advertising but increasing direct mail and trade show promotional activities	1	2	3	4
- Authorize the marketing manager to increase the number of salesmen in the field, but reduce the number of manufacturing engineers to maintain the same total cost	1	2	3	4
- Authorize an 8% salary increase for the manufacturing superintendent, allowed for in the budget and within the rate range for the job	1	2	3	4
- Authorize the factory to work overtime two Saturdays next month to reduce the backlog of overdue orders	1	2	3	4
- Cancel two engineering development projects	1	2	3	4
- Identify potential acquisition targets and approach them for discussions	1	2	3	4
- Set the division's annual budget at the start of a new fiscal year	1	2	3	4
- Change the division's annual budget in mid-year	1	2	3	4
- Approach financial institutions for financing division projects	1	2	3	4

7. (continued)

Please circle the appropriate response using the following scale:

    1 = The divisional manager can take action without any contact with corporate headquarters

    2 = Divisional manager takes action--informs headquarters later

    3 = Advise headquarters in advance of action he/she intends to take

    4 = The divisional manager has to get formal approval from headquarters before taking any action

Problem Requiring Action:

- Change the division's main supplier   1   2   3   4

- Set a new strategic direction for the division   1   2   3   4

- Authorize a $1 million R&D expense   1   2   3   4

- Authorize lawyers to represent the division in court   1   2   3   4

- Set the transfer price at which his/her division's
   products are sold to other divisions within the
   company   1   2   3   4

- Negotiate with environmental activists   1   2   3   4

8. To what degree are the following the responsibility of Corporate Headquarters or Groups?

    Please indicate the degree of responsibility as follows:

        1 = Always the responsibility of corporate headquarters and/or groups

        2 = Nearly always the responsibility of corporate headquarters and/or groups

        3 = A shared responsibility with operating divisions

        4 = Rarely the responsibility of corporate headquarters and/or groups

        5 = Never the responsibility of corporate headquarters and/or groups

PLEASE CIRCLE THE APPROPRIATE RESPONSE

Overall Financial Control	1	2	3	4	5
Setting the Price Levels of Major Products	1	2	3	4	5
Approval of Major Investments	1	2	3	4	5
Long-term Strategic Planning	1	2	3	4	5
Public Relations	1	2	3	4	5
Relations with Financial Institutions	1	2	3	4	5
Legal Functions	1	2	3	4	5
Identifying Acquisitions	1	2	3	4	5
Deciding Upon Acquisitions	1	2	3	4	5
Setting Annual Budgets	1	2	3	4	5
Setting Business Strategy for Divisions	1	2	3	4	5
R&D Decisions	1	2	3	4	5

9. What year did the present CEO take over? _____

10. What is the CEO's area of expertise and education:

☐ Finance

☐ Marketing

☐ Engineering

☐ Manufacturing

☐ Legal

☐ Other; please specify _____

11. In the period 1981-1987, did the company come under any <u>hostile</u> takeover attempt?

☐ Yes

☐ No

If NO, did the management of the firm feel that the firm was a likely takeover target in 1981-87?

☐ Yes

☐ No

12. In the period 1981-87, did the firm undertake any restructuring?

☐ Yes

☐ No

If YES, please provide some details _____

_____

_____

_____

_____

COMPANY NAME: _____

RESPONDENT'S POSITION: _____

Once again--thank you for your cooperation: **FULL CONFIDENTIALITY IS GUARANTEED**

Would you like a copy of the findings?   ☐ Yes

                                              ☐ No

9 Summary and Future Research

The purpose of this research was to study the extent and effects of corporate refocusing in the period 1981 to 1987. The refocusing phenomenon in this period seemed to be significantly large and widespread, with far-reaching implications, to merit careful study and exploration. The objective was therefore to understand the root causes of this phenomenon and explore its effects on firm performance and behavior.

The major findings from the study are the following:

• More firms were refocusing in the 1980s than in the 1960s. For example, in the 1960s only 1 percent of the top American companies were refocusing, while fully 25 percent were diversifying. By contrast, in the 1980s more than 20 percent of these firms were refocusing, while only 8 percent were diversifying. As a result the trend toward diversification that began more than fifty years ago is now reversing itself. In particular, there was a significant increase in the single-business firms, and a decrease in the unrelated-business firms within the population of Fortune 500 firms. This represents a major evolutionary change for the American corporation.

• Even though many firms refocused, a large number of firms continued to diversify. Consistent with profit-maximizing behavior, the firms that refocused were the "overdiversified" firms, while the firms that diversified were the "underdiversified" firms. The net effect of some firms diversifying and some refocusing was a relatively small change in average diversification and concentration levels in the economy as a whole. Thus the fear that all the restructuring of the 1980s would lead to higher concentration levels did not materialize.

• Firms refocused primarily by divesting unrelated businesses and acquiring related ones. For example, I estimated that the top 100 U.S. firms undertook 431 acquisitions and 302 divestitures in the period 1981–87. More than 65 percent of the acquisitions were related to the core business and almost 58 percent of the divestitures were unrelated to the core business.

• Significant refocusing activity was displayed by the conglomerates and the Fortune 100−200 firms.

• The firms that refocused were characterized by high diversification and poor performance relative to their industry counterparts. This implies that firms refocus in response to a performance crisis, possibly brought about by "excessive" diversification. In addition a firm is more likely to refocus the higher the profitability, size, concentration ratio, and advertising intensity of its core industry—that is, the higher the "attractiveness" of its core business. Firms whose managers feel they are a possible takeover target are also more likely to refocus, and this suggests that a lot of the restructuring of the 1980s was brought about by the threat of hostile takeovers. On the other hand, the higher the R&D intensity of the firm's core business, the lower is the likelihood that the firm will refocus. A change in the top management of the firm, as well as the firm's debt-to-equity ratio, have no effect on the refocusing decision.

• Refocusing announcements were associated with statistically significant positive abnormal returns, which implies that reductions in diversification create market value. On average, a firm's market value goes up by about 2 percent on the day it announces its refocusing. A firm's refocusing announcement is valued higher, if the firm is highly diversified and unprofitable. That is, the firms most in need of "surgery" gain the most from it. The capital market's expectation for improved performance after refocusing is not fulfilled in the short term, and this implies that it may take some time before refocusing's beneficial effects materialize.

• Consistent with event-study interpretations, refocusing by the over-diversified firms is associated with profitability improvements. The effect of refocusing on profitability is not fully realized until after three to four year.

• The relationship between diversification and profitability is curvilinear. At low levels of diversity there exists a positive relationship between diversification and profitability; at high levels of diversity, the relationship is negative. This means that a firm contemplating diversification can start from zero diversification and diversify *profitably* up its optimal limit. After this point the costs outweigh the benefits of additional diversification, so it doesn't pay for the firm to diversify any more. Every firm has a limit to how much it can diversify, but the optimal point differs according to a firm's resources.

• Refocusing is a necessary but not sufficient condition for improved performance: Firms must also adjust their organizational structure to accommodate the new strategy if the benefits of refocusing are to be fully realized. More specifically, refocused firms are better served by a centralized M-form structure, while high-diversity firms do better by adopting a more decentralized M-form structure, which facilitates the exploitation of the advantages of an internal capital market.

• Along with the trend toward reduced diversification, there is a trend away from the M-form structure, toward the CM-form structure.

These results are consistent with the notion that at any given point in time, every firm has a limit to how much it can diversify. This limit is a function of the firm's resources and its external environment. For a variety of reasons many firms have diversified beyond this limit. As a result their profitability and market value have suffered. Primarily because of a stronger market for corporate control, but also because of organizational learning, the overdiversified firms were reducing their diversification to return to equilibrium. As a result their profitability and market value increased. At the same time the underdiversified firms were following a profit-maximizing strategy by diversifying in order to approach their optimal diversification limit.

Future Research

As is always the case with any research project, more questions arise or remain unanswered than resolved. A research agenda that builds on this study will have to explore some of the following issues:

Actions Supporting Refocusing

Chapter 8 touched upon the issue that refocusing is a necessary but not sufficient condition for improved performance. In that chapter I explored the proposition that in addition to refocusing, firms must also adjust their organization structure if the benefits from refocusing are to be fully realized. However, it is possible that changing the organization structure may not be enough and that firms may need to do much more in order to achieve any significant improvements in performance. In this case the firm would need to identify what other actions in addition to, or in combination with refocusing, it must take in order to improve its performance.

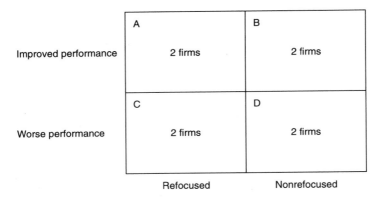

Figure 9.1
Research design for case studies

A priori we don't know exactly what these actions may be, and we have no guidance from past academic research, apart from some general propositions from the research on managing diversity (e.g., Allen 1979; Bettis et al. 1978; Dundas 1982; Finkelstein 1986; Govindarajan 1988; Grant et al. 1988; Gupta and Govindarajan 1984; Hitt and Ireland 1986; Kitching 1967; Lorsch and Allen 1973; Napier and Smith 1987; Pitts 1986). Since this means moving into an unexplored terrain, the best research policy may be to undertake a few exploratory field studies to learn as much as possible about the research issue, and then generate hypotheses that can be tested through large-sample studies. Specifically, the research design of figure 9.1 could be adopted: Focus on one industry to control for industry effects and study eight firms more carefully.

As the figure shows, by comparing the two firms in quadrant *A* with the two firms in quadrant *C*, we can identify some of the policies that the *A* firms followed and that may be necessary to make refocusing a successful strategy. Similarly, by comparing the two *A* firms with the two *B* firms, we can understand the circumstances where refocusing is not a necessary strategy. Finally, by comparing the two *C* firms with the two *D* firms, we can get a better feeling of the policies that failed to support the refocusing strategy of the *C* firms.

The Market for Corporate Control

The market for corporate control seems to be getting a lot of credit for a lot of good things happening in corporate America today, but no one really knows how this market has affected firm behavior and performance.

The supporters of this market point to the abnormal returns generated from takeovers as evidence of the beneficial effects of the market. This is hardly convincing evidence. First, the very existence of such abnormal returns can be and has been attacked (e.g., Mueller 1987). Second, the real source and meaning of such benefits can be and have been disputed (e.g., Caves 1989). Third, and most important, the assumed benefits of the market for corporate control that have been reported in the literature cannot be correct, since no one has bothered to define precisely what we mean by the market for corporate control and what kinds of activities this market encompasses.

In their review article Jensen and Ruback (1983) include every type of takeover as part of the market. But 95 percent of all takeovers are non-hostile, friendly transactions between management teams. How can any-one assume that these transactions are part of the market for corporate control?

Generally speaking, the market for corporate control is made up of two components: actual hostile takeovers and cases where no hostile attempt has been made but there is a credible and real threat that one could take place any minute. Since there is only a handful of actual hostile takeovers taking place (e.g., Bhide 1989), the bulk of the market for corporate control is made up of perceived threats of takeover. Since no one has studied how *firms that felt they were possible takeover targets* behaved or performed, no one can legitimately make any claims about the market.

What we need is to study firms whose management felt they were likely takeover targets and compare their actions and performance against a control group of firms that didn't feel like takeover targets. In the questionnaire I sent out for the purposes of chapter 8, I explicitly asked the CEO of each firm to state whether the top management team felt that the firm was a likely takeover target in the period 1981–87. Of the 149 replies on this question, 82 firms (55 percent) answered in the affirmative, and 67 firms answered no. Of those that felt a real threat of takeover, 76 percent restructured, and 24 percent did not. Of those that didn't feel a real threat of takeover, 35 percent restructured and 65 percent did not. The distribution of these answers is shown in figure 9.2.

In this distribution we have the perfect sample to study the effects of the market for corporate control. For example, we can compare the firms in quadrant *A* versus those in quadrant *C* to see how their performance differs before and after the takeover threat. We can also trace their invest-ment or restructuring activity over the period to see how the takeover targets differ from the rest. Another interesting test will be to examine the 20 quadrant *B* firms to see why they didn't respond to the perceived

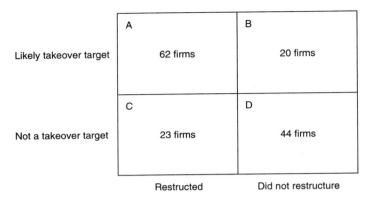

Figure 9.2
Questionnaire data on restructuring

takeover threat, and how well they fared relative to the 62 quadrant *A* firms that responded to the threat.

The Role of the Board of Directors

The behavior and performance of a firm is monitored by two regulatory forces: the outside regulator, which is really the market for corporate control, and the inside regulator, which is the firm's board of directors. The question is, In what circumstances does the inside force take the appropriate actions to improve the performance of a firm before the outside force intervenes? What is the composition and incentive structure of the boards that take the right actions versus those boards that let their firms fall prey to takeover artists?

Looking again at figure 9.2, we can get some answers to these questions by comparing the 62 *A* firms with the 20 *B* firms. Systematic differences in the composition of the boards of these firms could help us understand why the *A* firms responded to the takeover threat by restructuring voluntarily while the *B* firms did not. Additional insights could be obtained by comparing the *C* firms with the *D* firms. This stream of research could build upon the recent work of Gibbs (1993), Hoskisson, Johnson, and Moesel (1994), and Johnson, Hoskisson, and Hitt (1993).

Joint Ventures and Refocusing

Over the past few years we have witnessed a dramatic increase in the number of strategic alliances and joint ventures undertaken by U.S. firms.

Could these transactions be substitutes to diversification? Put differently, Could it be that instead of diversifying directly into a new industry, firms are now entering these same industries through alliances? If this is the case, Is this a more efficient form of diversification?

A very similar issue revolves around the international activities of U.S. firms. For example, international acquisitions—especially in Europe—are on the rise. Are firms substituting their domestic refocusing with international diversification? How does this alter the optimal level of diversification for each firm? These issues deserve some additional attention in the strategy field.

Managerial Implications

Refocusing turns out to be the natural response of firms to a more volatile external environment and a more competitive capital market. The most important managerial implication of this study is that refocusing has an underlying strategic logic: External changes over the past twenty years have caused the diversified corporation to become a less valuable institution than before. This means that many diversified firms will have to rethink their whole diversification strategy. Firms that have—for whatever reason—diversified beyond their optimal level need to reduce their diversification. The key question then becomes: How does a firm know that it has diversified beyond its optimal level? Although this is a difficult question to answer, a good indicator of overdiversification may be when the breakup value of a firm is bigger than its market value. This implies that firms need to estimate what their breakup value is and compare it to their current market value. If the two are not approximately equal, then firms should reduce their diversification.

Another important implication of this study is that corporate raiders exist (and become wealthy) for a very good reason. It is not because the capital market is undervaluing companies that they exist, and it is not because they are out to make a quick profit by destroying companies. Rather, they exist because many companies—through their overdiversification—allow them to exist. If there were no companies with breakup values bigger than their market value, we would not have corporate raiders around. Clearly then the surest way for corporate managers to protect their companies from raiders is for them to become inside-raiders, to take the corrective actions that will improve the market value of their firm before a raider strikes (e.g., Johnson, Hoskisson, and Hitt 1993).

The results of this study show that managers who take the appropriate actions to reduce the diversification level of their overdiversified firms stand to gain: Refocusing is associated with both profitability and market value improvements. However, refocusing is not a quick fix. It takes about two to three years for the beneficial effects of refocusing to materialize. And it requires additional changes within the firm—such as changing the firm's organizational structure—for refocusing to really have a positive impact.

It is important to stress that just because so many companies are reducing their diversification, it does not mean that diversification is a mistake for every firm. There are many benefits associated with diversification, and companies can still benefit by diversifying. However, the refocusing phenomenon of the 1980s suggests that (1) companies cannot and should not diversify to the same extent as in the 1960s, (2) companies will reap the biggest rewards from diversification if they diversify only in areas related to their core business—in this way they can apply their skills and assets effectively in the new areas—and (3) no matter what route to diversification they choose, they should realize that they cannot diversify forever and they should stand ready to stop their diversification when they reach their optimal level.

What if companies have diversified in a lot of unrelated businesses? What can they do then? This study suggests that the era of the conglomerate may be over and these companies will have to refocus. However, it is still possible to manage a conglomerate organization effectively. Even though such a task is extremely difficult, it is not impossible. The corporate center in a conglomerate organization needs to perform two important functions: act as an internal capital market to its divisions and act as a disciplinary "shareholder" to its divisions. This basically means that the conglomerate corporate center should decentralize the organization and restrict its activities to setting the overall strategic direction of the firm and providing the divisions with the necessary finances. It should not get involved in the operating decisions of the divisions or their day to day activities. These tasks should be left to the divisional managers who know their individual businesses better than the corporate center.

At a macro level the results of this study paint an optimistic picture for American business. They suggest that the massive restructuring of the past ten years has been "tonic and not poison" (*Business Week*, 1/12/87, p. 40) for the American corporation. Through refocusing, many firms have been able to streamline their operations and improve their competitiveness so that they are now more efficient global competitors. The results also highlight the endogenous dynamism of the modern corporation and the American corporate marketplace. Through entirely market forces—and at the expense of no government interference—firms have responded to the challenges of a new environment and positioned themselves for another round of competitive warfare. Just like in any other evolutionary battle, casualties have been incurred and excesses have been committed. But the end result has been the revitalization of the American corporation. This suggests that reports of the death of the American public corporation (e.g., Jensen 1989) were greatly exaggerated. Indeed pleas by business academics and executives for a U.S. industrial policy to save the American corporation were unnecessary. The system seems to be doing just fine on its own.

The results also highlight the dynamic nature of competition: Competitive strengths erode, and new sources of competitive advantage arise as conditions change; people make mistakes, and people learn from their mistakes and adjust their behavior; "sustainable" strengths disappear over night, and new competitors emerge to challenge established dinosaurs. Competitive renewal is a continuous process, and only managers and companies that make it a way of life rather than a one-shot affair can expect to be alive in the long run.

Limitations

It may be worthwhile to highlight a few of the most serious limitations of this work. Most of them derive from the fact that the emphasis of the book has been on the empirics rather than theory development. I was more concerned with discovering empirically whether refocusing is associated with profitability improvements or with market value increases than with an understanding of the exact reasons why firms overdiversified in 1950 to 1980 or why they were refocusing in the 1980s. This means that at the end of the empirical analysis I can only offer a possible story and not a theory as to why firms refocus. My proposed "story" seems to be consistent with a lot of empirical findings but it is still only a story, not a theory.

At the beginning of this book I stated that I intend to provide answers for the following questions:

1. Is there more refocusing taking place in the 1980s as compared to the 1960s? How prevalent is this phenomenon?

2. What are the characteristics of the firms that are refocusing?

3. Why are firms refocusing, and why do we observe this behavior now?

4. What is the effect of refocusing on firm value?

5. What is the effect of refocusing on firm profitability?

6. How do firms adjust their organizational structure to accommodate the new strategy of refocusing?

I believe that the empirical analyses in this book have reasonably answered five of these questions; however, my answer to question 3 may meet with some criticism. The "story" I have proposed as an answer to question 3 goes like this:

At any given point in time, every firm has a limit to how much it can diversify. This limit is a function of the firm's resources and its external environment. For a variety of reasons many firms have diversified beyond this limit. As a result their profitability and market value have suffered. Primarily because of a stronger market for corporate control (but also because of organizational learning) the over-diversified firms are now reducing their diversification to return to equilibrium. As a result their profitability and market value increase.

This story can be attacked from a variety of angles:

1. First, the proposition that every firm has a limit to how much it can diversify has not been fully verified. Nor has it been definitely established that (assuming a limit does exist) a firm faces one rather than multiple limits. In addition no effort has been made to examine in detail what determines this limit (if it actually exists), or how firms could identify their limit. In response to these shortcomings, I made the following points in chapter 2:
Presenting the marginal cost (MC) and marginal benefit (MB) curves as monotonically rising and declining, respectively, is probably an over-simplification. It is possible that as a firm learns over time how to manage diversification, MB can curve upward before coming down again while MC can curve downward before rising again. This raises the possibility of multiple optimal points for a firm. Furthermore, if learning by the firm leads to continual shifts in the curves (rather than simply affecting their slopes), a firm may actually have no optimal diversification limit. Finally, given that both MB and MC are path-dependent, it is possible that a firm does not just have one (or multiple) optimal diversification points but rather a continually evolving (with time and experience) frontier of optimal diversification. Overall, therefore, there are possibilities of (1) multiple equilibria, (2) no equilibrium, and (3) a continually shifting frontier of equilibria (which ultimately implies no equilibrium).

Although all three scenarios are theoretically possible, I do not believe that they affect the empirical analyses in this book. First, the existence of multiple equilibria do not prevent the outcome of overdiversified firms. All I wanted was to identify firms that have overdiversified and examine what happened when they reduced their diversification. I was not particularly concerned if they were overdiversified because they went past their first, second, or third optimal point. Second, at a given point in time a firm has an optimal limit even if over time this limit shifts. Since this study is cross-sectional, I may have captured at least some firms in an overdiversified position (even if in a few years time their optimal point increases and they become optimally diversified again). Finally, even if theoretically some firms have infinite learning abilities and manage to continually shift their optimal limit (and hence have no optimal limit), it is highly unlikely that too many such firms exist in practice. Hence I am confident that the sample contains enough overdiversified firms for us to examine what happens when overdiversified firms refocus.

In response to the criticism that I have not made an effort to examine in detail what determines the optimal diversification limit of a firm, I can only remark about the immensity of such a task. Every firm has a different optimal limit depending on its resources, its external environment, the type of diversification it is following (i.e., related versus unrelated), the caliber of its management team, its past diversification experiences, whether any learning occurred from other diversification experiences, and so on. Clearly a firm that has tried diversification in the past and has learned something from the experience is able to manage more diversity (and hence have a bigger optimal diversification level D^*) than a novice diversifier. Likewise a firm that has good managers is able to manage diversification better than a firm with bad managers. Identifying a firm's exact optimal diversification level is an impossible task—the optimal diversification limit for a firm is really a theoretical concept, much like the utility concept in economics, and it cannot be measured precisely.

2. A second possible attack on my proposed "story" of refocusing is that I have not really established why so many firms overdiversified in 1950 to 1980. In chapter 2 I gave several reasons why I would expect some firms to have overdiversified, but in my empirical analyses I have made no attempt to distinguish between these possible reasons for overdiversification. Hence I do not know the actual reasons why firms overdiversified. This means that it is still unclear whether the existence of overdiversified firms can be explained as non-profit-maximizing behavior by the managers of these firms (e.g., Jensen 1986; Mueller 1972) or whether these firms were profit maximizing but found themselves in this position after their optimal level of diversification had been lowered by external events.

The existing literature has identified several possible reasons why firms may have overdiversified in the past twenty years. These include, among others, agency reasons, stock market inefficiencies, tax incentives, changes in the capital market, and increased globalization. This book has not explicitly tested which of these reasons are valid: My focus has not been to explain why firms overdiversified but to determine if refocusing by these overdiversified firms is associated with ex post profitability improvements or ex ante market value improvements. However, recent empirical work has begun to address this question. For example, Hoskisson, Johnson, and Moesel (1993) have found that restructuring intensity is directly related to firm performance and strategy which in turn are preceded by weak corporate governance; this points to an agency explanation of overdiversification. On the other hand, Liebeskind and Opler (1992) have found that refocusing during the 1980s was primarily a response to changing competitive forces in the U.S. economy; this points to a downward-shifting optimal diversification level as the primary cause of overdiversification. Finally, Morck et al. (1990) have found that in the 1960s the stock market reacted positively to diversifying acquisitions which, with hindsight, appears to have been a mistake; this suggests that capital market inefficiencies may also have a role to play in overdiversification. The evidence from this research suggests that all the reasons proposed in chapter 2 may have something to do with overdiversification. However, the relative importance of these reasons is still unclear.

3. Finally, my story of refocusing can be attacked for emphasizing the market for corporate control (at the expense of product-market discipline or active board monitoring) as the main reason why firms refocus. Again my research has not really distinguished between the various possible drivers of refocusing (but see Jensen 1993 for a vigorous defense of the market for corporate control).

My focus on the market for corporate control was not meant to deny the importance of product-market discipline or the influence of the board of directors on restructuring. In fact in a recent paper Gibbs (1993, p. 66) argues that "... since firms with strong governance restructured, it does indicate that factors in addition to agency costs are driving restructuring." It can therefore be argued that as global competition intensified in the 1980s, more and more firms were forced to refocus (in response to poor financial results) by their boards of directors. However, my questionnaire results seem to suggest that even in cases where the restructuring appears to be voluntary (e.g., brought about by the board), the fear of takeover may have been the primary catalyst for the board to act (e.g., Markides and Singh 1994). In addition there is no reason to expect that my empirical results would be any different if I assumed that refocusing is voluntary rather than takeover induced. However, this is something that requires further exploration.

Over and above the shortcomings with the theory in this book, there may be a few shortcomings with the empirics:

1. The fact that the sample is drawn from the Fortune 500 list means that the firms under study are the biggest firms in the United States. This sample bias implies that the findings in this book may be applicable only for the big firms rather than the whole of the U.S. economy.

2. If (as I argued in chapter 2) the capital market acted inefficiently in the 1960s, then can we be totally sure that its behavior in the 1980s is not also inefficient? In this repsect the results of chapter 6, which are based on the assumption of capital market efficiency (in the semistrong form), may be viewed with suspicion. Nevertheless, one can argue that the capital market in the 1960s did not act inefficiently: Given the information it had at the time, it viewed diversification in a positive way. When it received additional information on the ex post performance of diversification, it adjusted its behavior accordingly. Hence there was nothing inefficient with the behavior of the capital market. In addition one can argue that the functionings of the capital market have improved enormously over the past twenty years (for a variety of reasons given in chapter 2), so its behavior in the 1980s must have been more efficient than its behavior in the 1960s.

3. The empirical analysis might be criticized for not addressing several interesting questions associated with refocusing. For example, why do some firms choose to refocus on anything other than their core business? What happens to the divisions that get divested? Do they improve as well? Which divisions are more likely to be divested? Are there performance or behavior differences between those firms that refocus voluntarily versus those firms that refocus after a takeover threat? What internal changes (incentives, board composition, strategic controls, etc.) are introduced after a firm refocuses? All these questions require additional exploration.

Despite these shortcomings I am confident that the book has raised and successfully tackled a series of important questions related to refocusing. My goal was to learn as much as possible about the causes and consequences of refocusing. Whether I have been successful, only time will tell. However, at the very least I hope to have provided the basic platform from which more and better research on diversification and refocusing can be launched.

Bibliography

Aaker, A. D., and Jacobson, R. 1987. The role of risk in explaining differences in profitability. *Academy of Management Journal* 30:277–96.

Adams, W. 1986. *The Structure of American Industry*. 7th ed. New York: Macmillan.

Alchian, A., and Demsetz, H. 1972. Production, information costs, and economic organization. *American Economic Review* 62:777–95.

Alexander, G. J., Benson, P. G., and Kampmeyer, J. M. 1984. Investigating the valuation effects of announcements of voluntary corporate sell-offs. *Journal of Finance* 39:503–17.

Alexander, G. J., Benson, P. G., and Gunderson, E. W. 1986. Asset redeployment: Trans-World Corporation's spin-off of TWA. *Financial Management* (summer):50–58.

Allen, S. A. 1979. Understanding reorganizations of divisionalized companies. *Academy of Management Journal* 22:641–71.

Amihud, Y., and Lev, B. 1981. Risk reduction as a managerial motive for conglomerate mergers. *Bell Journal of Economics* 12:605–17.

Amihud, Y., Kamin, J. Y., and Ronen, J. 1983. Managerialism, ownerism, and risk. *Journal of Banking and Finance* 7:189–96.

Amit, R., and Livnat, J. 1988. Diversification strategies, business cycles, and economic performance. *Strategic Management Journal* 9:99–110.

Amit, R., and Livnat, J. 1988a. Diversification and the risk-return trade-off. *Academy of Management Journal* 31:154–66.

Amit, R., and Livnat, J. 1988b. Efficient corporate diversification: Methods and implications. Unpublished manuscript. Northwestern University.

Andrews, K. R. 1980. *The Concept of Corporate Strategy*. 2d ed. Homewood, IL: Irwin.

Armour, H. O., and Teece, D. J. 1978. Organizational structure and economic performance: A test of the multidivisional hypothesis. *Bell Journal of Economics* 9:106–22.

Arnould, R. J. 1969. Conglomerate growth and public policy. In L. Gordon, ed., *Economics of Conglomerate Growth*. Oregon State University, Department of Agricultural Economics, Corvallis, pp. 72–80.

Aron, J. D. 1988. Ability, moral hazard, firm size, and diversification. *Rand Journal of Economics* 19:72–87.

Attaran, M., and Zwick, M. 1987. The effect of industrial diversification on employment and income: A case study. *Quarterly Review of Economics and Business* 27:38–54.

Baird, I. S., and Thomas, H. 1985. Toward a contingency theory of strategic risk-taking. *Academy of Management Review* 10:230–44.

Baker III, G. P. 1987. Management compensation and divisional leveraged buy-outs. Ph.D. dissertation. Harvard University, Cambridge.

Barnea, A., and Logue, D. E. 1973. Stock market-based measures of corporate diversification. *Journal of Industrial Economics* 22:51–60.

Barney, J. B. 1988. Returns to bidding firms in mergers and acquisitions: Reconsidering the relatedness hypothesis. *Strategic Management Journal* 9:71–78.

Barton, S. L. 1988. Diversification strategy and systematic risk: Another look. *Academy of Management Journal* 31:166–75.

Bass, F. M., and Parsons, L. J. 1969. Simultaneous-equation regression analysis of sales and advertising. *Applied Economics* 1:103–24.

Bass, F. M., Cattin, P. J., and Wittink, D. R. 1977. Market structure and industry influence on profitability. In H. B. Thorelli, ed., *Strategy + Structure = Performance*. Bloomington: Indiana University Press, pp. 181–97.

Baumol, W. J. 1967. *Business Behavior, Value and Growth*, rev. ed. New York: Harcourt, Brace.

Baumol, W. J., Heim, P., Malkiel, B. G., and Quandt, R. E. 1970. Earnings retention, new capital and the growth of the firm. *Review of Economics and Statistics* 52:345–55.

Baumol, W. J., Heim, P., Malkiel, B. G., and Quandt, R. E. 1973. Efficiency of corporate investment: Reply. *Review of Economics and Statistics* 55:128–31.

Baysinger, B. D., and Hoskisson, R. E. 1990. The composition of boards of directors and strategic control: Effects on corporate strategy. *Academy of Management Review* 15:72–87.

Beam, H. H. 1979. The new route to the top. *Advanced Management* 44:55–61.

Beattie, D. L. 1980. Conglomerate diversification and performance: A survey and time series analysis. *Applied Economics* 12:251–73.

Benston, G. J. 1985. The validity of profits-structure studies with particular reference to the FTC's line of business data. *American Economic Review* 75:37–67.

Berg, N. A. 1965. Strategic planning in conglomerate companies. *Harvard Business Review* 43:79–92.

Berg, N. A. 1973. Corporate role in diversified companies. In B. Taylor and K. MacMillan, eds., *Business Policy: Teaching and Research*. New York: Halsted Press.

Berry, C. H. 1971. Corporate growth and diversification. *Journal of Law and Economics* 14:371–83.

Berry, C. H. 1974. Corporate diversification and market structure. *Bell Journal of Economics and Management Science* 5:196–204.

Bethel, J. E., and Liebeskind, J. 1993. The effects of ownership structure on corporate restructuring. *Strategic Management Journal* 14 (special issue):15–31.

Bettauer, A. 1967. Strategy for divestments. *Harvard Business Review* (March–April):116–24.

Bettis, R. A. 1981. Performance differences in related and unrelated diversified firms. *Strategic Management Journal* 2:379–93.

Bettis, R. A. 1982. Risk considerations in modeling corporate strategy. In K. H. Chung, ed., *Academy of Management Proceedings '82*, New York, pp. 22–25.

Bettis, R. A. 1983. Modern financial theory, corporate strategy and public policy: Three conundrums. *Academy of Management Review* 8:406–15.

Bettis, R. A., and Hall, W. K. 1981. Strategic portfolio management in the multibusiness firm. *California Management Review* 24:23–38.

Bettis, R. A., and Hall, W. K. 1982. Diversification strategy, accounting-determined risk, and accounting-determined return. *Academy of Management Journal* 25:254–64.

Bettis, R. A., and Mahajan, V. 1985. Risk/return performance of diversified firms. *Management Science* 31:785–99.

Bettis, R. A., and Mahajan, V. 1985a. A managerially relevant approach to accounting-determined risk. Unpublished manuscript. Southern Methodist University, Dallas, TX.

Bettis, R. A., Hall, W., and Prahalad, C. K. 1978. Diversity and performance in the multibusiness firm. American Institute for Decision Sciences, *1978 Proceedings*. Austin, TX, pp. 210–12.

Bhagat, S., Shleifer, A., and Vishny, R. W. 1990. Hostile takeovers in the 1980s: The return to corporate specialization. In M. N. Baily and C. Winston, eds., *Brookings Papers on Economic Activity*, Microeconomics 1990: 1–84, Washington: Brookings Institution.

Bhargava, N. 1973. The impact of organization form on the firm: Experience of 1920–1970. Ph.D. dissertation. University of Pennsylvania, Philadelphia.

Bhide, A. 1989. The causes and consequences of hostile takeovers. Ph.D. dissertation. Harvard Business School, Boston.

Bhide, A. 1990. Reversing corporate diversification. *Journal of Applied Corporate Finance* 3:70–81.

Biggadike, R. 1979. The risky business of diversification. *Harvard Business Review* (May–June):103–11.

Black, B. S., and Grundfest, J. A. 1988. Shareholder gains from takeovers and restructurings between 1981 and 1986: $162 billion is a lot of money. *Journal of Applied Corporate Finance* 1:5–15.

Blackburn, V. L., and Lang, J. R. 1988. Pre-merger performance and returns to related and unrelated acquiring firms. Unpublished manuscript. Iowa State University, Ames.

Boddewyn, J. J. 1983. Foreign and domestic divestment and investment decisions: Like or unlike? *Journal of International Business Studies* (winter):23–35.

Bothwell, J. L., Cooley, T. F., and Hall, T. E. 1984. A new view of the market structure-performance debate. *Journal of Industrial Economics* 32:397–417.

Boudreaux, K. J. 1975. Divestiture and share price. *Journal of Financial and Quantitative Analysis* (November):619–26.

Bowman, E. H. 1980. A risk/return paradox for strategic management. *Sloan Management Review* 21:17−31.

Bowman, E. H. 1982. Risk seeking by troubled firms. *Sloan Management Review* 23:33−42.

Bradburd, R. M., and Caves, R. E. 1982. A closer look at the effect of market growth on industries' profits. *Review of Economics and Statistics* 64:635−45.

Brancato, C. K., and Winch, K. F. 1987. *Leveraged Buy-outs and the Pot of Gold: Trends, Public Policy, and Case Studies*. Washington: Congressional Research Service.

Brealey, R. A., Hodges, S. D., and Capron, D. 1976. The return on alternative sources of finance. *Review of Economics and Statistics* 58:469−77.

Brenner, M., and Downes, D. H. 1979. A critical evaluation of the measurement of conglomerate performance using the capital asset pricing model. *Review of Economics and Statistics* 61:292−96.

Browne, L. E., and Rosengren, E. S. 1988. The merger-boom: An overview. *New England Economic Review* (March−April):22−32.

Brozen, Y. 1982. *Mergers in Perspective*. Washington: American Enterprise Institute.

Budd, F. W. 1986. Hostile acquisitions and restructuring of corporate America. *The Freeman* 36:166−76.

Buell, S. G., and Schwartz, E. 1981. Increasing leverage, potential failure rates and possible effects on the macro-economy. *Oxford Economic Papers* 33:442−58.

Bühner, R. 1987. Assessing international diversification of West German corporations. *Strategic Management Journal* 8:25−37.

Business Week. 1985. Breakup value is Wall Street's new buzzword. July 8: 80−81.

Buxton, A. J., Davies, S. W., and Lyons B. R. 1984. Concentration and advertising in consumer and producer markets. *Journal of Industrial Economics* 32:451−64.

Buzzell, R. D., and Gale, B. T. 1987. *PIMS principles: Linking strategy to performance*. New York: Free Press.

Cable, J. R., and Dirrheimer, M. J. 1983. Hierarchies and markets: An empirical test of the multidivisional hypothesis in West Germany. *International Journal of Industrial Organization* 1:43−62.

Cable, J. R., and Yasuki, H. 1984. Internal organization, business groups and corporate performance: An empirical test of the multidivisional hypothesis. *Proceedings of 11th EARIE Meetings*, Rome, pp. 335−66.

Calman, R. F. 1987. Restructuring by divestment. In M. L. Rock, ed., *The Mergers and Acquisition Handbook*, New York: McGraw-Hill, pp. 373−81.

Calvo, G. A., and Wellisz, S. 1978. Supervision, loss of control, and the optimum size of the firm. *Journal of Political Economy* 86:943−52.

Capon, N., Hulbert, J. M., Farley, J. U., and Martin, L. E. 1988. Corporate diversity and economic performance: The impact of market specialization. *Strategic Management Journal* 9:61−74.

Cardozo, R. N., and Smith, D. K., Jr. 1983. Applying financial portfolio theory to product portfolio decisions: An empirical study. *Journal of Marketing* 47:110−19.

Carter, J. R. 1977. In search of synergy: A structure-performance test. *Review of Economics and Statistics* 59:279–89.

Caves, R. E. 1970. Uncertainty, market structure, and performance: Galbraith as conventional wisdom. In J. Markham and G. Papanek, eds., *Industrial Organization and Economic Development*. Boston: Houghton Mifflin.

Caves, R. E. 1971. International corporations: The industrial economics of foreign investment. *Economica* 38:1–28.

Caves, R. E. 1981. Diversification and seller concentration: Evidence from changes, 1963–72. *Review of Economics and Statistics* 68:289–93.

Caves, R. E. 1988. Effects of mergers and acquisitions on the economy: An industrial organization perspective. Working paper 88-031. Harvard Business School, Boston.

Caves, R. E. 1989. Mergers, takeovers, and economic efficiency: Foresight versus hindsight. *International Journal of Industrial Organization* 7:151–74.

Caves, R. E., and Yamey, B. S. 1971. Risk and corporate rates of return: Comment. *Quarterly Journal of Economics* 85:513–17.

Caves, R. E., and Porter, M. E. 1980. The dynamics of changing seller concentration. *Journal of Industrial Economics* 29:1–15.

Caves, R. E., Fortunato, M., and Ghemawat, P. 1984. The decline of dominant firms, 1905–1929. *Quarterly Journal of Economics* 99:523–46.

Caves, R. E., Gale, B. T., and Porter, M. E. 1977. Interfirm profitability differences: Comment. *Quarterly Journal of Economics* 91:667–75.

Caves, R. E., Porter, M. E., Spence, M. A., and Scott, J. T. 1980. *Competition in the Open Economy: A Model Applied to Canada*. Cambridge: Harvard University Press.

Chakravarthy, B. S. 1986. Measuring strategic performance. *Strategic Management Journal* 7:437–58.

Chandler, A. D., Jr. 1962. *Strategy and Structure*. Cambridge: MIT Press.

Chang, Y., and Thomas, H. 1987. The impact of diversification strategy on risk-return performance. In F. Hoy, ed., *Best Paper Proceedings*. Boston: Academy of Management, pp. 2–6.

Chatterjee, S., and Wernerfelt, B. 1988. Related or unrelated diversification: A resource-based approach. In F. Hoy, ed., *Best Papers Proceedings 1988*. Anaheim, CA: Academy of Management, pp. 7–11.

Chen, K. C., Cheng, D. C., and Hite, G. L. 1986. Systematic risk and market power: An application of Tobin's q. *Quarterly Review of Economics and Business* 26:58–72.

Child, J. 1982. Divisionalization and size: A Comment on the Donaldson/Grinyer debate. Discussion note. *Organization Studies* 3:351–53.

Chiplin, B., and Wright, M. 1980. Divestment and structural change in U.K. industry. *National Westminster Bank Quarterly Review* (February):42–51.

Choi, D., and Philippatos, G. C. 1983. An examination of merger synergism. *Journal of Financial Research* 6:239–56.

Chopra, J., Boddewyn, J. J., and Torneden, R. L. 1978. U.S. foreign divestment: A 1972–1975 updating. *Columbia Journal of World Business* (Spring):14–18.

Christensen, H. K., and Montgomery, C. A. 1981. Corporate economic performance: Diversification strategy versus market structure. *Strategic Management Journal* 2:327–43.

Christofides, L. N., and Tapon, F. 1979. Uncertainty, market structure and performance: The Galbraith-Caves hypothesis revisited. *Quarterly Journal of Economics* 93:719–26.

Clark, J. A. 1986. Market structure, risk, and profitability: The quiet life hypothesis revisited. *Quarterly Review of Economics and Business* 26:45–56.

Clarke, C. J., and Gall, F. 1987. Planned divestment—a five-step approach. *Long-Range Planning* 20:17–24.

Clarke, R., and Davies, S. W. 1982. Market structure and price-cost margins. *Economica* 49:277–87.

Clarke, R., Davies, S., and Waterson, M. 1984. The profitability-concentration relation: Market power or efficiency? *Journal of Industrial Economics* 32:435–50.

Comanor, W. S., and Wilson, T. A. 1967. Advertising, market structure and performance. *Review of Economics and Statistics* 49:423–40.

Comment, R., and Jarrell, G. A. 1991. *Corporate focus and stock returns*. Working paper MR 91-01. Graduate School of Business, University of Rochester, NY.

Conn, R. L. 1985. A reexamination of merger studies that use the capital asset pricing model methodology. *Cambridge Journal of Economics* 9:43–56.

Copeland, T. E., and Weston, J. F. 1988. *Financial Theory and Corporate Policy*, 3d ed. Reading, MA: Addison-Wesley.

Copeland, T. E., Lemgruber, E. F., and Mayers, D. 1987. Corporate spin-offs: Multiple announcement and ex-date abnormal performance. In T. E. Copeland, ed., *Modern Finance and Industrial Economics*. Cambridge, MA: Basil Blackwell, pp. 114–37.

Cowling, K., ed. 1972. *Market Structure and Corporate Behaviour*. London: Gray-Mills.

Cowling, K. 1976. On the theoretical specification of industrial structure-performance relationships. *European Economic Review* 8:1–14.

Cowling, K., and Waterson, M. 1976. Price-cost margins and market structure. *Economica* 43:267–74.

Coyne, J., and Wright, M., eds. 1986. *Divestment and Strategic Change*. Oxford: Philip Allan Publishers, Ltd.

Craig, C. S., and Douglas, S. P. 1982. Strategic factors associated with market and financial performance. *Quarterly Review of Economics and Business* 22:101–12.

Curley, A. J., Hexter, J. L., and Choi, D. 1982. The cost of capital and the market power of firms: A comment. *Review of Economics and Statistics* 64:519–25.

Curry, B., and George, K. D. 1983. Industrial concentration: A survey. *Journal of Industrial Economics* 31:203–55.

Cyert, R. M., and Hedrick, C. L. 1972. Theory of the firm: Past, present, and future; an interpretation. *Journal of Economic Literature* 10:398–412.

Daems, H. 1988. Determinants of changes in industrial diversification: The experience of European industrial groups. Unpublished manuscript. Harvard Business School, Boston.

Dalton, D. R., Todor, W. D., Spendolini, M. J., Fielding, G. J., and Porter, L. W. 1980. Organization structure and performance: A critical review. *Academy of Management Review* 5:49–64.

Dann, L. Y., and DeAngelo, H. 1988. Corporate financial policy and corporate control: A study of defensive adjustments in asset and ownership structure. *Journal of Financial Economics* 20:87–127.

Davies, S. 1980. Minimum efficient size and seller concentration: An empirical problem. *Journal of Industrial Economics* 28:287–301.

Davidson, W. N., III, and Macdonald, J. L. 1987. Evidence of the effect on shareholder wealth of corporate spinoffs: The creation of royalty trusts. *Journal of Financial Research* 10:321–27.

DeAngelo, H., DeAngelo, L., and Rice, E. M. 1984. Going private: Minority freezeouts and stockholder wealth. *Journal of Law and Economics* 27:367–401.

DeAngelo, H., and DeAngelo, L. 1987. Management buy-outs of publicly traded corporations. *Financial Analysts Journal* (May–June):38–49.

DeAngelo, H., and DeAngelo, L. 1988. The role of proxy contests in the governance of publicly held corporations. Working paper 88-01. University of Rochester, NY.

DeAngelo, L. E. 1986. Accounting numbers as market valuation substitutes: A study of management buy-outs of public stockholders. *Accounting Review* 61:400–20.

DeAngelo, L. E. 1988. Managerial competition, information costs and corporate governance. *Journal of Accounting and Economics* 10:3–36.

Didrichsen, J. 1972. The development of diversified and conglomerate firms in the United States, 1920–1970. *Business History Review* 46:202–19.

Doi, N. 1985. Diversification and R&D activity in Japanese manufacturing firms. *Managerial and Decision Economics* 6:147–52.

Donaldson, G. 1990. Voluntary restructuring: The case of General Mills. Unpublished manuscript. Harvard Business School, Boston.

Donaldson, G. 1990. Voluntary restructuring: The case of General Mills. *Journal of Financial Economics* 27:117–41.

Donaldson, G. 1994. Corporate restructuring: Managing the change process from within. Boston: Harvard Business School Press.

Donaldson, L. 1982. Divisionalization and size: A theoretical and empirical critique. *Organization Studies* 3:321–37.

Donsimoni, M. P., Geroski, P., and Jacquemin, A. 1984. Concentration indices and market power: Two views. *Journal of Industrial Economics* 32:419–34.

Dubofsky, P., and Varadarajan, P. R. 1987. Diversification and measures of performance: Additional empirical evidence. *Academy of Management Journal* 30:597–608.

Dugger, W. M. 1985. Centralization, diversification, and administrative burden in U.S. enterprises. *Journal of Economic Issues* 19:687–701.

Duhaime, I. M., and Patton, G. R. 1980. Selling off. *Wharton Magazine* (Winter):43−47.

Duhaime, I. M., and Baird, I. S. 1987. Divestment decision making: The role of business unit size. *Journal of Management* 13:483−98.

Duhaime, I. M., and Grant, J. H. 1984. Factors influencing divestment decision making: Evidence from a field study. *Strategic Management Journal* 5:301−18.

Dundas, K. N. M., and Richardson, P. R. 1980. Corporate strategy and the concept of market failure. *Strategic Management Journal* 1:177−88.

Dundas, K. N. M., and Richardson, P. R. 1982. Implementing the unrelated product strategy. *Strategic Management Journal* 3:287−301.

Easterbrook, F. H., and Fischel, D. R. 1982. Corporate control transactions. *Yale Law Journal* (March):698−741.

Eckbo, B. E. 1983. Horizontal mergers, collusion, and stockholder wealth. *Journal of Financial Economics* 11:241−73.

Edwards, F. R., and Heggestad, A. A. 1973. Uncertainty, market structure, and performance: The Galbraith-Caves hypothesis and managerial motives in banking. *Quarterly Journal of Economics* 87:455−73.

Edwards, F. R., and Heggestad, A. A. 1979. Comment on uncertainty, market structure, and performance: The Galbraith-Caves hypothesis revisited. *Quarterly Journal of Economics* 93: 727−29.

Elgers, P. T., and Clark, J. J. 1980. Merger types and shareholder returns: Additional evidence. *Financial Management* 9:66−72.

Ellert, J. C. 1976. Mergers, antitrust law enforcement, and shareholder returns. *Journal of Finance* 31:715−32.

Engle, R. F., Hendry, D. F., and Richard J. F. 1983. Exogeneity. *Econometrica* 51:277−304.

Ezzamel, M. A. 1985. On the assessment of the performance effects of multidivisional structures: A synthesis. *Accounting and Business Research* 16:23−34.

Fama, E. 1976. *Foundations of Finance*. New York: Basic Books.

Fama, E. F. 1980. Agency problems and the theory of the firm. *Journal of Political Economy* 88:288−307.

Ferenbach, C. 1983. Leveraged buy-outs: A new capital market in evolution. *Midland Corporate Finance Journal* (winter):56−62.

Figenbaum, A., and Thomas, H. 1986. Dynamic and risk measurement: Perspectives on Bowman's risk-return paradox for strategic management; an empirical study. *Strategic Management Journal* 7:395−407.

Finkelstein, S. 1986. The acquisition integration process. In J. A. Pearce, II, and R. B. Robinson, Jr., eds., *Best Papers Proceedings 1986*. Chicago: Academy of Management, pp. 12−16.

Fisher, I. N., and Hall, G. R. 1969. Risk and corporate rates of return. *Quarterly Journal of Economics* 83:79−92.

Fisher, I. N., and Hall, G. R. 1971. Risk and corporate rates of return: Reply. *Quarterly Journal of Economics* 85:518−22.

Fisher, L., and Lorie, J. H. 1964. Rates of return on investments in common stocks. *Journal of Business* 37:1–21.

Fisher, F. M., and McGowan, J. J. 1983. On the misuse of accounting rates of return to infer monopoly profits. *American Economic Review* 73:82–97.

Fligstein, N., and Markowitz, L. 1994. Financial reorganization of American corporations in the 1980s. In W. J. Wilson, ed., *Sociology and Social Policy*. New York: Russell Sage.

Friend, I., and Husic, F. 1973. Efficiency of corporate investment. *Review of Economics and Statistics* 55:122–27.

Gabarro, J. J. 1985. When a new manager takes charge. *Harvard Business Review* 63:110–23.

Gahlon, J. M., and Stover, R. D. 1979. Diversification, financial leverage, and conglomerate systematic risk. *Journal of Financial and Quantitative Analysis* 24:999–1013.

Galai, D., and Masulis, R. 1976. The option pricing model and the risk factor of stock. *Journal of Financial Economics* 3:53–82.

Galbraith, C., Samuelson, B., Stiles, C., and Merrill, G. 1986. Diversification, industry research and development, and market performance. In J. A. Pearce, II, and R. B. Robinson, Jr., eds., *Best Papers Proceedings 1986*. Chicago: Academy of Management, pp. 17–20.

Gale, B. 1972. Market share and rate of return. *Review of Economics and Statistics* 54:412–23.

Gaskins, D. W. 1970. Optimal pricing by dominant firms. Unpublished Ph.D. dissertation. University of Michigan, Ann Arbor.

Geroski, P. A. 1981. Specification and testing the profits—Concentration relationship: Some experiments for the U.K. *Economica* 48:279–88.

Geroski, P. A. 1982a. Interpreting a correlation between market structure and performance. *Journal of Industrial Economics* 30:319–26.

Geroski, P. A. 1982b. Simultaneous equations models of the structure-performance paradigm. *European Economic Review* 19:145–58.

Geroski, P. A., and Gregg, P. 1994. Corporate restructuring in the UK during the recession. *Business Strategy Review* 5:1–19.

Gibbs, P. A. 1993. Determinants of corporate restructuring: The relative importance of corporate governance, takeover threat and free cash flow. *Strategic Management Journal* 14 (special issue):51–68.

Ginsberg, A. 1988. Measuring and modelling changes in strategy: Theoretical foundations and empirical directions. *Strategic Management Journal* 9:559–75.

Gorecki, P. K. 1975. An inter-industry analysis of diversification in the U.K. manufacturing sector. *Journal of Industrial Economics* 24:131–46.

Gorecki, P. K. 1980. A problem of measurement from plants to enterprises in the analysis of diversification: A note. *Journal of Industrial Economics* 28:327–34.

Gort, M. 1962. *Diversification and Integration in American Industry*. Princeton: National Bureau of Economic Research.

Goto, A. 1981. Statistical evidence on the diversification of Japanese large firms. *Journal of Industrial Economics* 29: 271–78.

Govindarajan, V. 1988. A contingency approach to strategy implementation at the business unit level: Integrating administrative mechanisms with strategy. *Academy of Management Journal* 31:828–53.

Grabowski, H. G., and Mueller, D. C. 1975. Life-cycle effects on corporate returns on retentions. *Review of Economics and Statistics* 57:400–409.

Grant, R. M. 1988. On dominant logic, relatedness and the link between diversity and performance. *Strategic Management Journal* 9:639–42.

Grant, R. M., and Thomas, H. 1988. Diversity and profitability: Evidence and future research directions. In A. M. Pettigrew, ed., *Competitiveness and the Management Process.* Oxford: Basil Blackwell, pp. 68–85.

Grant, R. M., and Jammine, A. P. 1988. Performance differences between the Wrigley/Rumelt strategic categories. *Strategic Management Journal* 9:333–46.

Grant, R., Jammine, A., and Thomas, H. 1986. The impact of diversification strategy upon the profitability of British manufacturing firms. In J. A. Pearce, II, and R. B. Robinson, Jr., eds., *Best Papers Proceedings 1986.* Academy of Management, Chicago, pp. 26–30.

Grant, R., Jammine, A., and Thomas, H. 1988. Diversity, diversification, and profitability among British manufacturing companies, 1972–84. *Academy of Management Journal* 31: 771–801.

Green, S. 1988. The incentive effects of ownership and control in management buy-outs. *Long-Range Planning* 21:26–33.

Grinyer, P. H. 1982. Divisionalization and size: A rejoinder. Discussion note. *Organization Studies* 3:339–50.

Grinyer, P. H., and Ardekani, M. Y. 1981. Strategy, structure, size, and bureaucracy. *Academy of Management Journal* 24:471–86.

Grinyer, P. H., Ardekani, M. Y., and Al-Bazzaz, S. 1980. Strategy, structure, the environment, and financial performance in 48 U.K. companies. *Academy of Management Journal* 23:193–220.

Gupta, A. K., and Govindarajan, V. 1982. An empirical examination of linkages between strategy, managerial characteristics, and performance. In K. H. Chung, ed., *Proceedings '82.* New York: Academy of Management, pp. 31–35.

Gupta, A. K., and Govindarajan, V. 1984. Business unit strategy, managerial characteristics, and business unit effectiveness at strategy implementation. *Academy of Management Journal* 27:25–41.

Guth, W. D. 1980. Corporate growth strategies. *Journal of Business Strategy* 1:56–62.

Hamermesh, R. G. 1977. Responding to divisional profit crises. *Harvard Business Review* (March–April):124–30.

Hall, M., and Weiss, L. W. 1967. Firm size and profitability. *Review of Economics and Statistics* 49:319–31.

Hannah, L., and Kay, J. A. 1981. The contribution of mergers to concentration growth: A reply to Professor Hart. *Journal of Industrial Economics* 29:305–13.

Harrigan, K. R. 1980. The effect of exit barriers upon strategic flexibility. *Strategic Management Journal* 1:165–76.

Harrigan, K. R. 1981. Deterrents to divestiture. *Academy of Management Journal* 24:306—23.

Harris, B. C. 1983. *Organizations: The effect on large corporations.* Ann Arbor: UMI Research Press.

Hassid, J. 1977. Diversification and the firm's rate of growth. *Manchester School of Economic and Social Studies* 45:16—28.

Hayes, R. H. 1972. New emphasis on divestment opportunities. *Harvard Business Review* (July—August):55—64.

Healy, P. M., and Palepu, K. G. 1988a. Earnings and risk information from primary stock offers. Mimeo. MIT and Harvard University. September.

Healy, P. M., and Palepu, K. G. 1988b. Earnings information conveyed by dividend initiations and omissions. *Journal of Financial Economics* 21:149—75.

Hearth, D., and Zaima, J. K. 1984. Voluntary corporate divestitures and value. *Financial Management* (spring):10—16.

Hilke, J. C., and Nelson, P. B. 1988. Diversification and predation. *Journal of Industrial Economics* 37:107—11.

Hill, C. W. L. 1983. Conglomerate performance over the economic cycle. *Journal of Industrial Economics* 32:197—211.

Hill, C. W. L. 1985a. Internal organization and enterprise performance: Some U.K. evidence. *Managerial and Decision Economics* 6:210—16.

Hill, C. W. L. 1985b. Oliver Williamson and the M-form firm: A critical review. *Journal of Economic Issues* 19:731—51.

Hill, C. W. L. 1988. Internal capital market controls and financial performance in multidivisional firms. *Journal of Industrial Economics* 37:67—83.

Hill, C. W. L., Hitt, M. A., and Hoskisson, R. E. 1992. Cooperative versus competitive structures in related and unrelated diversified firms. *Organization Science* 3:501—21.

Hill, C. W. L., and Hoskisson, R. E. 1987. Strategy and structure in the multiproduct firm. *Academy of Management Review* 12:331—41.

Hill, C. W. L., and Pickering, J. F. 1986. Divisionalization, decentralization and performance of large U.K. companies. *Journal of Management Studies* 23:26—50.

Hill, C. W. L., and Snell, S. A. 1988. External control, corporate strategy, and firm performance in research-intensive industries. *Strategic Management Journal* 9:577—90.

Hiller, J. R. 1978. Long-run profit maximization: An empirical test. *Kyklos* 31:475—90.

Hite, G. L. 1977. Leverage, output effects, and the M-M theorems. *Journal of Financial Economics* 5:177—202.

Hite, G. L., and Owers, J. E. 1983. Security price reactions around corporate spin-off announcements. *Journal of Financial Economics* 12:409—36.

Hite, G. L., Owers, J. E., and Rogers, R. C. 1987. The market for interfirm asset sales: Partial sell-offs and total liquidations. *Journal of Financial Economics* 18:229—52.

Hitt, M. A., and Ireland, R. D. 1986. Relationships among corporate level distinctive competencies, diversification strategy, corporate structure and performance. *Journal of Management Studies* 23:401—16.

Hofmann, R. 1989. Continental group. *Directors and Boards* (winter):13.

Holl, P. 1983. Discretionary behavior and the M-form hypothesis in large U.K. firms. Unpublished manuscript. University of Nottingham.

Hopkins, H. D. 1984. Acquisition strategy and market structure. In J. A. Pearce, II, and R. B. Robinson, Jr., eds., *Proceedings 1984*. Boston: Academy of Management, pp. 17−21.

Hopkins, H. D. 1987. Acquisition strategy and the market position of acquiring firms. *Strategic Management Journal* 8:535−47.

Hoskisson, R. E. 1987. Multidivisional structure and performance: The diversification strategy contingency. In F. Hoy, ed., *Best Paper Proceedings 1987*. Boston: Academy of Management, pp. 36−40.

Hoskisson, R. E. 1987b. Multidivisional structure and performance: The contingency of diversification strategy. *Academy of Management Journal* 30:625−44.

Hoskisson, R. E., and Galbraith, C. G. 1985. The effect of quantum versus incremental M-form reorganization on performance: A time series exploration on intervention dynamics. *Journal of Management* 11:55−70.

Hoskisson, R. E., and Hitt, M. A. 1988. Strategic control systems and relative R&D investment in large multiproduct firms. *Strategic Management Journal* 9:605−21.

Hoskisson, R. E., and Hitt, M. A. 1990. Antecedents and performance outcomes of diversification: A review and critique of theoretical perspectives. *Journal of Management* 16:461−509.

Hoskisson, R. E., Hitt, M. A., and Hill, C. W. L. 1991. Managerial risk taking in diversified firms: An evolutionary perspective. *Organization Science* 2:296−314.

Hoskisson, R. E., Hitt, M. A., and Hill, C. W. L. 1993. Managerial incentives and investment in R&D in large multiproduct firms. *Organization Science* 4:325−41.

Hoskisson, R. E., and Johnson, R. A. 1992. Corporate restructuring and strategic change: The effect of diversification strategy and R&D intensity. *Strategic Management Journal* 13:625−34.

Hoskisson, R. E., Johnson, R. A., and Moesel, D. D. 1993. Antecedents of corporate restructuring intensity. Paper presented at the 13th Annual International Conference, Strategic Management Society, Chicago.

Hoskisson, R. E., Johnson, R. A., and Moesel, D. D. 1994. Corporate divestiture intensity in restructuring firms: Effects of Governance, Strategy and Performance. *Academy of Management Journal* 37:1207−51.

Hoskisson, R. E., and Turk, T. A. 1990. Corporate restructuring: Governance and control limits of the internal capital market. *Academy of Management Review* 15:459−77.

Huntsman, B., and Hoban, J. P., Jr. 1980. Investment in new enterprise: Some empirical observations on risk, return, and market structure. *Financial Management* 9:44−51.

Hurdle, G. J. 1974. Leverage, risk, market structure, and profitability. *Review of Economics and Statistics* 56:478−85.

Ikeda, K., and Doi, N. 1983. The performances of merging firms in Japanese manufacturing industry: 1964−75. *Journal of Industrial Economics* 31:257−66.

Ittner, C. D., and Markides, C. C. 1990. Restructuring and corporate control: The impact of defensive divestiture on shareholder wealth. Unpublished manuscript. Harvard Business School, Boston. February.

Jacobsen, R. 1988. The persistence of abnormal returns. *Strategic Management Journal* 9: 415–30.

Jacoby, N. 1969. The conglomerate corporation. *Center Magazine* 2:7–15.

Jacquemin, A. P., and Berry, C. H. 1979. Entropy measure of diversification and corporate growth. *Journal of Industrial Economics* 27:359–69.

Jahera, J. S., Jr., Lloyd, W. P., and Page, D. E. 1987. Firm diversification and financial performance. *Quarterly Review of Economics and Business* 27:51–62.

Jain, P. C. 1985. The effect of voluntary sell-off announcements on shareholder wealth. *Journal of Finance* 40:209–24.

Jarrell, G. A. 1991. For a higher share price, Focus your business. *Wall Street Journal*, May 13.

Jarrell, G. A., Brickley, J. A., and Netter, J. M. 1988. The market for corporate control: The empirical evidence since 1980. *Journal of Economic Perspectives* 2:49–68.

Jensen, M. C. 1986. Agency costs of free cash flow, corporate finance, and takeovers. *American Economic Review* (May):323–29.

Jensen, M. C. 1988. Takeovers: Their causes and consequences. *Journal of Economic Perspectives* 2:21–48.

Jensen, M. C. 1989. Eclipse of the public corporation. *Harvard Business Review* 67:61–74.

Jensen, M. C. 1993. The modern industrial revolution: Exit and the failure of internal control systems. *Journal of Finance* 48:831–80.

Jensen, M. C., and Meckling, W. H. 1976. Theory of the firm: Managerial behavior, agency costs and ownership structure. *Journal of Financial Economics* (October):305–60.

Jensen, M. C., and Ruback, R. S. 1983. The market for corporate control: The scientific evidence. *Journal of Financial Economics* 11:5–50.

Joehnk, M. D., and Nielsen, J. F. 1974. The effects of conglomerate merger activity on systematic risk. *Journal of Financial and Quantitative Analysis* 9:215–25.

Johnson, R. A., Hoskisson, R. E., and Hitt, M. A., 1993. Board of director involvement in restructuring: The effects of board versus managerial controls and characteristics. *Strategic Management Journal* 14 (special issue):33–50.

Johnson, T. H., and Kaplan, R. S. 1987. *Relevance Lost: The Rise and Fall of Management Accounting.* Boston: Harvard Business School Press.

Jones, G. R., and Hill, C. W. L. 1988. Transaction cost analysis of strategy-structure choice. *Strategic Management Journal* 9:159–72.

Kallapur, S. 1990. Estimating the rate of return on retained earnings. Unpublished manuscript. Harvard Business School, Boston. February.

Kaplan, R. S. 1983. Measuring manufacturing performance: A new challenge for managerial accounting research. *Accounting Review* 58:686–705.

Kaplan, S. N. 1988. Sources of value in management buy-outs. Ph.D. dissertation. Harvard University, Cambridge.

Kaplan, S. N., and Weisbach, M. S. 1990. The success of acquisitions: Evidence from divestitures. NBER Working paper 3231. Cambridge, MA.

Kardasz, S. W., and Stollery, K. R. 1982. Profits and advertising in Canadian manufacturing: A simultaneous model. *Quarterly Review of Economics and Business* 22:105–15.

Kazanjian, R. K., and Drazin, R. 1987. Implementing internal diversification: Contingency factors for organization design choices. *Academy of Management Review* 12:342–54.

Keren, M., and Levhari, D. 1983. The internal organization of the firm and the shape of average costs. *Bell Journal of Economics* 14:474–86.

Kerr, J. L. 1985. Diversification strategies and managerial rewards: An empirical study. *Academy of Management Journal* 28:155–79.

Kim, E. H., and Schatzberg, J. D. 1987. Voluntary corporate liquidations. *Journal of Financial Economics* 19:311–28.

Kitching, J. 1967. Why do mergers miscarry? *Harvard Business Review* (November–December):22–33.

Klein, A. 1986. The timing and substance of divestiture announcements: Individual, simultaneous and cumulative effects. *Journal of Finance* 41:685–97.

Kudla, R. J., and McInish, T. H. 1981. The microeconomic consequences of an involuntary corporate spin-off. *Sloan Management Review* (summer):41–46.

Kudla, R. J., and McInish, T. H. 1983. Valuation consequences of corporate spin-offs. *Review of Business Economic Research* 18:71–77.

Kudla, R. J., and McInish, T. H. 1988. Divergence of opinion and corporate spin-offs. *Quarterly Review of Economics and Business* 28:20–29.

Kummer, D. R. 1976. Stock price reaction to announcements of forced divestiture proceedings. *Journal of the Midwest Finance Association*: 99–123.

Kummer, D. R. 1978. Valuation consequences of forced divestiture announcements. *Journal of Economics and Business* (winter):130–36.

Kwoka, J. E., Jr. 1981. Does the choice of concentration measure really matter? *Journal of Industrial Economics* 29:445–53.

Lamont, B. T., and Anderson, C. R. 1985. Mode of corporate diversification and economic performance. *Academy of Management Journal* 28:926–34.

Lauenstein, M. C. 1985. Diversification—The hidden explanation of success. *Sloan Management Review* 27:49–55.

Laughhunn, D. J., Payne, J. W., and Crum, R. 1980. Managerial risk preferences for below-target returns. *Management Science* 26:1238–49.

Lawrence, P. R., and Lorsch, J. W. 1967. *Organization and Environment*. Boston: Division of Research, Harvard Business School.

Lecraw, D. J. 1984. Diversification strategy and performance. *Journal of Industrial Economics* 33:179–98.

Lee, W. B., and Cooperman, E. S. 1989. Conglomerates in the 1980s: A performance appraisal. *Financial Management* 18:45−54.

Lehn, K., and Poulsen, A. 1987. Sources of value in corporate going private transactions. Mimeo. Washington University. February.

Leibenstein, H. 1966. Allocation efficiency and X-efficiency. *American Economic Review* 56: 392−416.

Leibenstein, H. 1976. *Beyond Economic Man*. Cambridge: Harvard University Press.

Leibenstein, H. 1987. *Inside the Firm: The Inefficiencies of Hierarchy*. Cambridge: Harvard University Press.

Lemelin, A. 1982. Relatedness in the Patterns of Interindustry Diversification. *Review of Economics and Statistics* 44:646−57.

Lenz, R. T. 1981. Determinants of organizational performance: An interdisciplinary review. *Strategic Management Journal* 2:131−54.

Leontiades, M. 1986. The rewards of diversifying into unrelated businesses. *Journal of Business Strategy* 6:81−87.

Lev, B., and Sunder, S. 1979. Methodological issues in the use of financial ratios. *Journal of Accounting and Economics* 1:187−210.

Levy, D. T., and Haber, L. J. 1986. An advantage of the multiproduct firm: The transferability of firm-specific capital. *Journal of Economic Behavior and Organization* 7:291−302.

Levy, H., and Sarnat, M. 1970. Diversification, portfolio analysis and the uneasy case for conglomerate mergers. *Journal of Finance* 25:795−802.

Lewellen, W. 1971. A pure financial rationale for the conglomerate merger. *Journal of Finance* 26:521−37.

Lewis, T. R. 1983. Preemption, divestiture, and forward contracting in a market dominated by a single firm. *American Economic Review* 73:1092−1101.

Lewis, W. W. 1990. Strategic restructuring: A critical requirement in the search for corporate potential. In M. L. Rock and R. H. Rock, eds., *Corporate Restructuring*. New York: McGraw-Hill, pp. 43−55.

Lichtenberg, F. R. 1990. Want more productivity? Kill that conglomerate. *Wall Street Journal*, January 16.

Lichtenberg, F. R. 1992. Industrial de-diversification and its consequences for productivity. *Journal of Economic Behavior and Organization* 18:427−38.

Liebeskind, J., and Opler, T. C. 1992. The causes of corporate refocusing. Working paper. University of Southern California, Los Angeles.

Liebeskind, J., Opler, T. C., and Hatfield, D. E. 1992. Corporate restructuring and the consolidation of U.S. industry. Working paper. University of Southern California, Los Angeles.

Liebeskind, J., Wiersema, M., and Hansen, G. 1992. LBOs, corporate restructuring and the incentive-intensity hypothesis. *Financial Management* 21:73−88.

Light, J. O. 1989. The privatization of equity. *Harvard Business Review* 67:62−63.

Lindahl, F. W., and Ricks, W. E. 1988. Market reactions to announcements of write-offs. Unpublished manuscript. Duke University, Durham, NC.

Lindenberg, E. B., and Ross, S. A. 1981. Tobin's *q* ratio and industrial organization. *Journal of Business* 54:1–32.

Linn, S. C., and Rozeff, M. S. 1984. The corporate sell-off. *Midland Corporate Finance Journal* 2:428–36.

Linn, S. C., and Rozeff, M. S. 1985a. The effect of voluntary divestiture on stock prices: Sales of subsidiaries. Unpublished manuscript. University of Iowa, Iowa City.

Linn, S. C., and Rozeff, M. S. 1985b. The effect of voluntary spin-offs on stock prices: The Anergy hypothesis. *Advances in Financial Planning and Forecasting* 1:265–91.

Lorsch, J. W., and Allen, S. A. 1973. *Managing Diversity and Interdependence.* Boston: Division of Research, Harvard Business School.

Lowenstein, L. 1985. Management buy-outs. *Columbia Law Review* (May):730–80.

Lowenstein, L. 1986. No more cozy management buy-outs. *Harvard Business Review* (January–February):147–56.

Lubatkin, M. 1987. Merger strategies and stockholder value. *Strategic Management Journal* 8:39–53.

Lubatkin, M., and O'Neill, H. M. 1987. Merger strategies and capital market risk. *Academy of Management Journal* 30:665–84.

Lubatkin, M., and Shrieves, R. E. 1986. Towards reconciliation of market performance measures to strategic management research. *Academy of Management Review* 11:497–512.

MacDonald, J. M. 1985. R&D and the directions of diversification. *Review of Economics and Statistics* 47:583–90.

Mancke, R. B. 1974. Interfirm profitability differences: A new interpretation of the evidence. *Quarterly Journal of Economics* 88:181–93.

Mancke, R. B. 1977. Interfirm profitability differences: Reply. *Quarterly Journal of Economics* 91:677–80.

Mariotti, S., and Ricotta, E. 1987. Diversification: The European versus the U.S. experience. *Multinational Business* (spring):23–32.

Markham, J. W. 1973. *Conglomerate Enterprise and Public Policy.* Boston: Harvard Business School.

Markides, C. C. 1988. Corporate divestitures: A neglected topic in business policy research. Unpublished manuscript. Harvard University, Cambridge.

Markides, C. C. 1990. Diversification, refocusing and economic performance. D.B.A. dissertation. Harvard Business School, Boston.

Markides, C. C. 1991. Back to basics: Reversing corporate diversification. *Multinational Business* (winter):12–25.

Markides, C. C. 1992a. The economic characteristics of de-diversifying firms. *British Journal of Management* 2:91–100.

Markides, C. C. 1992b. The consequences of corporate refocusing: Ex-ante evidence. *Academy of Management Journal* 35:398–412.

Markides, C. C. 1993. Corporate refocusing. *Business Strategy Review* 4:1–15.

Markides, C. C. 1995. Diversification, restructuring and economic performance. *Strategic Management Journal* 16:101–18.

Markides, C. C., and Berg, N. 1988. Corporate divestitures: Survey of the literature and future research directions for business policy. Working paper 89-011. Harvard Business School, Boston. August.

Markides, C. C., and Singh, H. 1994. Takeover threats, internal controls and corporate restructuring. Unpublished manuscript. London Business School.

Markides, C. C., and Williamson, P. J. 1994a. Related diversification, core competences and corporate performance. *Strategic Management Journal*, special issue, ed. by C. K. Prahalad and G. Hamel (summer):149–65.

Markides, C. C., and Williamson, P. J. 1994b. Corporate diversification and organizational structure: A resource-based view. Unpublished manuscript. London Business School.

Marris, R. 1964. *The Economic Theory of Managerial Capitalism*. Glencoe, IL: Free Press.

Marris, R., and Mueller, D. C. 1980. The corporation, competition, and the invisible hand. *Journal of Economic Literature* 18:32–63.

Marsh, T. A., and Swanson, D. S. 1984. Risk-return trade-offs for strategic management. *Sloan Management Review* 25:35–51.

Marshall, W. J., Yawitz, J. B., and Greenberg, E. 1984. Incentives for diversification and the structure of the conglomerate firm. *Southern Economic Journal* 51:1–23.

Martin, S. 1979. Advertising, concentration, and profitability: The simultaneity problem. *Bell Journal of Economics* 10:639–47.

Martin, S. 1988. Market power and/or efficiency? *Review of Economics and Statistics* 70:331–35.

Matsusaka, J. G. 1990. Takeover motives during the conglomerate merger wave. Working paper. University of Chicago.

Maupin, R. J. 1987. Financial and stock market variables as predictors of management buy-outs. *Strategic Management Journal* 8:319–27.

McDougall, F. M., and Round, D. K. 1984. A comparison of diversifying and nondiversifying Australian industrial firms. *Academy of Management Journal* 27:384–98.

McFetridge, D. G. 1978. The efficiency implications of earnings retentions. *Review of Economics and Statistics* 60:218–24.

Meeks, G., and Meeks, J. G. 1981. Profitability measures as indicators of post-merger efficiency. *Journal of Industrial Economics* 29:335–43.

Melicher, R. W., Rush, D. F., and Winn, D. N. 1976. Degree of industry concentration and market risk-return performance. *Journal of Financial and Quantitative Analysis* 11:627–35.

Merchant, K. A., and Bruns, W. J., Jr. 1986. Measurements to cure management myopia. *Business Horizons* (May–June):56–64.

Michel, A., and Shaked, I. 1984. Does business diversification affect performance? *Financial Management* 13:18–25.

Miles, J. A., and Rosenfeld, J. D. 1983. The effect of voluntary spin-off announcements on shareholder wealth. *Journal of Finance* 38:1597–1606.

Miller, R. A. 1969. Market structure and industrial performance: Relation of profit rates to concentration, advertising intensity, and diversity. *Journal of Industrial Economics* 17:104–18.

Mitchell, M. L., and Lehn, K. 1990. Do bad bidders become good targets? *Journal of Political Economy* 98:372–98.

Montgomery, C. A. 1979. Diversification, market structure, and firm performance: An extension of Rumelt's model. Ph.D. dissertation. Purdue University, West Lafayette, IN.

Montgomery, C. A. 1982. The measurement of firm diversification: Some new empirical evidence. *Academy of Management Journal* 25:299–307.

Montgomery, C. A. 1985. Product-market diversification and market power. *Academy of Management Journal* 28:789–98.

Montgomery, C. A., and Singh, H. 1984. Diversification strategy and systematic risk. *Strategic Management Journal* 5:181–91.

Montgomery, C. A., and Thomas, A. R. 1988. Divestment: Motives and gains. *Strategic Management Journal* 9:93–97.

Montgomery, C. A., and Wernerfelt, B. 1988. Diversification, Ricardian rents, and Tobin's Q. *Rand Journal of Economics* 19:623–32.

Montgomery, C. A., and Wilson, V. A. 1986. Mergers that last: A predictable pattern? *Strategic Management Journal* 7:91–96.

Montgomery, C. A., Thomas, A. R., and Kamath, R. 1984. Divestiture, market valuation, and strategy. *Academy of Management Journal* 27:830–40.

Morck, R., Schleifer, A., and Vishny, R. W. 1989. Do managerial objectives drive bad acquisitions? Unpublished manuscript. University of Chicago. September.

Morck, R., Shleifer, A., and Vishny, R. W. 1990. Do managerial objectives drive bad acquisitions? *Journal of Finance* 45:31–48.

Mueller, D. C. 1972. A life cycle theory of the firm. *Journal of Industrial Economics* 20:199–219.

Mueller, D. C. 1977. The effects of conglomerate mergers. *Journal of Banking and Finance* 1:315–47.

Mueller, D. C. 1985. Mergers and market share. *Review of Economics and Statistics* 67:259–67.

Mueller, D. C. 1987. *The Corporation: Growth, Diversification and Mergers: Fundamentals of Pure and Applied Economics*. London: Harwood Academic Publishers.

Mullins, D. W., Jr. 1982. Does the capital asset pricing model work? *Harvard Business Review* (January–February):105–14.

Murphy, K. J. 1985. Corporate performance and managerial remuneration: An empirical analysis. *Journal of Accounting and Economics* (April):11–42.

Murphy, K. J. 1986. Top executives are worth every nickel they get. *Harvard Business Review* (March–April):125–31.

Myers, S., and Majluf, N. 1984. Corporate finance and investment decisions when firms have information that investors do not have. *Journal of Financial Economics* 13:187–222.

Napier, N. K., and Smith, M. 1987. Product diversification, performance criteria and compensation at the corporate manager level. *Strategic Management Journal* 8:195–201.

Nathanson, D. A. 1986. The strategic diversity classification system: A framework for decision making. In W. D. Guth, ed., *Handbook of Business Strategy, 1985–1986*.

Nathanson, D. A., and Cassano, J. S. 1982. Organization, diversity, and performance. *Wharton Magazine* 6:19–26.

Nees, D. B. 1979. The divestment decision process in large- and medium-sized diversified companies: A descriptive model based on clinical studies. *International Studies of Management and Organization* (winter):67–95.

Nees, D. B. 1981. Increase your divestment effectiveness. *Strategic Management Journal* 2:119–30.

Neumann, M., Böbel, I., and Haid, A. 1982. Innovations and market structure in West German industries. *Managerial and Decision Economics* 3:131–39.

Nieman, J. L., ed. 1987. *Mergerstat Review 1987*. W. T. Grimm & Co. Chicago.

Pagoulatos, E., and Sorenson, R. 1981. A simultaneous equation analysis of advertising, concentration, and profitability. *Southern Economic Journal* 47:728–41.

Palepu, K. 1985. Diversification strategy, profit performance, and the entropy measure. *Strategic Management Journal* 6:239–55.

Payne, J. W., Laughhunn, D. J., and Crum, R. 1981. Further tests of aspiration level effects in risky choice behavior. *Management Science* 27:953–58.

Penrose, E. 1959. *The Theory of the Growth of the Firm*. Oxford: Basil Blackwell.

Phillips, A. 1976. A critique of empirical studies of relations between market structure and profitability. *Journal of Industrial Economics* 24:241–49.

Pickering, J. F., and Cockerill, T. A. J. 1984. *The Economic Management of the Firm*. Totowa, NJ: Barnes & Noble.

Pitts, R. A. 1976. Diversification strategies and organizational policies of large diversified firms. *Journal of Economics and Business* (spring–summer):181–88.

Pitts, R. A., and Hopkins, H. D. 1982. Firm diversity: Conceptualization and measurement. *Academy of Management Review* 7:620–29.

Plott, C. R. 1982. Industrial organization theory and experimental economics. *Journal of Economic Literature* 20:1485–1527.

Porter, M. E. 1976a. *Interbrand Choice, Strategy, and Bilateral market Power*. Cambridge: Harvard University Press.

Porter, M. E. 1976b. Please note location of nearest exit: Exit barriers and planning. *California Management Review* 19:21–33.

Porter, M. E. 1979. The structure within industries and companies' performance. *Review of Economics and Statistics* 61:214–27.

Porter, M. E. 1980. *Competitive Strategy: Techniques for Analyzing Industries and Competitors*. New York: Free Press.

Porter, M. E. 1985. *Competitive Advantage: Creating and Sustaining Superior Performance.* New York: Free Press.

Porter, M. E. 1987. From competitive advantage to corporate strategy. *Harvard Business Review* (May–June):43–60.

Prahalad, C. K., and Bettis, R. A. 1986. The dominant logic: A new linkage between diversity and performance. *Strategic Management Journal* 7:485–501.

Rappaport, A. 1981. Selecting strategies that create shareholder value. *Harvard Business Review* (May–June):139–49.

Ravenscraft, D. J. 1983. Structure-profit relationships at the line of business and industry level. *Review of Economics and Statistics* 65:22–31.

Ravenscraft, D. J., and Scherer, F. M. 1987a. *Mergers, Sell-Offs and Economic Efficiency.* Washington: Brookings Institution.

Ravenscraft, D. J., and Scherer, F. M. 1987b. Life after takeover. *Journal of Industrial Economics* 36:147–56.

Ravenscraft, D. J., and Scherer, F. M. 1987c. Divisional sell-off: A hazard function analysis. Unpublished manuscript. University of North Carolina, Chapel Hill. February.

Reed, R. 1991. Bimodality in diversification: An efficiency and effectiveness rationale. *Managerial and Decision Economics* 12:57–66.

Reed, R., and Luffman, G. A. 1986. Diversification: The growing confusion. *Strategic Management Journal* 7:29–35.

Rhoades, S. A. 1973. The effect of diversification on industry profit performance in 241 manufacturing industries: 1963. *Review of Economics and Statistics* 55:146–55.

Rhoades, S. A., and Rutz, R. D. 1982. Market power and firm risk. *Journal of Monetary Economics* 9:73–85.

Robichek, A. A., and Van Horne, J. C. 1967. Abandonment value and capital budgeting. *Journal of Finance* 22:577–88.

Roll, R. 1977. A critique of the asset pricing theory's tests. *Journal of Financial Economics* 4:129–76.

Roll, R. 1983. The hubris hypothesis of corporate takeovers. Unpublished manuscript. UCLA School of Management.

Roll, R. 1986. The hubris hypothesis of corporate takeovers. *Journal of Business* 59:197–216.

Rosenberg, J. B. 1977. Diversification and market structure: A note. *Review of Business and Economic Research* 12:79–83.

Rosenfeld, J. D. 1984. Additional evidence on the relation between divestiture announcements and shareholder wealth. *Journal of Finance* 39:1437–48.

Ruback, R. S. 1983. The cities service takeover: A case study. *Journal of Finance* 38:319–30.

Rumelt, R. 1974. *Strategy, Structure, and Economic Performance.* Boston: Division of Research, Harvard Business School.

Rumelt, R. 1982. Diversification strategy and profitability. *Strategic Management Journal* 3:359–69.

Salter, M. S., and Weinhold, W. A. 1979. *Diversification through Acquisition: Strategies for Creating Economic Value.* New York: Free Press.

Salter, M. S., and Weinhold, W. A. 1982. What lies ahead for merger activities in the 1980s. *Journal of Business Strategy* (spring):66–99.

Samuels, J. M., and Smyth, D. J. 1968. Profits, variability of profits and firm size. *Economica* 35:127–39.

Sawyer, M. C. 1982. On the specification of structure-performance relationships. *European Economic Review* 17:295–306.

Schendel, D. E., and Hofer, C. W., eds. 1979. *Strategic Management: A New View of Business Policy and Planning.* Boston: Little, Brown.

Schendel, D., and Patton, G. R. 1978. A simultaneous equation model of corporate strategy. *Management Science* 24:1611–21.

Scherer, F. M. 1980. *Industrial Market Structure and Economic Performance,* 2d ed. Boston: Houghton Mifflin.

Scherer, F. M. 1988. Corporate takeovers: The efficiency arguments. *Journal of Economic Perspectives* 2:69–82.

Scherer, F. M., Beckenstein, A., Kaufer, E., and Murphy, R. D. 1975. *The Economics of Multiplant Operation.* Cambridge: Harvard University Press.

Schipper, K. 1983. The evidence on divestitures, going private proposals, and spin-offs. *Midland Corporate Finance Journal* 1:51–55.

Schipper, K., and Smith, A. 1983. Effects of recontracting on shareholder wealth: The case of voluntary spin-offs. *Journal of Financial Economics* 12:437–67.

Schipper, K., and Smith, A. 1986. A comparison of equity carve-outs and seasoned equity offerings: Share price effects and corporate restructuring. *Journal of Financial Economics* 15: 153–86.

Schleifer, A., and Vishny, R. W. 1988. Management buy-outs as a response to market pressure. In A. J. Auerback, ed., *Mergers & Acquisitions.* Chicago: University of Chicago Press, pp. 87–103.

Scott, B. R. 1973. The industrial state: Old myths and new realities. *Harvard Business Review* 51 (March–April):133–48.

Scott, J. T. 1982. Multimarket contact and economic performance. *Review of Economics and Statistics* 64:368–75.

Shefrin, H., and Statman, M. 1985. The disposition to sell winners too early and ride losers too long: Theory and evidence. *Journal of Finance* 40:777–92.

Shepherd, W. G. 1972. The elements of market structure. *Review of Economics and Statistics* 54:25–37.

Shepherd, W. G. 1979. *The Economics of Industrial Organization.* Englewood Cliffs, NJ: Prentice-Hall.

Shleiffer, A., and Vishny, R. W. 1990. The takeover wave of the 1980s. *Science* 249:745–49.

Shleiffer, A., and Vishny, R. W. 1991. Takeovers in the '60s and the '80s: Evidence and implications. *Strategic Management Journal* 12:51–59.

Sicherman, N. W., and Pettway, R. H. 1987. Acquisition of divested assets and share-holders' wealth. *Journal of Finance* 42:1261–73.

Singh, A. 1972. *Takeovers: Their Relevance to the Stock Market and the Theory of the Firm.* Cambridge: Cambridge University Press.

Singh, H, and Chang, S. 1992. Corporate reconfiguration: A resource perspective. Unpublished manuscript. Wharton School, University of Pennsylvania, Philadelphia.

Singh, H., and Montgomery, C. A. 1987. Corporate acquisition strategies and economic performance. *Strategic Management Journal* 8:377–86.

Skantz, T. R., and Marchesini, R. 1987. The effect of voluntary corporate liquidation on shareholder wealth. *Journal of Financial Research* 10:65–75.

Slater, M. 1980. The managerial limitations to the growth of firms. *Economic Journal* 90: 520–28.

Slovic, P., and Lichtenstein, S. 1971. Comparison of Bayesian and regression approaches to the study of information processing in judgement. *Organizational Behavior and Human Performance* 6:649–744.

Slovic, P., Fischhoff, B., and Lichtenstein, S. 1977. Behavioral decision theory. *Annual Review of Psychology* 28:1–39.

Slusser, W. P. 1987. Liquidating the company to realize value. In S. J. Lee and R. D. Colman, eds., *Handbook of Mergers, Acquisitions and Buy-outs*, pp. 559–63.

Smirlock, M., Gilligan, T., and Marshall, W. 1984. Tobin's q and the structure-performance relationship. *American Economic Review* 74:1051–60.

Smith, K. V., and Weston, J. F. 1977. Further evaluation of conglomerate performance. *Journal of Business Research* 5:5–14.

Solomon, E. 1970. Alternative rate of return concepts and their implications for utility regulation. *Bell Journal of Economics and Management Science* 1:65–81.

Song, J. H. 1982. Diversification strategies and the experience of top executives of large firms. *Strategic Management Journal* 3:377–80.

Spencer, D. E., and Berk, K. N. 1981. A limited information specification test. *Econometrica* 49:1079–85.

Springate, D. J., and Miller, R. D. 1978. Managerial determinants of economic performance within an industry. *1978 Proceedings*. Austin, TX: American Institute of Decision Sciences, pp. 213–14.

Stauffer, T. R. 1971. The measurement of corporate rates of return: A generalized formulation. *Bell Journal of Economics and Management Science* 2:434–69.

Steer, P., and Cable, J. 1978. Internal organization and profit: An empirical analysis of large U.K. firms. *Journal of Industrial Economics* 27:13–30.

Steward, J. F., Harris, R. S., and Carleton, W. T. 1984. The role of market structure in merger behavior. *Journal of Industrial Economics* 32:293–312.

Stewart, G. B., III and Glassman, D. M. 1987–88. Why restructuring adds value? *Cash Flow* (November 1987):42–47, (December 1987):44–47, (January 1988):36–43, (February 1988): 46–48, and (March 1988):38–43.

Stillman, R. 1983. Examining antitrust policy towards horizontal mergers. *Journal of Financial Economics* 11:225–40.

Strickland, A. D. 1985. Conglomerate mergers, mutual forbearance behavior, and price competition. *Managerial and Decision Economics* 6:153–59.

Strickland, A. D., and Weiss, L. W. 1976. Advertising, concentration, and price-cost margins. *Journal of Political Economy* 84:1109–21.

Strong, J. S., and Meyer, J. R. 1987. Asset writedowns: Managerial incentives and security returns. *Journal of Finance* 42:643–63.

Subrahmanyam, M. G., and Thomadakis, S. B. 1980. Systematic risk and the theory of the firm. *Quarterly Journal of Economics* 94:437–51.

Sullivan, T. G. 1977. A note on market power and returns to stockholders. *Review of Economics and Statistics* 59:108–13.

Sullivan, T. G. 1982. The cost of capital and the market power of firms: Reply and correction. *Review of Economics and Statistics* 64:523–25.

Sutherland, J. W. 1980. A quasi-empirical mapping of optimal scale of enterprise. *Management Science* 26:963–81.

Sutton, C. J. 1980. *Economics and Corporate Strategy*. Cambridge: Cambridge University Press.

Teece, D. J. 1980. Economies of scope and the scope of the enterprise. *Journal of Economic Behavior and Organization* 1:223–47.

Teece, D. J. 1981. Internal organization and economic performance: An empirical analysis of the profitability of principal firms. *Journal of Industrial Economics* 30:173–99.

Teece, D. J. 1982. Towards an economic theory of the multiproduct firm. *Journal of Economic Behavior and Organization* 3:39–63.

Tehranian, H., Travlos, N. G., and Waegelein, J. F. 1987. The effect of long-term performance plans on corporate sell-off-induced abnormal returns. *Journal of Finance* 42:933–42.

Thomadakis, S. B. 1976. A model of market power, valuation and the firm's returns. *Bell Journal of Economics* 7:150–62.

Thomadakis, S. B. 1977. A value-based test of profitability and market structure. *Review of Economics and Statistics* 59:179–85.

Thompson, J. D. 1967. *Organizations in Action*. New York: McGraw-Hill.

Thompson, R. S. 1981. Internal organization and profit: A note. *Journal of Industrial Economics* 30:201–11.

Thompson, R. S. 1984. Diversification strategy and systematic risk: An empirical inquiry. *Managerial and Decision Economics* 5:98–103.

Tiao, G. C., and Box, G. E. P. 1981. Modeling multiple time series with applications. *Journal of the American Statistical Association* 76:802–16.

Torabzadeh, K. M., and Berlin, W. J. 1987. Leveraged buyouts and shareholder returns. *Journal of Financial Research* 10:313–19.

Turk, T. A., and Baysinger, B. 1989. The impact of public policy on corporate strategy:

Taxes, antitrust policy and diversification clienteles. Working paper. Department of Management, Texas A&M University, College Station.

Tversky, A., and Kahneman, D. 1981. The framing of decisions and the psychology of choice. *Science* 211:453–58.

Vancil, R. 1979. *Decentralization: Managerial Ambiguity by Design*. Homewood, IL: Dow-Jones Irwin.

Varadarajan, P. R. 1986. Product diversity and firm performance: An empirical investigation. *Journal of Marketing* 50:43–57.

Varadarajan, P. R., and Ramanujam, V. 1987. Diversification and performance: A reexamination using a new two-dimensational conceptualization of diversity in firms. *Academy of Management Journal* 30:380–93.

Wall Street Journal. 1985. Shifting strategies: Surge in restructuring is profoundly altering much of US industry. August 12, p. 1.

Waterson, M. 1984. *Economic Theory of the Industry*. Cambridge: Cambridge University Press.

Weiss, L. W. 1974. The concentration-profits relationship and antitrust. In D. Goldschmid et al., eds., *Industrial Concentration: The New Learning*, Boston: Little Brown.

Wernerfelt, B., and Montgomery, C. A. 1986. What is an attractive industry? *Management Science* 32:1223–30.

Wernerfelt, B., and Montgomery, C. A. 1988. Tobin's q and the importance of focus in firm performance. *American Economic Review* 78:246–50.

Weston, F. J. 1970. The nature and significance of conglomerate firms. *St. John's Law Review* 44 (special ed.):66–80.

White, L. J. 1981. What has been happening to aggregate concentration in the United States? *Journal of Industrial Economics* 29:223–30.

Wier, P. 1983. The costs of antimerger lawsuits: Evidence from the stock market. *Journal of Financial Economics* 11:207–24.

Wiersema, M. F. 1985. Strategic redirection. Ph.D. dissertation. University of Michigan, Ann Arbor.

Williams, J. R., Paez, B. L., and Sanders, L. 1988. Conglomerates revisited. *Strategic Management Journal* 9:403–14.

Williamson, O. E. 1964. *The Economics of Discretionary Behavior: Managerial Objectives in a Theory of the Firm*. Englewood Cliffs, NJ: Prentice-Hall.

Williamson, O. E. 1965. Managerial discretion and business behavior. *American Economic Review* 53:1032–57.

Williamson, O. E. 1967. Hierarchical control and optimum firm size. *Journal of Political Economy* 75:123–38.

Williamson, O. E. 1970. *Corporate Control and Business Behavior*. Englewood Cliffs, NJ: Prentice-Hall.

Williamson, O. E. 1975. *Markets and Hierarchies: Analysis and Antitrust Implications*. New York: Free Press.

Williamson, O. E., and Bhargava, N. 1972. Assessing and classifying the internal structure and control apparatus of the modern corporation. In R. Marris and A. Wood, eds., *The Corporate Economy*. London: Macmillan.

Winn, D. N. 1977. On the relations between rates of return, risk, and market structure. *Quarterly Journal of Economics* 91:157–63.

Wolf, B. M. 1977. Industrial diversification and internationalization: Some empirical evidence. *Journal of Industrial Economics* 26:177–91.

Worcester, D. 1967. *Monopoly, Big Business and Welfare in the Postwar United States*. Seattle: University of Washington Press.

Wright, M. 1985. Divestment and organizational adaptation. *European Management Journal* 3:85–93.

Wright, M. 1986. The make-buy decision and managing markets: The case of management buy-outs. *Journal of Management Studies* 23:443–64.

Wright, M., and Thompson, S. 1987. Divestment and the control of divisionalized firms. *Accounting and Business Research* 17:259–67.

Wrigley, L. 1970. Divisional autonomy and diversification. Ph.D. dissertation. Harvard Business School, Boston.

Yavitz, B., and Newman, W. H. 1982. What the corporation should provide its business units. *Journal of Business Strategy* 3:14–19.

Yip, G. S. 1982. Diversification entry: Internal development versus acquisition. *Strategic Management Journal* 3:331–45.

You, V., Caves, R., Smith, M., and Henry, J. 1986. Mergers and bidders' wealth: Managerial and strategic factors. In L. G. Thomas, III, ed., *Economics of Strategic Planning*. Lexington, MA: Lexington Books.

Zaima, J. K., and Hearth, D. 1985. The wealth effects of voluntary sell-offs: Implications for divesting and acquiring firms. *Journal of Financial Research* 8:227–36.

Index